Biotechnology
Changing Life Through Science

■■■

Biotechnology
Changing Life Through Science

Volume 1
Medicine

K. Lee Lerner and
Brenda Wilmoth Lerner, Editors

U·X·L
An imprint of Thomson Gale, a part of The Thomson Corporation

THOMSON
GALE

Detroit • New York • San Francisco • New Haven, Conn. • Waterville, Maine • London

Biotechnology: Changing Life Through Science

K. Lee Lerner and Brenda Wilmoth Lerner, Editors

Project Editor
Kristine Krapp

Editorial
Kathleen Edgar, Madeline Harris, Melissa Hill, Elizabeth Manar, Kim McGrath, Paul Lewon

Indexing Services
Factiva, a Dow Jones & Reuters Company

Rights and Acquisitions
Margaret Chamberlain-Gaston, Shalice Caldwell-Shah

Imaging and Multimedia
Randy Bassett, Lezlie Light, Michael Logusz, Christine O'Bryan, Robyn Young

Product Design
Jennifer Wahi

Composition
Evi Seoud, Mary Beth Trimper

Manufacturing
Wendy Blurton, Dorothy Maki

LIBRARY OF CONGRESS CATALOGING-IN-PUBLICATION DATA

Biotechnology : changing life through science / K. Lee Lerner and Brenda Wilmoth Lerner, editors.
    p. cm.
  Includes bibliographical references and index.
  ISBN-13: 978-1-4144-0151-5 (set hardcover : alk. paper)
  ISBN-10: 1-4144-0151-5 (set hardcover : alk. paper)
  ISBN-13: 978-1-4144-0152-2 (vol. 1 hardcover : alk. paper)
  ISBN-10: 1-4144-0152-3 (vol. 1 hardcover : alk. paper)
  [etc.]
  1. Biotechnology–Juvenile literature. I. Lerner, K. Lee. II. Lerner, Brenda Wilmoth.
  TP248.218.B56 2007
  660.6–dc22
                                  2006029356

ISBN-13:	ISBN-10:
978-1-4144-0151-5 (set)	1-4144-0151-5 (set)
978-1-4144-0152-2 (vol. 1)	1-4144-0152-3 (vol. 1)
978-1-4144-0153-9 (vol. 2)	1-4144-0153-1 (vol. 2)
978-1-4144-0154-6 (vol. 3)	1-4144-0154-X (vol. 3)

This title is also available as an e-book.
ISBN-13: 978-1-4144-0465-3, ISBN-10: 1-4144-0465-4
Contact your Thomson Gale sales representative for ordering information.
Printed in China
10 9 8 7 6 5 4 3 2 1

Contents

CONTENTS

CONTENTS

■ ■ ■

Introduction

Biotechnology: Changing Life Through Science is devoted to helping younger students and general readers understand the fast-developing science and issues related to technologies touching on the most intimate and fundamental mechanisms of life.

This book is a collection of more than 165 entries on topics covering biotechnology applications ranging across medicine, agriculture, and industry. To be sure, the topics are often challenging to younger students—but in such challenges lie the opportunity to place their early studies of basic science into a context that both motivates them toward science and that enhances their critical thinking skills as they evaluate news and issues related to science, technology, and ethics.

Toward this goal, *Biotechnology: Changing Life Through Science* entries are designed to instruct, challenge, and excite less-experienced students, while providing a solid foundation and reference for students already captivated by biotechnology.

At the core of the advances in biotechnology lies the science of molecular biology and genetics. Because *Biotechnology: Changing Life Through Science* is designed for younger students, the editors have attempted to include simple explanations of sometimes advanced scientific principles. Despite the complexities of genetics, along with the fast pace of research and innovation, every effort has been made to set forth entries in everyday language and to provide generous explanations of the most important terms used by professional scientists.

Essential features of *Biotechnology: Changing Life Through Science*

Written by experts, teachers, and expert writers in fields of physics, molecular biology, genetics, and microbiology, every effort has been taken to explain scientific concepts clearly and simply, without sacrificing fundamental accuracy. The articles in the book are meant to be understandable by anyone with a curiosity about biotechnology.

Entries are arranged alphabetically within volumes devoted to applications generally (but not exclusively) related to biomedical, agricultural, and industrial biotechnologies. *See also* references at the end of entries alert the readers to related entries across the three-volume set that may provide additional resources or insights each topic.

Each entry contains a *Words to Know* section to help students understand important or complex terms. A general compendium of these terms is also included in the book. A *Timeline* allows students to place events in context to significant advances in science and biotechnology.

A *Where To Learn More* section lists generally usable print material and Web sites, while a comprehensive *General Index* guides the reader to topics and terms mentioned in the book.

Photos and color illustrations created for this title are included throughout the book where they might stimulate interest or understanding.

Advisors and Contributors

While compiling this volume, the editors relied on the expertise and contributions of the following scholars, teachers, and writers:

William Arthur Atkins, M.S.
Physics and science writer
Normal, Illinois

Antonio Farina, M.D., Ph.D.
Department of Embryology, Obstetrics, and Gynecology
University of Bologna. Italy

Larry Gilman, Ph.D.
Electrical engineerr
Sharon, Vermont

Amit Gupta, M.S.
Science and technology writer
Ahmedabad, India

Brian D. Hoyle, Ph.D.
Microbiologist
Nova Scotia, Canada

Alexander I. Ioffe, Ph.D.
Senior Scientist
Russian Academy of Sciences. Moscow, Russia

Kelli Miller Stacey
Science and technology writer (Ms. Miller Stacy is winner of the American Medical Writers Association's 2006 Eric W. Martin Award for excellence in medical writing)
Canton, GA

Maysoun Shomali, M.S. (molecular biology)
Biotechnology specialist
Cambridge, MA

Stephanie Watson
Science and technology writer
Smyrna, GA

The editors are deeply grateful to Christine Jeryan, Stacey Chamberlin, and John Krol for their copyediting skills. Their efforts greatly contributed to our overall effort to ensure that the language used in this book was as accessible as possible to younger students without sacrificing accuracy. Their collective efforts added significant readability to this book. The editors also wish to acknowledge and thank Adrienne Wilmoth Lerner and Alicia Cafferty for their research efforts.

The editors gratefully acknowledge and extend thanks to Debra Kirby at Thomson Gale for her faith in the project and for their sound content advice. We also offer special thanks to the Thomson Gale imaging teams for their skilled work in collecting and editing images.

This book would not have been possible without the efforts of project manager Kristine Krapp. Her clear thoughts, insights, patience, and sound editorial judgments added significantly to the quality of all aspects of *Biotechnology: Changing Life Through Science*.

K. Lee Lerner and Brenda Wilmoth Lerner, editors
London, U.K., and Cairo, Egypt
October 2006

K. Lee Lerner is a physicist, lecturer, and director of more than two dozen books and films related to science and technology. Brenda Wilmoth Lerner is former nurse and infection control expert who has edited or written more than a dozen books related to the history and applications of medical science.

Timeline

1947 Nuremberg Code issued regarding voluntary consent of human subjects.

1948 Barbara McClintock publishes her research on transposable regulatory elements ("jumping genes") in maize. Her work was not appreciated until similar phenomena were discovered in bacteria and fruit flies in the 1960s and 1970s. McClintock was awarded the Nobel Prize in Medicine or Physiology in 1983.

1952 Alfred Hershey and Martha Chase publish a paper suggesting that DNA (deoxyribonucleic acid) is the genetic material.

1952 Renato Dulbecco develops a practical method for studying animal viruses in cell cultures.

1952 Rosalind Franklin completes a series of x-ray crystallography studies of two forms of DNA. Her colleague, Maurice Wilkins, gives information about her work to James Watson.

1953 James D. Watson and Francis H. C. Crick publish two landmark papers in the journal *Nature*. Watson and Crick propose a double helical model for DNA and call attention to the genetic implications of their model. Their model is based, in part, on the x ray crystallographic work of Rosalind Franklin and the biochemical work of Erwin Chargaff. Their model explains how the genetic material is transmitted.

1953 Jonas Salk begins testing a polio vaccine comprised of a mixture of killed viruses.

1953 Stanley Miller produces amino acids from inorganic compounds similar to those in Earth's primitive atmosphere with electrical sparks that simulate lightning.

1955   Fred L. Schaffer and Carlton E. Schwerdt report on their successful crystallization of the polio virus. Their achievement is the first successful crystallization of an animal virus.

1955   National Institutes of Health organizes a Division of Biologics Control within the U.S. Food and Drug Administration (FDA), following deaths from a faulty polio vaccine.

1957   Alick Isaacs and Jean Lindenmann publish their pioneering report on the drug interferon, a protein produced by interaction between a virus and an infected cell that can interfere with the multiplication of viruses.

1957   Francis Crick proposes that during protein formation each amino acid is carried to the RNA template by an "adapter molecule" containing nucleotides and that the adapter is the part that actually fits on the RNA template. Later research demonstrates this "adapter molecule" is transfer RNA.

1958   FDA publishes its first list of substances generally recognized as safe.

1958   Frederick Sanger is awarded the Nobel Prize in chemistry for his work on the structure of proteins, especially for determining the primary sequence of insulin.

1958   George W. Beadle, Edward L. Tatum, and Joshua Lederberg were awarded the Nobel Prize in Medicine or Physiology. Beadle and Tatum were honored for the work with a group of fungi called *Neurospora* that led to the one gene-one enzyme theory. Lederberg was honored for discoveries concerning genetic recombination and the organization of the genetic material of bacteria.

1959   English biochemist Rodney Porter begins studies that lead to the discovery of the structure of antibodies. Porter receives the 1972 Nobel Prize in Physiology or Medicine for this research.

1959   Severo Ochoa and Arthur Kornberg are awarded the Nobel Prize in Medicine or Physiology for their discovery of the mechanisms in the biological creation (synthesis) of ribonucleic acid (RNA) and deoxyribonucleic acid (DNA).

1959   Sydney Brenner and Robert W. Horne develop a method for studying viruses using the electron microscope.

1961   Francis Crick, Sydney Brenner, and others propose that a molecule called transfer RNA uses a three-base code in the manufacture of proteins.

1961 Marshall Warren Nirenberg and J. Heinrich Matthaei establish the relationship between the sequence of nucleotides in the genetic material and amino acids in the gene product.

1962 United States Congress passes Kefauver-Harris Drug Amendments that shift the burden of proof of clinical safety to drug manufacturers. For the first time, drug manufacturers had to prove their products were safe and effective before they could be sold.

1965 Anthrax vaccine adsorbed (AVA), is approved for use in the United States.

1965 François Jacob, André Lwoff, and Jacques Monod are awarded the Nobel Prize in Medicine or Physiology for their discoveries concerning genetic control of enzymes and virus synthesis.

1965 James M. Schlatter, American chemist, combines two amino acids and obtains a sweet-tasting substance. This chemical is about 200 times sweeter than sugar and is named aspartame. In 1983, it is approved for use in carbonated beverages. It becomes a widely used artificial sweetener.

1966 Bruce Ames develops a test to screen for compounds that cause mutations, including those that are cancer causing. The so-called Ames test utilizes the bacterium *Salmonella typhimurium*.

1966 Marshall Nirenberg and Har Gobind Khorana lead teams that decipher the genetic code. All of the 64 possible triplet combinations of the four bases (the codons) and their associated amino acids are determined and described.

1967 Charles Yanofsky demonstrates that the sequence of codons in a gene determines the sequence of amino acids in a protein.

1967 Thomas Brock discovers the heat-loving bacterium *Thermus aquaticus* from a hot spring in Yellowstone National Park. The bacterium yields the enzyme that becomes the basis of the DNA polymerase reaction.

1968 Werner Arber discovers that bacteria defend themselves against viruses by producing DNA-cutting enzymes. These enzymes quickly become important tools for molecular biologists.

1969 By executive order of the President, the United States renounces first-use of biological weapons and restricts future weapons research programs to issues concerning defensive responses (e.g., immunization, detection, etc.).

1969 Jonathan R. Beckwith, American molecular biologist, and colleagues isolate a single gene.

1969 Max Delbrück, Alfred D. Hershey, and Salvador E. Luria are awarded the Nobel Prize in Medicine or Physiology for their discoveries concerning the replication mechanism and the genetic structure of viruses.

1970 Howard Martin Temin and David Baltimore independently discover reverse transcriptase in viruses. Reverse transcriptase is an enzyme that speeds the reaction in which RNA can be transcribed into DNA.

1972 Biological and Toxin Weapons Convention first signed. BWC prohibits the offensive weaponization of biological agents (e.g., anthrax spores). The BWC also prohibits the transformation of biological agents with established legitimate and sanctioned purposes into agents of a nature and quality that could be used to effectively induce illness or death.

1972 Paul Berg and Herbert Boyer produce the first recombinant DNA molecules by splicing together pieces of DNA from different sources to form recombinant genes. Recombinant technology emerges as one of the most powerful techniques of molecular biology.

1973 Concerns about the possible hazards posed by recombinant DNA technologies, especially work with tumor viruses, leads to the establishment of a meeting at Asilomar, California. The proceedings of this meeting are subsequently published by the Cold Spring Harbor Laboratory as a book entitled *Biohazards in Biological Research.*

1975 César Milstein and George Kohler create monoclonal antibodies, which are explored as drug treatments for cancer and other diseases.

1977 Frederick Sanger develops a method to sequence the genome of a microorganism.

1977 The first known human fatality from H5N1 avian flu (bird flu) occurs in Hong Kong.

1977 The last reported smallpox case is recorded. Ultimately, the World Health Organization (WHO) declares the disease eradicated.

1978   Louise Brown, the world's first "test-tube baby," is born.

1978   Scientists clone the gene for human insulin.

1980   Researchers successfully introduce a human gene, which codes for the protein interferon, into a bacterium.

1981   AIDS (acquired immune deficiency syndrome) is recognized and tracked as an epidemic.

1983   *Escherichia coli* O157:H7 is identified as a human pathogen.

1983   Luc Montagnier and Robert Gallo discover the human immunodeficiency virus that is believed to cause acquired immunodeficiency syndrome.

1983   The United States Congress passes the Orphan Drug Act, which allowed the FDA to research and market drugs necessary for treating rare diseases.

1985   Alec Jeffreys develops "genetic fingerprinting," a method of using DNA polymorphisms (unique sequences of DNA) to identify individuals. The method, which has been used in paternity, immigration, and murder cases, is generally referred to as "DNA fingerprinting."

1987   Maynard Olson creates and names yeast artificial chromosomes (YACs), which provided a technique to clone long segments of DNA.

1987   The idea to use patterns of the iris of the eye as an identification marker was patented, along with the algorithms necessary for iris identification.

1988   The Human Genome Organization (HUGO) is established by scientists in order to coordinate international efforts to sequence the human genome. The Human Genome Project officially adopts the goal of determining the entire sequence of DNA comprising the human chromosomes.

1989   Sidney Altman and Thomas R. Cech are awarded the Nobel Prize in chemistry for their discovery of ribozymes (RNA molecules with catalytic activity). Cech proves that RNA could function as a biocatalyst as well as an information carrier.

1989   The Internet revolution begins with the invention of the World Wide Web.

1991   The gender of a mouse is changed at the embryo stage.

1992   American and British scientists develop a technique for testing embryos in the womb for genetic abnormalities such as cystic fibrosis and hemophilia.

1993   George Washington University researchers clone human embryos and nurture them in a Petri dish for several days. The project provokes protests from ethicists, politicians, and critics of genetic engineering.

1994   Geneticists determine that DNA repair enzymes perform several vital functions, including preserving genetic information and protecting the cell from cancer.

1994   The Genetic Privacy Act, the first United States Human Genome Project legislative product, proposed regulation of the collection, analysis, storage, and use of DNA samples and genetic information obtained from them.

1995   After thwarting U.N. weapons inspectors, the government of Iraq admits to producing over 200 gallons (8,000 liters) of concentrated anthrax as part of the nation's biological weapons program.

1995   Religious leaders and biotechnology critics protest the patenting of plants, animals, and human body parts.

1996   Dolly, the world's first cloned sheep, is born. Several European countries ban human cloning. U.S. Congress debates a bill to ban human cloning.

1996   H5N1 avian flu virus is identified in Guangdong, China.

1996   Researchers C. Cheng and L. Olson demonstrate that the spinal cord can be regenerated in adult rats. Experimenting on rats with a severed spinal cord, Cheng and Olson use peripheral nerves to connect white matter and gray matter.

1996   Scientists discover a link between apoptosis (cellular suicide, a natural process whereby the body eliminates useless cells) gone awry and several neurodegenerative conditions, including Alzheimer's disease.

1997   Ian Wilmut of the Roslin Institute in Edinburgh, Scotland, announces the birth of a lamb called Dolly, the first mammal cloned from an adult cell (a cell in a pregnant ewe's mammary gland).

1997   Microscopic analysis of the Murchison meteorite led some scientists to argue evidence of ancient life on other planets.

Later studies cast doubt that the changes in the meteorite must be due to biological processes.

1997 Researchers identify a gene that plays a crucial role in establishing normal left-right configuration during organ development.

1997 The National Center for Human Genome Research (NCHGR) at the National Institutes of Health becomes the National Human Genome Research Institute (NHGRI).

1997 While performing a cloning experiment, Christof Niehrs, a researcher at the German Center for Cancer Research, identifies a protein responsible for the creation of the head in a frog embryo.

1997 William Jacobs and Barry Bloom create a biological entity that combines the characteristics of a bacterial virus and a plasmid (a DNA structure that functions and replicates independently of the chromosomes).

1998 DNA fingerprinting is used to identify remains of Russian Imperial Romanov family.

1998 The U.S. Department of Energy (DOE) funds bacterial artificial chromosome and sequencing projects.

1998 Dolly, the first cloned sheep, gives birth to a lamb that had been conceived by a natural mating with a Welsh Mountain ram. Researches said the birth of Bonnie proved that Dolly was a fully normal and healthy animal.

1998 Ian Wilmut announced the birth of Polly, a transgenic lamb containing human genes.

1998 Immunologist Ellen Heber-Katz, researcher at the Wistar Institute in Philadelphia, reports that a strain of laboratory mice can regenerate tissue in their ears, closing holes which scientists had created for identification purposes. This discovery reopens the discussion on possible regeneration in humans.

1998 Two research teams succeed in growing embryonic stem cells.

1999 Scientists announce the complete sequencing of the DNA making up human chromosome 22. The first complete human chromosome sequence is published in December 1999.

2000 On June 26, 2000, leaders of the public genome project and Celera, a biotech company, announce the completion of a working draft of the entire human genome sequence.

2000 U.S. President Clinton signed an executive order prohibiting federal departments and agencies from using genetic information in hiring or promoting workers.

2000 The first volume of *Annual Review of Genomics and Human Genetics* is published. Genomics is defined as the new science dealing with the identification and characterization of genes and their arrangement in chromosomes. It defines human genetics as the science devoted to understanding the origin and expression of human individual uniqueness.

2001 In February 2001, the complete draft sequence of the human genome is published. The public sequence data is published in the British journal *Nature*, and the Celera sequence is published in the American journal *Science*. Increased knowledge of the human genome allows greater specificity in pharmacological research and drug interaction studies.

2001 Letters containing a powdered form of *Bacillus anthracis*, the bacteria that causes anthrax, are mailed by an unknown terrorist or terrorist group (foreign or domestic) to government representatives, members of the news media, and others in the United States. More than 20 cases and five deaths are eventually attributed to the terrorist attack.

2001 The company Advanced Cell Technology announces that its researchers have created cloned human embryos that grew to the six-cell stage.

2001 The United States announces that the National Institutes of Health (NIH) will fund research on only 64 embryonic stem cell lines already created from human embryos.

2002 Following September 11, 2001, terrorist attacks on the United States, the Public Health Security and Bioterrorism Preparedness and Response Act of 2002 is passed in an effort to improve the ability to prevent and respond to public health emergencies.

2002 Severe acute respiratory syndrome (SARS) virus is found in patients in China, Hong Kong, and other Asian countries. The newly discovered virus is not identified until early 2003. The spread of the virus reaches epidemic proportions in Asia and expands to the rest of the world.

2002 The agricultural chemical atrazine, used in weed control, is thought to be partially responsible for the dramatic global decline in amphibians, as it is found to disturb male frog sex hormones, altering their reproductive organs.

2002 The Best Pharmaceuticals for Children Act is passed in an effort to improve safety and efficacy of patented and off-patent medicines for children.

2002 The Defense Advanced Research Projects Agency (DARPA) initiates the Biosensor Technologies program in 2002 to develop fast, sensitive, automatic technologies for the detection and identification of biological warfare agents.

2002 The planned destruction of stocks of smallpox-causing variola virus at the two remaining depositories in the United States and Russia is delayed over fears that large-scale production of vaccine might be needed in the event of a bioterrorist action.

2003 "Smart passports" fitted with a microchip that will allow immigration officials to identify the facial biometric features of the passport holder are under development and scheduled for introduction by early 2005.

2003 FDA requires food labels to include trans fat content. Trans fats are believed to raise cholesterol levels in the blood. This is the first major change to the nutrition facts panel on foods since 1993.

2003 Dolly, the first cloned sheep, dies of a chronic lung disease.

2003 United States invades Iraq and finds chemical, biological, and nuclear weapons programs, but no actual weapons.

2004 Food Allergy Labeling and Consumer Protection Act requires the labeling of food containing a protein derived peanuts, soybeans, cow's milk, eggs, fish, crustacean shellfish, tree nuts, and wheat that accounts for a majority of food allergies.

2004 Project BioShield Act of 2004 authorizes U.S. government agencies to expedite procedures related to rapid distribution of treatments as countermeasures to chemical, biological, and nuclear attack.

2005 U.S. FDA Drug Safety Board is founded.

2006 Mad cow disease confirmed in Alabama cow as third reported case in the United States.

2006 H5N1 virus, responsible for avian flu, spreads from Asia to Europe. The World Health Organization (WHO) attempts to coordinate multinational disaster and containment plans. Some nations begin to stockpile antiviral drugs.

2006   U.S. Center for Biologics Evaluation and Research (CBER) launches a new Genetic Modification Clinical Research Information System (GeMCRIS)—an Internet database related to human gene transfer trials. The database allows access to information about human gene transfer research.

■ ■ ■

Words To Know

A

Acidic: Having the qualities of an acid, one of which is that it will chemically react with and neutralize metallic oxides.

Acquired immune deficiency syndrome (AIDS): An epidemic disease caused by an infection with the human immunodeficiency virus (HIV).

Acromegaly: A disease caused by the release of excess growth hormone, resulting in excessive growth of some bones.

Adhesive: A substance that causes a physical attraction between different types of molecules; glue.

Adrenal glands: Two glands located next to the kidneys. The adrenal glands produce the hormones epinephrine and norepinephrine and the corticosteroid hormones.

Adult stem cell: A renewable and unspecialized cell found among specialized cells in a tissue or organ.

Aerobic reaction: Chemical reaction that requires oxygen or that take place in the presence of oxygen.

Aerodynamics: The study of forces associated with air moving over airfoil shapes (airplane or bird wings).

Algae: A group of tiny aquatic plants (including seaweed and pond scum) with chlorophyll and colored pigments.

Alkali: A water-soluble material (a material that can be dissolved in water) that comes from ash after plant material or wood is burned.

Allele: Any of two or more alternative forms of a gene that occupy the same location on a chromosome.

Allogenic: Of the same species.

Allograft: Transplanted tissues or organs from donors of the same species.

Alzheimer's disease: A degenerative disease of the central nervous system that generally afflicts elderly people and that can lead to memory loss and death.

Amino acids: Compounds whose molecules are one of the building blocks of a protein.

Ammonia: A chemical composed of molecules containing one nitrogen and three hydrogen atoms.

Amniocentesis: A method of detecting genetic abnormalities in a fetus; in this procedure, amniotic fluid is sampled through a needle placed in the uterus; fetal cells in the amniotic fluid are then analyzed for genetic defects.

Amniotic fluid: The fluid that surrounds the developing fetus in the womb.

Amputate: To cut off a limb or part of the body.

Anabolic: To build the body. Often used to describe a group of hormones sometimes abused by athletes in training to temporarily increase the size of their muscles.

Anaerobic reaction: Chemical reaction that takes place in the absence of oxygen.

Analgesic: A drug that relieves pain without loss of consciousness.

Anaphylactic shock: A violent, sometimes fatal, response to an allergen after initial contact.

Anesthesia: A drug that induces sleep so that an individual can undergo surgery or remain unconscious until a crucial and painful period of a surgical procedure has passed.

Anode: A positively charged electrode.

Antennae: Small sensory projections on the front section of the head of insects and other animals.

Anthrax: A deadly disease caused by anthrax bacteria. Used more often as a biological weapon than any other bacterium or virus.

Antibacterial: A substance that kills or inhibits the growth of germs (bacteria and other microorganisms, but not viruses). Also often a term used to describe a drug used to treat bacterial infections.

Antibiotics: Drugs that target and kill bacteria, but are ineffective against viruses.

Antibodies: Molecules created by the immune system in response to the presence of an antigen (a foreign substance or particle). Antibodies mark foreign microorganisms in the body for destruction by other immune cells.

Anticoagulant: A subtance that prevents blood from clotting.

Antifreeze protein: In nature, antifreeze proteins (AFPs) help animals and plants living in extreme winters cope with extreme cold. AFPs prevent formation of ice crystals so the fluids within an organism do not freeze.

Antifreeze: A substance that lowers the freezing temperature.

Antigen: A molecule, usually a protein, that the body identifies as foreign and toward which it directs an immune response.

Antimicrobial: A material that slows the growth of bacteria or that is able to to kill bacteria. Includes antibiotics (which can be used inside the body) and disinfectants (which can only be used outside the body).

Antioxidant: A chemical compound that has the ability to prevent the oxidation of substances with which it is associated. Oxidation can damage cells.

Apoptosis: Programmed cell death in which a controlled sequence of events (or program) leads to the elimination of cells without releasing harmful substances into the surrounding area. Many types of cell damage can trigger apoptosis, and it also occurs normally during development.

Arrhythmia: Any abnormal rhythm of the heart, which can be too rapid, too slow, or irregular in pace; one of the symptoms of anxiety disorder.

Arthritis: Inflammation of the joints.

Artificial insemination: The process of placing male sperm into the reproductive tract of the female to increase the chances of fertilization. AI is one of the treatments for infertility among humans. With animals, AI is used as a means of producing superior offspring by selecting healthy parents with desired traits.

Artificial intelligence: Devices that attempt to reproduce or exhibit human-like intelligence and behavior.

Artificial selection: Selective breeding, carried out by humans, to produce desired traits in domestic animals and plants.

Aspartame: A low-calorie artificial (synthetic) sweetener.

Atherosclerosis: Abnormal narrowing of the arteries of the body that generally originates from the buildup of fatty plaque on the artery wall.

Atom: Small, indestructible particles, composed of protons, neutrons, and electrons, from which all elements are made.

Autograft: A type of skin graft that uses tissue from another part of the patient's own body, and therefore has cells with the same genes.

Autoimmune disorder: Disorders that are caused by misdirected immune response in which lymphocytes mount an attack against normal body cells.

Autologous: A transfusion or transplant of a patient's own blood, bone marrow, or tissue.

Autologous blood transfusion: A transfusion from a patient's own blood.

B

Bacteria: Microscopic, usually one-celled, organisms whose activities range from the development of disease to fermentation.

Bacterial resistance: Immunity evolved by a certain strain of bacteria to one or more antibiotics.

Bacterium: (Singular of bacteria.) A single-celled microorganism that is often parasitic.

Base pair: Two bases bonded together—either A with T, or C with G—to bridge the two spirals of a DNA molecule, much as a rung connects the two uprights of a ladder.

Base: One of the four chemical letters in the DNA code. There are four kinds, called A, C, G, and T (short for adenine, cytosine, guanine, and thymine).

Batik: A method of dyeing cloth in which areas are covered with substances that keep dyes from penetrating in order to make patterns.

Benign: A growth that does not spread to other parts of the body. Recovery is favorable with treatment.

Bioactive: An artificial material that has an effect on a natural, living organism, cell, or tissue.

Bioballistic method: The shooting of tiny DNA-coated metal bullets into cells as part of the genetic engineering process.

Biochemist: A scientist who studies biochemistry (the study of the molecules and chemical reactions in living things).

Biocompatible: Able to live or exit together. Not harmful or mutually beneficial.

Biodegradable: Able to be broken down by natural processes.

Biodetectors: Devices that can detect biological molecules and substances.

Biodiesel: An environmentally friendly fuel made from a combination of plant and animal fat. It can be safely mixed with petro diesel.

Biodiversity: Literally, "life diversity": the number of different kinds of living things. The more different kinds, the greater the biodiversity.

Bioengineered: The process of using engineering to solve medical problems.

Biofortify: To genetically engineer a crop plant so that it produces more of a certain nutrient, such as iron or a vitamin.

Biogas: Methane produced by rotting excrement or other biological sources. It can be burned as a fuel.

Biological and Toxic Weapons Convention: Treaty dating to the early 1970s that forbids the use of biological weapons.

Biological weapon: A weapon that uses bacteria, viruses, or poisonous substances made by bacteria or viruses.

Biologist: A scientist who studies biology (the science of living things).

Biomass: Any biological material used to produce energy (such as wood by burning).

Biometrics: Computerized identification of persons using traits or behaviors that are unique to each individual.

Biopharming: The practice of growing genetically engineered plants or animals to produce chemicals that can be used as drugs.

Bioprocessing: The use of microorganisms to produce a desired end product.

Bioreactor: A container used for bioprocessing.

Bioremediation: The use of living organisms to help repair environmental damage, such as from an oil spill.

Biorobotics: The use of living organisms to create or modify robots or robotic devices.

Biosafety: The safe handling of bacteria and viruses. Four levels of biosafety are officially defined for laboratories that handle bacteria and viruses.

Biosafety cabinet: A box in which biological laboratory work may be done safely. It either sucks air in to keep germs from escaping, or is completely sealed against the outside air.

Biosynthesis: Production of a chemical compound by a living organism, as in metabolism.

Biotechnology: Any technique that uses parts of living organisms to create or modify products, plants, animals, or microorganisms for specific uses.

Bioterrorism: Terrorism using biological weapons such as bacteria or viruses.

Blastocyst: A cluster of cells resulting from multiple cell divisions after successful fertilization of an ovum by a sperm. This is the developmental form that must implant itself in the uterus to achieve pregnancy.

Bone marrow: A spongy tissue located in the hollow centers of certain bones, such as the skull and hip bones. Bone marrow is the site of blood cell generation.

Bone: Composed primarily of a non-living matrix of calcium salts and a living matrix of collagen fibers, bone is the major component that makes up the human skeleton. Bone produces blood cells and functions as a storage site for elements such as calcium and phosphorus.

Brackish: A mixture of fresh and salt water.

Bradycardia: A heartbeat that is too slow.

Bronchodilators: Drugs, either inhaled or taken orally, that widen lung airways by relaxing the chest muscles.

Bt: Short for *Bacillus thuringiensis*, a kind of bacteria. Genes from Bt bacteria have been added to the DNA of some genetically engineered plants, including corn and cotton, to make them resistant to certain insects.

C

Cadaver: A dead body.

Calcium: An essential macro mineral necessary for bone formation and other metabolic functions.

Calorie: The amount of energy obtained from food. The number of calories needed daily is based on a person's age, gender, weight, and activity level.

Cambium: A layer of actively dividing cells in plants, from which tissues used for conducting water and nutrients are derived.

Carbohydrates: Carbon-containing compounds that form the supporting tissues of plants. Found in abundance in foods made from grains.

Carbon dioxide: A heavy, colorless gas that dissolves in water.

Carbonation: Bubbling in a liquid caused by carbon dioxide.

Cardiac: Having to do with the heart.

Cartilage: A connective tissue found in the knees, tip of the nose, and outside of the ears; it provides flexibility and resilience to these structures.

Catabolic: To break down. The break down of complex molecules into simpler molecules.

Catalyst: Any agent that accelerates a chemical reaction without entering the reaction or being changed by it.

Catalyze: To accelerate a chemical reaction without entering the reaction or being changed by it.

Cathode: A negatively charged electrode.

Cell line: Series of cells descended from each other like the generations of a family.

Cells: The smallest living units of the body which together form tissues.

Cellulose: The main ingredient of plant tissue and fiber.

Cellulosic fermentation: The production of ethanol by the fermentation of cellulose rather than of starches and sugars.

Centers for Disease Control: Department of the U.S. government devoted to understanding and preventing the spread of infectious disease. Often referred to as the CDC.

Ceramic: A hard, brittle substance produced by strongly heating a nonmetallic mineral or clay.

Chemotherapy: Use of powerful drugs to kill cancer cells in the human body.

Chlorophyll: Green pigment in a plant leaf that is involved in the process of photosynthesis.

Cholesterol: A common type of steroid in the body, which is made in the liver. High levels are associated with cardiovascular disease.

Chorionic villus sampling: Testing a sample of cells from the tissue surrounding the embryo. It can be used to determine a child's paternity before he or she is born.

Chromosome: A thread-shaped structure that carries genetic information in cells.

Circumcision: Removal of the foreskin of the penis.

Clinical trial: A government-approved experiment using human volunteers to see if a new drug or other treatment for a disease is safe and effective.

Clone: A cell or organism which contains the identical genetic information of the parent cell or organism.

Cloning: The production of multiple genetically identical cells or organisms.

Clotting: The solidification of blood in response to a wound: coagulation.

Coagulation: The solidifying or clotting of blood. Beneficial when used by the body to seal a wound; harmful if it occurs inside blood vessels.

Cocklebur: A flowering plant whose seeds are produced in a spiny, double-chambered burr.

Coding sequence: A gene that produces a protein when triggered by a promoter gene.

Collagen: A type of protein that makes up connective tissue in the body.

Combination therapy: The use of more than one drug at the same time in treating a disease. Combination therapy is standard in both AIDS and cancer.

Complementary DNA: DNA that is created (transcribed) from an RNA template. This is the reverse of the normal process and so is called reverse transcription.

Compost: A mixture of decaying organic matter, such as manure and leaves, that can be used as fertilizer.

Cortisol: A hormone involved with reducing the damaging nature of stress.

Cosmetic: Preparation or procedure intended for beautifying the body.

C-reactive protein: A protein which is released during inflammation. Used as a measure of risk for heart attack and stroke.

Crop: Agricultural plant grown on a farm. Also: part of an ant's digestive tract that expands to form a sac in which liquid food is stored.

Cross-pollination: Transport of pollen from the flower of one plant to the flower of a different plant of the same species.

Cryonic suspension: Storing or preserving organisms (or parts of organisms) at very low temperatures.

Cryonicists: Scientists who study cryonics, the science of storing or preserving organisms (or parts of organisms) at very low temperatures.

Culture medium: A substance that supports the growth of bacteria so they may be identified.

Curdle: To coagulate milk (create curds) with acidic substances.

Curds: The lumps obtained by the mixing and coagulating milk with acidic substances and then draining off the liquid (whey).

Cushing syndrome: A disorder in which too much of the adrenal hormone, cortisol, is produced; it may be caused by a pituitary or adrenal gland tumor.

Custody: The legal right of a parent to care for and make decisions regarding their child.

Cystic fibrosis: A fatal disease in which a single defective gene prevents the body from making a protein called cystic fibrosis transmembrane conductance regulator.

Cytokine: Molecule produced by cells to control reactions between other cells.

D

Database: A collection of data in a computer.

Dead zone: An area of ocean where nothing can live except bacteria that flourish on fertilizer from agricultural runoff.

Defoliation: Removal of leaves from a tree.

Deforestation: Removal of trees from an area.

Deoxyribonucleic acid (DNA): The double-helix shaped molecule that serves as the carrier of genetic information for humans and most other organisms.

Dermis: The innermost layer of skin. It is made up of connective tissue that gives skin its strength.

Desiccation: The process of removing water; drying out.

Dextrose: A naturally occurring form of glucose. Also one of the two main sugars found in honey.

Diabetes: A disease in which the body cannot make or properly use the hormone insulin.

Dialysis: The mechanical filtering of blood to replace the functioning of kidneys or liver.

Diesel engine: An internal combustion engine that burns diesel oil as fuel.

Differentiate: To become a specialized type of cell.

Diffusion: Random movement of molecules which leads to a net movement of molecules from a region of high concentration to a region of low concentration.

Digital: Information processed as encoded on or off data bits.

Distill: Collecting and condensing the vapor from a boiling solution. Each distinct, volatile chemical compound boils off individually at a specific temperature, so distillation is a way of purifying the volatile compounds in a mixture.

DNA (deoxyribonucleic acid): A double-helix shaped molecule inside cells that holds the genetic information.

DNA polymerase: A chemical that turns a single-sided piece of DNA into a double-sided piece (if nucleotides are available in the solution). Found in nature and used in the polymerase chain reaction (PCR).

DNA sequence: The sequence of base pairs in a DNA molecule.

DNA template: In the polymerase chain reaction used to copy DNA, the DNA template is the piece of DNA that is to be copied.

Drought: A prolonged and abnormal shortage of rain.

E

Ecosystem: A group of organisms and the environment they inhabit.

Elastomer: An organic polymer that has rubber-like, elastic qualities.

Electric field: An invisible physical influence that exerts a force on an electric charge. All electric charges produce electric fields. Magnetic fields that are changing (getting weaker or stronger) also produce electric fields.

Electricity: An electric current produced by the repulsive force produced by electrons of the same charge.

Electrochemical: The study of chemical change involving electricity.

Electrode: A conductor by which electricity enters or leaves.

Electrolyte: A chemical compound that separates into ions (charged particles) in a solution and is then able to conduct electricity.

Electron: A fundamental particle of matter carrying a single unit of negative electrical charge.

Electrophoresis: Separation of nucleic acid or protein molecules in an electric field.

Elements: Pure substances that cannot be changed chemically into a simpler substance.

Embryo: A stage in development after fertilization of an egg by a sperm.

Embryologist: A scientist who studies embryos and their development.

Embryonic stem cell: A stem cell found in embryos about a week old. Descendants of one of these cells can be any kind of tissue. These cells can reproduce indefinitely in the laboratory.

Emissions: The generation of photons of light from an electronically excited atomic or molecular species in order to reduce its total energy.

Encryption: The converting of text into difficult-to-understand code so that it is only readable by specific people.

Enteric: Involving the intestinal tract or relating to the intestines.

Enzymes: Proteins that help control the rate or speed of chemical reactions in the cell.

Epidermis: The outer layer of the skin consisting of dead cells. It is the primary protective barrier against sunlight, chemicals, and other possible harmful agents. The epidermal cells are constantly being shed and replenished.

Epithelium: The layer of cells that covers external and internal surfaces of the body. The many types of epithelium range from flat cells to long cells to cubed cells.

Escherichia coli: *E. coli,* a species of bacteria that live in the intestinal tract and that are often associated with fecal contamination.

Essential acid: Acids that cannot be synthesized by the body and must be obtained from the diet.

Ethanol: A type of alcohol having different forms that can be drunk or used as fuel.

Ethical: Having to do with morality, or what is perceived as being the right thing to do.

Ethics: The study of what is right or wrong.

Ethyl alcohol: A drinkable alcohol, also called ethanol, which is produced by the fermentation of sugar.

Ethylene: A gas used to make tomatoes ripen quickly.

Eugenics: A social movement in which the population of a society, country, or the world is to be improved by controlling the passing on of hereditary information through selective breeding.

Eukaryotes: Cells whose genetic material is carried on chromosomes inside a nucleus encased in a membrane. All organisms except bacteria are eukaryotes.

Evolution: In biology, inheritable changes occurring over a time span greater than one generation.

Ex situ: A Latin term meaning "from the place" or removed from its original place.

Expression (of gene):   In cell biology, to make a protein according to the recipe in a DNA molecule. A gene that is used to make a protein is said to be expressed.

Extraterrestrial: Beyond Earth.

F

Fat substitute: A substance that feels like fat or help foods feel like they contain fat.

Fats: Waxy or oily substances found in many plant and animals tissues. An oil is a fat that is liquid at room temperature.

Fatty acid: An acid made of carbon, hydrogen, and oxygen that is found in body fat.

Feces: Solid waste of a living body.

Feedstock: The source of starting material for a chemical reaction.

Fermentation: The process of breaking down sugar without oxygen into simpler substances, commonly alcohol and carbon dioxide.

Fertilizer: An agricultural chemical that is added to soil to provide nutrients and increase crop productivity.

Fibrin: A protein that functions in the blood-clotting mechanism; forms mesh-like threads that trap red blood cells.

Fibroblast cells: Cells in the dermis layer of the skin that give rise to connective tissue.

Fixative: A substance used to bind dye to a fabric.

Fluorescence: Emission of light at one wavelength in response to light at another wavelength. For example, a substance that glows visibly when exposed to ultraviolet light is fluorescing.

Fossil fuel: A fuel that is derived from the decay of plant or animal life; coal, oil, and natural gas are the fossil fuels.

Fouling: A term to describe the buildup of organisms (plants, algae, small animals, etc.) on a ship's hull, slowing its speed.

Free radical: An unstable particle that can cause damage in cells.

G

Gel electrophoresis: A laboratory test that separates molecules based on their size, shape, or electrical charge.

Gene gun: A device that shoots tiny metal bullets coated with DNA fragments into cells in order to alter their DNA permanently.

Gene therapy: Treating disease by replacing nonfunctional genes or supplying genes that do function properly.

Gene: A discrete unit of inheritance, represented by a portion of DNA located on a chromosome. The gene is a code for the production of a specific kind of protein or RNA molecule, and therefore for a specific inherited characteristic.

Gene use restriction technology (GURT): A form of genetic engineering that allows traits in plants to be turned on or off using chemicals or other means. Terminator technology is a form of GURT.

Genetic discrimination: The denial of rights or privileges to people because of the nature of their genes (DNA).

Genetic disease: An inherited disease.

Genetic disorder: An inherited disorder.

Genetic engineering: The manipulation of genetic material to produce specific results in an organism.

Genetic mutation: A change in the genes caused by a random change in the base sequence. This results in a trait not seen in either parent.

Genetic screening: Examination of a person's genes to see if they contain any tendencies for disease or other defects.

Genetically modified food: A food product that contains a genetically modified plant or animal as an ingredient.

Geneticist: A scientist who studies genes.

Genetics: The science of genes and heredity.

Genome: A complete set of the DNA for a species.

Genotropin: An artificial form of human growth hormone made in a laboratory.

Germ cell: A cell that can pass its DNA on to future generations, including egg and sperm cells.

Germline cells: Cells that can pass their DNA on to future generations, including egg and sperm cells.

Germline gene therapy: The introduction of genes into reproductive cells or embryos to correct inherited genetic defects that can cause disease.

Gigantism: A rare disease caused by the release of too much growth hormone while a child is still developing.

Glass: A ceramic material consisting of a uniformly dispersed mixture of silica, soda ash, and lime; and often combined with metallic oxides.

Global warming: A projected increase in Earth's surface temperature caused by an increase in the concentration of greenhouse gases, which absorb infrared energy emitted by Earth's surface, thereby slowing its rate of cooling.

Glucose: A simple sugar that exists in plant and animal tissues. When it occurs in blood, it is known as blood sugar.

Gluten: A mass of waste protein obtained from wheat or corn that is used as a raw material for producing MSG.

Glycolysis: A set of reactions in living organisms that use sugars and produce ATP, a molecule that provides cellular energy.

Glyphosate: A weed-killing chemical; the world's most-used herbicide.

Golden Rice: A kind of genetically engineered rice that is yellow because it contains substances that the body can use to make vitamin A.

Graft: A transplanted tissue.

Grafting: A method of propagation of woody plants whereby a shoot, known as a scion, is taken from one plant and inserted into a rootstock of another plant. Plants with the desired traits of the scion can be readily and quickly developed.

Gram-negative: Those cells that lose the color of the stain after they are washed with an alcohol solution during the staining process.

Gram-positive: Those cells that retain the color of the stain after they are washed with an alcohol solution during the staining process.

Greenhouse gas: A gas that contributes to the warming of the Earth's atmosphere. Examples include carbon dioxide, HCFCs, CFCs, and HFCs.

Growth hormone deficiency: A condition in which the body makes too little growth hormone.

H

Haplotype: A group of genes that are inherited together by some people.

Heart attack: Blockage of an artery bringing blood to part of the heart. May injure or kill part or all of the heart.

Hematopoietic cell: A cells in the bone marrow that gives rise, by splitting, to all the various kinds of blood cells. *Hemato-* means blood and *-poietic* means making.

Hemodialysis: A method of mechanically cleansing the blood outside of the body, used when an individual is in relative or complete kidney failure, in order to remove various substances which would normally be cleared by the kidneys.

Hemophilia: A genetic disorder in which one or more clotting factors are not released by the platelets; causes severe bleeding from even minor cuts and bruises.

Hepatitis: General inflammation of the liver; may be caused by viral infection or by excessive alcohol consumption.

Herbicide: A chemical substance used to kill weeds or undesirable plants.

HIV: Human immunodeficiency virus, the virus that causes AIDS (acquired immune deficiency syndrome).

Hormone: A chemical messenger produced by the body. Hormones are created by one organ of the body, but they usually carry out functions in other organs or parts of the body.

Horticulturalist: A person whose job it is to grow plants in a garden or greenhouse.

Human Genome Project: The joint project for designed to decode the entire human genome (hereditary information).

Human immunodeficiency virus (HIV): The virus that causes AIDS (acquired human immunodeficiency syndrome).

Human leukocyte antigens (HLA): A type of antigen present on white blood cells; divided into several distinct classes; each individual has one of these distinct classes present on their white blood cells.

Hybridize: When two lengths of a one-sided DNA molecule with mirror-matching codes lock or zip together to form a single piece of two-sided DNA, they are said to hybridize.

Hydrogenation: A chemical reaction in which hydrogen is added to a compound.

Hygroscopic: A compound which has a tendency to absorb water molecules.

Hypertension: High blood pressure.

I

Immune rejection: Immune system rejection of a foreign substance, such as a donated organ.

Immune system: A system in the human body that fights off foreign substances, cells, and tissues in an effort to protect a person from disease.

Immunosensor: Drugs or radiation used to reduce the immune system's ability to function.

Immunosuppression: The act of reducing the efficiency of the immune system.

Immunosuppressive drugs: Medicines that turn off the body's defense (immune) system. They are used to fight organ transplant rejection.

In situ: A Latin term meaning "in place" or in the body or other natural system.

In vitro fertilization: Combining an egg and a sperm in the laboratory to create an embryo that is then implanted in the mother's uterus.

Incinerator: An industrial facility used for the controlled burning of waste materials.

Inflammation: A complex series of events associated with injury or disease that, when combined, serve to isolate, dilute, or destroy the agent responsible and the injured tissue.

Inorganic: Composed of minerals that are not derived from living plants and animals.

Insect resistance: The ability, possessed by some kinds of genetically engineered plants, to make a substance that is poisonous to insects.

Insecticide: A chemical that kills insects. Used in agriculture to kill insects that eat crops.

Insulin: A substance made by the body (or by genetically engineered bacteria) that the body needs to regulate the amount of sugar in the blood.

Insulin-like growth factor: A substance called IGF-1 for short, that is found in milk. More IGF-1 is found in milk from cows treated with recombinant bovine growth hormone and may increase the rate of twin births in women who drink such milk.

Interferon: A chemical messenger (cytokine) that plays a role in immune response.

Ion: An atom or molecule which has acquired electrical charge by either losing electrons (resulting in a positively charged ion) or gaining electrons (resulting in a negatively charged ion).

Iris: Colored portion of the eye.

Irrigation: The transport of water through ditches or pipes to fields to water crops.

J

Joint: A place in the body where bones meet.

K

Keratinocytes: Skin cells that make a protein called keratin, which protects the skin.

L

Lactic acid: A carboxylic acid formed during the metabolism of sugar in muscle cells. A buildup of lactic acid leads to a feeling of fatigue.

Lactobacillus: Bacteria that create lactic acid.

Lamarckism: The belief that acquired characteristics can be inherited, that is, that changes to an organism that happen during its life can be passed on to offspring.

Landfill: An area of land that is used to dispose of solid waste and garbage.

Leaching: The movement of dissolved chemicals with water percolating through soil.

Leaven: Yeast, baking soda, or baking powder that causes bread to rise by producing carbon dioxide gas.

Leukemia: A cancer of the blood-producing cells in bone marrow.

Ligaments: Structures that hold the bones of joints in the proper position.

Lipid: A family of compounds that are oily, fatty, or waxy, and cannot dissolve in water.

Liposome: A sphere composed of lipid, or fats.

Lymphocyte: A cell that functions as part of the lymphatic and immune systems by attacking specific invading substances.

Lymphoma: A cancer of the blood cells that are part of the active immune system.

Lysenkoism: A type of pseudoscience that arose in the Soviet Union in the 1930s and destroyed Soviet biology for decades. Lysenkoists denounced modern evolutionary biology and genetics.

M

Magnetic resonance imaging (MRI) scanners: A machine that uses magnetic fields and computer interpretation to produce images of the body's tissues.

Magnetism: The force that attracts or repels various substance, especially metals, which is due to the motion of electric charges.

Maize: Another word for corn, a cereal grain.

Menopause: The time in a woman's life when the chemical environment of her body changes, resulting in the cessation (stopping) of her menstrual period.

Metabolic: Related to the chemical processes of an organ or organism.

Metabolism: Chemical changes in body tissue that convert nutrients into energy for use by all vital bodily functions.

Metabolize: Any cellular chemical activity that converts nutrients to energy.

Metal: A shiny elemental chemical substance that is a good conductor of heat and electricity, and when polished, a good reflector of light.

Metastasize: The spread of cancer from one part of the body to another.

Methane: A gas resulting from the anaerobic digestion of organic matter by bacteria.

Methanol: An alcohol, used as an antifreeze, fuel, or solvent.

Microarray: A regular grid of spots containing biological molecules or living cells on the surface of a biochip.

Microbe: A microorganism or germ.

Microorganism: A tiny organism, too small to be seen without a microscope, such as a virus or bacterium.

Milling: Chewing and pulverizing hard seed into a powdery texture.

Mineral: A naturally occurring solid substance of nonbiological origin, having definite chemical composition and crystal structure.

Mitochondria: An organelle that specializes in ATP formation, the "powerhouse" of the cell.

Molecule: A chemical combination of atoms, and the smallest amount of a chemical substance.

Monoclonal antibodies: Antibodies produced from a single cell line that are used in medical testing and, increasingly, in the treatment of some cancers.

Monomer: A substance composed of molecules that are capable of joining together to form a polymer.

Mutation: A change in a gene's DNA that is not present in the parents' DNA. Whether a mutation is harmful is determined by the effect on the product for which the gene codes.

N

Nanometer: The distance equal to one-billionth of a meter.

Narcotic: A drug that depresses the central nervous system and is usually addictive.

Nectar: The sweet liquid that flowering plants make to attract insects and small birds, which help to pollinate those plants.

Neuron: A nerve cell. Neurons may be either sensory (involving the senses) or motor (involved in motion).

Neurotransmitters: Biochemical substances that transmit nerve impulses between nerve cells.

Nuclear transfer: Transfer of the central portion of living cells (those that contain a nucleus) that contains the genetic material. Technique used in cloning.

Nucleotide: Molecular unit that is the building block of DNA.

Nucleus: A compartment in the cell which is enclosed by a membrane and which contains cellular genetic information.

Nutrient: A substance that provides nourishment.

O

Oil: Animal or vegetable fat that is liquid at room temperature.

Oleochemicals: Chemicals derived from vegetable oils.

Opium: A natural product of the opium poppy, *Papaver somniferum*. Cutting the immature pods of the plant allows milky liquid to seep out and be collected. Air-dried, this is crude opium.

Organ Procurement and Transplantation Network (OPTN): A program that promotes organ donation and oversees the national distribution of organ transplants.

Organic farming: Farming that uses no artificial chemicals or genetically engineered plants or animals.

Organic materials: Any biomass of plants or animals, living or dead. The most important form of organic matter in soil is dead or decaying.

Organic: A term used to describe molecules containing carbon atoms.

Organism: Any living thing.

Ovaries: Female reproductive organs that contain unfertilized eggs.

Oxidation: A biochemical process which is part of metabolism. It involves the steady but relatively slow release of energy from food molecules for cell activity.

Ozone: A gas made up of three atoms of oxygen. Pale blue in color, it is a pollutant in the lower atmosphere, but essential for the survival of life on Earth's surface when found in the upper atmosphere because it blocks dangerous ultraviolet solar radiation.

P

Parallelism: The performance by a computer of two or more calculations at the same time.

Parkinson's disease: Disease of the nerves that causes the patient to gradually lose control of their muscles. Loss of a chemical in the brain called dopamine causes shaking and muscle stiffness.

Pasteurization: A method for treating milk and other liquids by heating them to a high enough temperature for a long enough period of time to kill or inactivate any microorganisms present in the liquid.

Patent: A grant given by a governmental body that allows a person or company sole rights to make, use or sell a new invention.

Paternity testing: Genetic testing to determine the father of an offspring.

Paternity: The genetic father of an offspring.

Pathogen: A disease-causing agent, such as a bacteria, virus, fungus, etc.

PCR: Polymerase chain reaction. A method of making many copies of a short piece of DNA quickly in a laboratory.

Penicillin: First antibiotic discovered (1928). Initially obtained from mold extracts.

Peritoneal dialysis: An alternative to hemodialysis in cases of kidney failure. Instead of pumping blood out of the body, dialysis fluid is drained into and out of the abdomen to absorb toxins.

Pesticide: A chemical meant to kill plants or insects that hurt crops.

pH: A measurement of the concentration of hydrogen ions in a solution of water. A neutral solution with equivalent amounts of hydrogen and hydroxyl ions has a pH of 7.0 at room temperature. Acidic solutions have a pH of less than 7.0 and basic (alkaline) solutions have a pH of more than 7.0.

Pharmaceutical: A drug, medicine, or vaccine.

Pharmacogenetics: The study of how a person's genetic makeup affects his or her response to medications.

Pharmacogenomics: The study of how human genetic variations affect responses to medications.

Pharmacology: The science of the properties, uses, and effects of drugs.

Phenylketonuria: A genetic disorder in which human body fails to produce the enzyme that breaks down phenylalanine. Accumulation of phenylalanine causes brain damage.

Pheromone: Smell-producing chemical that provides communication between animals.

Phospholipids: A molecule consisting of a phosphate head and two fatty acid chains that dangle from the head; the component of the plasma membrane.

Photosynthesis: Biological conversion of light energy into chemical energy by plants.

Physiologist: A person who studies living plants.

Pituitary gland: In humans, a structure (organ) below the brain that releases human growth hormone.

Plant propagation: The process of spreading plants either artificially or naturally.

Plasma: The liquid part of the blood. Contains clotting elements.

Plasmid: A circular piece of DNA that exists outside of the bacterial chromosome and copies itself independently. Scientists often use bacterial plasmids in genetic engineering to carry genes into other organisms.

Plasticizer: Substances added to plastics to make them flexible. For example, polystyrene by itself is hard and brittle.

Plastics: A group of natural or synthetic polymers that are capable of being softened and molded by heat and pressure; also sometimes used to include other structural materials, films, and fibers.

Platelets: Irregularly shaped disks found in the blood of mammals that aid in clotting the blood.

Pluripotent: Pertaining to a cell that has the capacity to develop into any of the various tissues and organs of the body.

Polio: A disease (poliomyelitis) caused by a virus that can result in muscle weakness, paralysis, or death.

Pollen: Cells of a plant that contain male DNA.

Pollination: Movement of pollen from the male reproductive organ to the female reproductive organ, usually followed by fertilization.

Pollution: An undesired substance that contaminates another system (air, ground, water, etc.).

Polychlorinated biphenyls (PCBs): A compound of biphenyl and chlorine that is considered a hazardous pollutant.

Polymer: A chemical compound formed by the combination of many smaller units.

Polymerase chain reaction (PCR): A method of making many copies of a short piece of DNA quickly in a laboratory.

Polymerizing: The process by which smaller chemical units are linked into a chain to form a polymer.

Polysaccharide: A molecule composed of many glucose subunits arranged in a chain.

Polystyrene: A type of rigid plastic used for making CD jewel cases, disposable cutlery, and other plastic objects that need to be stiff.

Polyunsaturated fat: A fat missing two or more hydrogen atoms from the maximum number that can be bonded to carbon atoms of a compound. These fats can remain liquid at room temperatures.

Predator: An insect or animal that kills and eats other insects or animals.

Preservative: A compound added to food products to ensure they do not spoil.

Primary graft dysfunction: A severe lung injury that occurs in some lung transplant patients.

Primer: In the polymerase chain reaction used to copy DNA, primers are short lengths of DNA that attach to the single-stranded DNA template and tell DNA polymerase where to start copying and where to stop.

Progesterone: Hormone secreted by the female reproductive organs; used in birth control.

Promoter: A gene that makes the cell produce the protein described by a second gene.

Prostaglandin: A fatty acid in the stomach that protects it from ulcerating.

Prosthetic: An artificial replacement for a lost limb or other body part. An artificial leg is a prosthesis, as is a replacement heart valve.

Protein: Complex molecules that cells use to form most of the structures and control chemical reactions within a cell.

Pseudoscience: Any system of beliefs that claims to be scientific but does not follow the scientific method by which scientific knowledge is produced.

Purify: To make something clean by getting rid of any impurities.

R

Radar: A method of detecting distant objects based on the reflection of radio waves from their surfaces.

Radiation: Energy in the form of waves, or particles.

Radioactive: The production of high-energy rays as a result of changes in the atomic structure of matter.

Reagent: A chemical added to a suspect material to produce a known reaction response. If the reaction response is observed as expected, the identity of the material is assumed to be known.

Recombinant bovine growth hormone: Bovine growth hormone made using genetically engineered (recombinant) bacteria. Called rbGH for short. Given to cows to increase milk production.

Recombinant DNA: DNA that is cut using specific enzymes so that a gene or DNA sequence can be inserted.

Recombinant DNA technology: A technique for cutting and splicing together DNA from different sources.

Recombinant proteins: Proteins that are produced when DNA from two different organisms is combined.

Red blood cells: Hemoglobin-containing blood cell that transports oxygen from the lungs to tissues. In the tissues, the red blood cells exchange their oxygen for carbon dioxide, which is brought back to the lungs to be exhaled.

Regeneration: The ability of an organism to reproduce a part of itself completely.

Rejection: An event that occurs when the body's defense (immune) system attacks a transplanted organ.

Rennet: An enzyme extracted from animal stomachs, used to curdle milk while making cheese.

Reproductive cells: Specialized cells capable uniting in the sexual cycle; female gametes are termed egg cells; male gametes may be zoospores or sperm cells.

Resistance: An immunity developed within a species (especially bacteria) via evolution to an antiobiotic or other drug.

Restriction enzyme: A special type of protein that can recognize and cut DNA at certain sequences of bases to help scientists separate out a specific gene.

Restriction length fragment polymorphism (RFLP): A variation in the DNA sequence, identifiable by restriction enzymes.

Retina: An extremely light-sensitive layer of cells at the back part of the eyeball. Images formed by the lens on the retina are carried to the brain by the optic nerve.

Retrovirus: A virus whose genetic material is RNA (ribonucleic acid), not DNA.

RNA: Ribonucleic acid. Used by most cells to copy protein recipes from DNA; in retroviruses, RNA is the primary genetic material.

S

Salinity: The amount of dissolved salts in water.

Sanitization: Cleaning or disinfecting to remove living material, like germs.

Saponifiation: A chemical reaction involving the breakdown of triglycerides to component fatty acids, and the conversion of these acids to soap.

Saturated fat: A fat containing the maximum number of hydrogen atoms that can be bonded to carbon atoms in the compound.

Scanning tunneling microscope: A device that emits a focused beam of electrons to scan the surface of a sample. Secondary electrons released from the sample are used to produce a signal that can, in turn, produce an image.

Scion: The upper or transferred component of a grafted plant.

Sediment: Soil and rock particles that wash off land surfaces and flow with water and gravity toward the sea. On the sea floor, sediment can build up into thick layers. When it compresses under its own weight, sedimentary rock is formed.

Septic tank: An underground tank, usually outside of a home, in which bacteria are used to break down and treat wastewater.

Sequencing: Finding the order of chemical bases in a section of DNA.

Silicone: A controversial substance that has been used in breast and other types of implants. It is classified as a high-risk category material by the FDA.

Single nucleotide polymorphisms (SNPs): Changes to a single nucleotide (A, C, T, or G) in a DNA sequence.

Skin: The largest organ of the body that provides a protective covering for internal structures and helps regulate body temperature.

Smallpox: A deadly viral disease that was eradicated in the 1970s. Today the virus only exists in closely-guarded samples held by the American and Russian governments.

Solvent: A substance (usually liquid) that can dissolve another substance.

Somatic cell gene therapy: The introduction of genes into tissue or cells to treat a genetic related disease in an individual.

Somatic cell: Cells that are part of the body but are not in the germline (able to pass their DNA on to future generations). Any type of cell in the body that is not a sperm or egg cell.

Sonar: SOund Navigation And Ranging. A device utilizing sound waves to determine the range and direction to an underwater object.

Spore-like stem cell: An unspecified cell that remains in a dormant state in the body until they are stimulated to divide and form specialized cells.

Stanol ester: A group of chemical compounds that reduce the amount of low-density lipoprotein (LDL) cholesterol in blood.

Stem cell: An unspecialized cell that can divide to form other types of specialized cells in the body. Stem cells give rise to cells that have specialized form and function such as nerve or muscle cells.

Sterilization: An operation that makes a person unable to have children. Usually this is done by cutting or tying off the tubes that convey eggs or sperm to the sexual organs.

Steroid: A group of organic compounds that belong to the lipid family and that include many important biochemical compounds including the sex hormones, certain vitamins, and cholesterol.

Stimuli: An agent, action, or condition that elicits a response.

Stock: The lower part of a graft, which generally turns into the root system of the resulting plant (also called a rootstock or understock).

Stoichiometry: Deals with determining proportions of elements and compounds in chemical reactions.

Stroke: Blockage of an artery bringing blood to part of the brain. May injure or kill part or all of the brain.

Styrofoam: The brand name for specially treated polystyrene. Commonly used to manufacture packing peanuts and food packaging material.

Substrate: The foundation material on which integrated circuits are built; usually made of silicon.

Surrogate: A female who carries another animal's genetic offspring.

Sustainable agriculture: Agricultural use that meets the needs and aspirations of the present generation, without compromising those of future ones.

Synthetic: Referring to a substance that either reproduces a natural product or that is a unique material not found in nature, and which is produced by means of chemical reactions.

T

Tachycardia: An elevated heart rate due to exercise or some condition such as an anxiety attack.

Technology agreement: A contract signed by a farmer in order to buy seed from a genetic engineering company. The farmer agrees to not use seed harvested from the genetically engineered crop.

Tendons: Strong pieces of tissue that connect muscles to bones.

Terminal: Causing, ending in, or approaching death; fatal.

Thermal cycler: A machine used to precisely heat and cool the mixture used in the PCR (polymerase chain reaction).

Thorax: The area just below the head and neck; the chest.

Three-dimensional: A visual representation in terms of height, width, and depth, as opposed to a "flat" image that represents only height and width.

Tissue engineering: Artificial products that are made from natural biological materials.

Tissue: Groups of cells with a similar function.

Toxic: Something that is poisonous and that can cause illness or death.

Toxin: A poison that is produced by a living organism.

Transfusion: A technique used to replace blood lost during an accident, illness, or surgery.

Transgene: A gene from one organism that is inserted into the genome of another organism.

Transgenic plant: A plant that has successfully incorporated a transferred gene or constructed piece of DNA into its genome.

Transgenic: A genetically engineered animal or plant that contains genes from another species.

Transplantation: Moving cells or tissues from their point of origin in one organism to a secondary site in the same or a different organism.

Triclocarban: A chemical that kills bacteria.

Triclosan: A chemical that kills bacteria. Most antibacterial soaps use this chemical.

Triglyceride: Natural fat in tissue, which comes from animal and plant fats and oils, that is considered dangerous to human health.

Tumor: An uncontrolled growth of tissue, either benign (non-cancerous) or malignant (cancerous).

Turbine: A device consisting of a series of baffles mounted on a wheel around a central shaft used to convert the energy of a moving fluid into the energy of mechanical rotation.

Turing machine: Imaginary general-purpose computer that reads instructions from one infinite tape and writes output symbols on another. Named after its inventor, British mathematician Alan Turing (1912–1954).

U

Udder: The milk-secreting organ of a cow, sheep, or goat.

Ultrasound imaging: Computer-generated images of ultrasonic waves passed into the body.

United Network for Organ Sharing (UNOS): A Richmond, Virginia company that runs the Organ Procurement and Transplantation Network.

Unsaturated fat: Fats found in vegetable oils including canola, peanut, olive, sunflower, safflower, soybean, corn, and cottonseed. Unsaturated fats are healthier than saturated fats.

Uterus: Organ in female mammals in which the embryo and fetus grow to maturity.

V

Vaccine: A product that produces immunity by inducing the body to form antibodies against a particular agent. Usually made from dead or weakened bacteria or viruses. Vaccines cause an immune system response that makes the person immune to (safe from) a certain disease.

Vascular constriction: The muscular contraction or narrowing of blood vessels in response to injury.

Vector: A vehicle that delivers foreign genes to another organism's DNA.

Virus: A very simple microorganism, much smaller than bacteria, that enters and multiplies within cells. Viruses often exchange or transfer their genetic material (DNA or RNA) to cells and can cause diseases such as chickenpox, hepatitis, measles, and mumps.

Vitamin A: A substance found in food (or made by the body from substances found in food) that is needed for metabolism (a body's chemical reactions). Lack of vitamin A can cause blindness.

Vitamin E: Substance that occurs naturally in human beings and is responsible for maintaining youthful skin.

W

Whey: The liquid part of milk that is separated from the curd when making cheese and other products that curdle milk.

White blood cells: Leukocytes. Cells that help fight infection and disease.

Whooping cough: An acute infectious disease caused by *Bordetella pertussis* that causes spasms of coughing and convulsions.

Woad: A blue dye obtained from the woad plant.

Wort: The sugar-water solution made when malted barley is steeped in water and its complex sugars break down into simple sugars.

X

X ray: Electromagnetic radiation of very short wavelength, and very high energy. Used for medical imaging.

Xenograft: Tissues and organs used for transplantation that come from different animal species, like pigs or baboons.

Xenotransplantation: Transplantation of tissue or an organ from one species to another, for example from pig to human.

Y

Yeast: A microorganism of the fungus family that promotes alcoholic fermentation, and is also used as a leavening (agent that makes dough rise) in baking.

Z

Zygote: The cell resulting from the union of the male sperm and the female egg. Normally the zygote has double the chromosome number of either the sperm or egg, and gives rise to a new embryo.

■■■

Antibiotics, Biosynthesized

Description

Antibiotics are drugs that kill bacteria living inside an animal without harming the animal.

Bacteria are single-celled life forms that can be either helpful or harmful. The human body needs many billions of the bacteria called *Escherichia coli* in the intestines to be healthy, but other bacteria, such as *Streptococci pyogenes*, can cause sickness or even death. *Streptococci pyogenes* causes strep throat; other bacteria can cause other diseases.

The word "antibiotic" is often reserved for a drug that kills bacteria. A drug that kills viruses (which are smaller and simpler than bacteria) is called an antiviral, and a drug that kills parasites inside the body is an antiparasitic. Substances that kill bacteria and viruses outside the body, but that would be poisonous inside the body, are called disinfectants, antimicrobials, or antibacterials. For example, ordinary household bleach (sodium hypochlorite) is a disinfectant, but it is not an antibiotic because it cannot be used to kill bacteria inside the body. Bleach is poisonous to people as well as to bacteria.

Most antibiotics are produced by special bacteria or fungi. These bacteria or fungi are grown in large cultures; the substances they produce are then harvested and purified for medical use. Antibiotics produced in this way are called biosynthesized antibiotics. *Bio* means "life" and *synthesize* means "to make," so biosynthesized means made by living things. There are also synthetic antibiotics, which are chemicals made in factories without the help of living things. Most antibiotics are still biosynthesized.

Antibiotics can be either swallowed in pill form or injected directly into the bloodstream using a needle. Direct injection is used only for more serious infections.

Scientific Foundations

Antibiotics kill bacteria without harming other cells by attaching themselves to complex molecules called enzymes. Enzymes, which are found inside bacteria as well as on their outer shell, help chemical reactions to happen in the bacterial cell. Each enzyme participates in a different chemical reaction. By attaching to an enzyme, an antibiotic can stop the enzyme from doing its job. Depending on which enzyme is targeted, the bacterial cell can be affected in several different ways. Its outer shell (cell wall) may break up, for example, or it may be unable to reproduce.

Enzymes can be different in different cells, such as bacteria and body cells, and still do the same job. Antibiotics interfere only with the kinds of enzymes that bacteria use.

Development

In the 1920s, a Scottish biologist named Sir Alexander Fleming (1881–1955) discovered that tears and sweat contain a substance he called lysozyme. Lysozyme slows bacterial growth, but is not strong enough to work as an antibiotic. In 1928, however, Fleming accidentally discovered that a kind of mold called *Penicillium*—which can grow on old bread—produces a substance that kills bacteria. Fleming left some dishes intended to grow bacteria sitting around his laboratory so long that they got moldy. As he was cleaning the dishes he noticed that the mold had killed the bacteria near it on the dish. He isolated the substance that killed the bacteria and called it penicillin, after the type of mold that made it. Penicillin was the first true antibiotic. Since it is made by a mold, it is one of the biosynthesized antibiotics.

It was not until 1940 that researchers at Oxford University in England discovered how to produce enough penicillin for it to be practical as a medicine. During World War II (1939–45), penicillin saved many soldiers' lives by fighting infections in wounds.

Current Issues

Scientists are always looking for new antibiotics because bacteria become resistant or immune to the old ones. Bacteria become resistant because they evolve. Not all bacteria are exactly alike; some of them make slightly different enzymes than others of their kind. In any large group of a certain kind of bacteria, a few individuals are likely, by chance, to have enzymes that are so different that a given antibiotic does not kill them. If the whole population is attacked with an antibiotic, these different, resistant

New, Improved—and Dangerous?

Today, most household hand soaps are labeled "antimicrobial." This means that they contain a substance that kills bacteria. Some scientists worry that subjecting the bacteria in all the kitchens and bathrooms of the country to these antimicrobial chemicals will force them to evolve resistance. "We are creating an environment of bacteria that are resistant to these products," says Dr. Stuart Levy, a researcher at Tufts University, "and they may well be resistant to antibiotics as well . . . . [T]here is an unfortunate mounting rage for antibacterial chemicals added to normal cleansings. And I think that this will create a changed microbiology and very likely, at least in the laboratory, contribute to the propagation of resistant bacteria." Yet other researchers say that there is no sign of such resistance developing because of antimicrobial soaps.

bacteria will survive. The next generation of bacteria will resemble the survivors, so when the population grows again, the same antibiotic will not work.

In the real world, bacterial resistance does not evolve quite so simply. Nevertheless, it does evolve over time, and it is a serious medical problem. A resistant strain of bacteria is often resistant to only one or two antibiotics, and can be treated simply by switching to a different antibiotic. However, a person can be infected by a type of bacteria that has evolved resistance to all known antibiotics. Some strains of the most dangerous bacteria, such as the bacterium that causes tuberculosis, have already evolved resistance to all known antibiotics. Resistant tuberculosis bacteria first appeared in the 1980s. The World Health Organization (WHO, the United Nations agency for health) declared in 1992 that resistant tuberculosis was a world health emergency.

Resistance is also the reason why some scientists question the use of antibiotics in raising animals for food. Antibiotics are fed to cows, chickens, turkeys, and pigs in order to make them grow faster by killing off most of the bacteria in their bodies. About fifty million pounds of antibiotics are produced in the United States every year, and about sixteen million pounds are fed to livestock to make them grow faster. However, many scientists think that dumping so many antibiotics into the environment may be helping antibiotic-resistant strains of bacteria to become more common.

Scientists are constantly looking for new antibiotics to stay one jump ahead of the ever-evolving, disease-causing bacteria of the world. One method of producing new antibiotics is to try to

Words to Know

Antibiotics: Drugs that target and kill bacteria, but are ineffective against viruses.

Antimicrobial: A material that slows the growth of bacteria or that is able to to kill bacteria. Includes antibiotics (which can be used inside the body) and disinfectants (which can only be used outside the body).

Biosynthesis: Production of a chemical compound by a living organism, as in metabolism.

Enzyme: A protein that helps control the rate or speed of chemical reactions in the cell.

Penicillin: First antibiotic discovered (1928). Initially obtained from mold extracts.

Resistance: An immunity developed within a species (especially bacteria) via evolution to an antiobiotic or other drug.

genetically engineer antibiotic-making bacteria—to actually change the bacteria's genes to force them to make new antibiotics. The goal is to create new antibiotics faster than bacteria can evolve resistance to them.

■ ■ ■

For More Information

Levy, Stuart. "The Challenge of Antibiotic Resistance." *Scientific American* 278 (March 1998): 32–39.

Lightman, Alan P. *The Discoveries: Great Breakthroughs in 20th Century Science.* New York: Pantheon Books, 2005.

McManus, Rick. "Feeling Sick? Stay Home! CDC's Gerberding Warns of Anti-Microbial-Resistant Infections." *National Institutes of Health,* March 2, 2004. <http://www.nih.gov/news/NIH-Record/03_02_2004/story01.htm> (accessed June 3, 2006).

Thompson, Kimberly M., and Debra Fulghum Bruce. *Overkill: How Our Nation's Abuse of Antibiotics and Other Germ Killers Is Hurting Your Health and What You Can Do About It.* Emmaus, PA: Rodale, 2002.

[See Also **Vol. 3, Antimicrobial Soaps; Vol. 2, Genetic Engineering; Vol. 1, Penicillins.**]

Anti-Rejection Drugs

Description

Anti-rejection drugs, called immunosuppressants, are used to prevent rejection in someone who has had an organ transplant. This is when doctors take an organ from a donor's body and implant it into a recipient's body, where it replaces a failing organ. Anti-rejection drugs help block the immune system to keep it from rejecting the transplanted organ, but still allow the person's immune system to fight off diseases.

Doctors have known for many years how to transplant organs. The remaining challenge is the immune system, which protects the body by fighting off bacteria and other substances that it sees as foreign. When the immune system detects something as foreign, it sends white blood cells called T-lymphocytes to attack it. The immune system usually considers a transplanted organ as foreign and tries to destroy it. This is called rejection. A person who rejects his or her new organ can become very sick and can even die.

When people start taking anti-rejection drugs, they take them in very high doses. After a few months, the risk of rejection goes down as the body gets used to the new organ. The patient can then take lower doses of the anti-rejection drugs.

Scientific Foundations

Anti-rejection drugs work by blocking the immune response from attacking the new organ. Some anti-rejection drugs limit the number of T-lymphocyte cells, so there are fewer of them to attack the organ. Others slow the production of substances in the body that are used to make T-lymphocyte cells. Steroid drugs such as prednisone reduce the swelling that occurs with an immune response.

This person's arm shows drug-induced photosensitivity from taking cyclosporine. Photosensitivity means that a person is more sensitive to sunlight, and being in the sun caused the redness and blisters on the arm.
Dr. P. Marazzi/Photo Researchers, Inc.

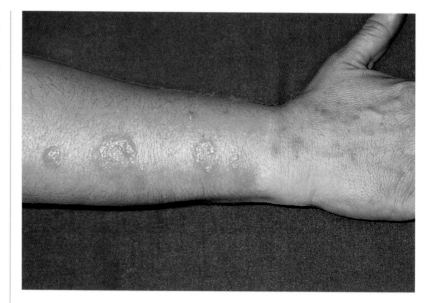

The most common anti-rejection drugs are:
- Cyclosporine—This drug comes from a fungus. It stops the activation of T-lymphocytes to prevent them from attacking the organ. Patients take it once or twice a day. Its side effects include high blood pressure, shaking, kidney or liver damage, and tender gums.
- Prednisone—This drug is a steroid. The body naturally makes steroids. Steroids reduce the swelling that occurs with an immune response. This drug is often used with cyclosporine.
- Tacrolimus—This drug works like cyclosporine. It prevents immune cells from causing rejection. Its side effects include high blood pressure, shaking, headache, and nausea.
- Sirolimus—This drug blocks the action of T-lymphocytes to prevent them from attacking the organ. It is usually combined with prednisone and cyclosporine. Its side effects include upset stomach, infection, shaking, and some kinds of cancer.
- Azathioprine (brand name Imuran)—This drug blocks production of white blood cells that cause rejection. Its side effects include nausea, rash, muscle pain, and infection.
- Mycophenolate mofetil (brand name CellCept)—This drug also holds back the immune system so that it does not reject the new organ. Its side effects include loose stools (diarrhea), lower numbers of white blood cells, blood infection, and other kinds of infections.

Souvenir Soils

Several pharmaceutical companies encourage their employees to collect and bring back soil samples during their vacation travels. Anti-rejection drugs such as drugs cyclosporine and tacrolimus are made from fungi found in soils in different parts of the world.

Development

Doctors have been able to transplant an organ from one person to another since the early 1900s. But in those days, every time they transplanted an organ, the person who received it would reject the organ and eventually die.

In the 1950s, doctors performed the first successful kidney transplant. The patients were identical twins. Because their tissue matched so closely, the risk for rejection was lower.

Once doctors understood the immune response that caused a patient's body to reject the new organ, they tried to use high-energy rays (radiation) all over the patient's body to reduce the rejection. However, radiation is toxic and did not prevent rejection of the transplanted organ.

In the early 1960s, Roy Calne of Peter Bent Brigham Hospital (now Brigham and Women's Hospital) in Boston, Massachusetts, studied drugs that blocked the immune response to prevent rejection. He experimented with a drug called azathioprine. Azathioprine worked well to prevent rejection, especially when combined with prednisone, a steroid drug.

The turning point for organ transplants came in 1983, when the U.S. Food & Drug Administration (FDA) approved cyclosporine as an anti-rejection drug. A Swiss biochemist named Jean-François Borel discovered the drug cyclosporine in 1972. He made this drug from a fungus. Cyclosporine blocked the actions of T-lymphocyte immune cells. It helped stop the immune system from rejecting transplanted organs and improved the survival rate after organ transplants. Doctors found that cyclosporine worked best with prednisone or azathioprine. This allowed more people to have successful organ transplants.

In the 1990s, the FDA approved three new anti-rejection drugs: tacrolimus, sirolimus, and mycophenolate mofetil. These drugs improved transplant survival rates even more.

Words to Know

Bacteria: Microscopic organisms whose activities range from the development of disease to fermentation.

Biochemist: A scientist who studies biochemistry (the study of the molecules and chemical reactions in living things).

Immunosuppressants: Drugs or radiation used to reduce the immune system's ability to function.

Radiation: Energy in the form of waves, or particles.

Rejection: An event that occurs when the body's defense (immune) system attacks a transplanted organ.

Steroid: A group of organic compounds that belong to the lipid family and that include many important biochemical compounds including the sex hormones, certain vitamins, and cholesterol.

Most transplant patients take anti-rejection drugs once or twice a day. Each drug works in a different way and has different side effects. Sometimes people take more than one drug at a time.

Current Issues

Researchers are evaluating several new anti-rejection drugs that are anticipated to work as well as the existing drugs, but with fewer side effects. One of these new drugs is called belatacept. In research studies, belatacept worked as well on kidney transplant patients as cyclosporine.

Other new anti-rejection drugs that are being studied trick the patient's body into not rejecting the new organ. One treatment method involves putting small pieces of tissue from the donor into the patient's body before the organ is transplanted.

Taking anti-rejection drugs in different ways may help them work better. In January 2006, scientists studied lung transplant patients who breathed in (inhaled) cyclosporine instead of swallowing it. The study found that people who inhaled cyclosporine were less likely to reject their new organ than people who took the drug by mouth.

Scientists are also looking at ways to prevent rejection with fewer or no drugs. In the 1990s, doctors discovered that some people could slowly stop taking anti-rejection drugs and still not reject their organ. This is because their immune system eventually accommodates the new organ. Scientists are trying to figure out the best way to safely have people stop taking their anti-rejection drugs.

For More Information

Altman, Lawrence K. "The Ultimate Gift: 50 Years of Organ Transplants." *The New York Times* (December 21, 2004).

"Inhaled Drug Boosts Survival After Lung Transplant." *CBC News* <http://www.cbc.ca/story/science/national/2006/01/11/inhale-transplant2006011.html> Updated January 11, 2006 (accessed March 26, 2006).

McVicar, Nancy. "Scientists Seek Ways to Prevent Organ Transplant Rejections Without Drugs." *South Florida Sun-Sentinel*, August 26, 2002.

National Kidney Foundation "Immunosuppressants." <http://www.kidney.org/atoz/atozltem.cfm?id=77> Updated May 13, 2004 (accessed March 24, 2006).

Rowland, Christopher. "Anti-Rejection Drugs for Transplant Patients Offer Protection, Risks." *The Boston Globe* (February 23, 2004).

[*See Also* **Vol. 1, Organ Transplants.**]

■■■

Arthritis Drugs

Description

Arthritis is the name given to a group of diseases in which the joints located between adjacent bones become stiff and sore. The stiffness and soreness is partially due to a process called inflammation—swelling of tissue that occurs when the body's immune system reacts against a molecule. (The immune system is designed to recognize and attack foreign substances in the body.) The joint pain, swelling, and stiffness of arthritis can make daily life hard. Over time, as inflammation continues, the joint can become less and less capable of movement. One example is the increasing stiffness of fingers that can occur in some people. Even simple tasks like holding a knife and fork can become difficult.

As of 2006 there was no cure for arthritis. However, some drug treatments can lessen the discomfort or slow the progress of some forms of the disease.

Scientific Foundations

Arthritis drugs work in different ways. Some drugs target a molecule of the immune system called a cytokine that directly triggers inflammation. These drugs are designed to attach to the molecule. This stops the molecule from stimulating inflammation.

Other drugs are more indirect in their activity. Instead of binding directly to the target molecule (one that causes inflammation), they stop the target from binding (attaching) to sites on other cells in the body. These binding sites are called receptors. Binding of a target molecule to the receptor can send a signal that starts other reactions that can lead to arthritis. By preventing the binding to the receptor, the signal is prevented from forming, and so the arthritis process is blocked.

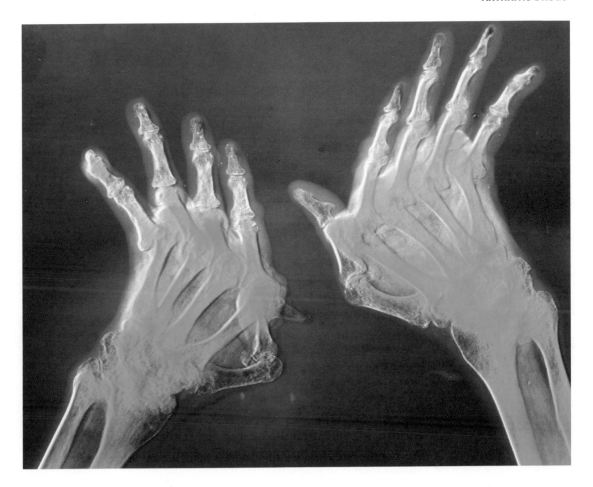

False-color x ray of hands deformed by severe arthritis. © CNRI/Photo Researchers, Inc.

The receptor strategy is a race between the arthritis drug and the target molecule for the receptor site. If there are more drug molecules present, they will be more likely to bind to the receptor and block the binding of the target molecule.

One type of arthritis that has benefited from the use of arthritis drugs is rheumatoid arthritis. This form of arthritis occurs when the body's immune system somehow recognizes components of the body as being foreign, and so attempts to dispose of the invader. The body attacks itself. Over time, this increasingly destroys joints.

Development

Monoclonal antibodies are drugs that have been developed to combat arthritis.

The basis of the monoclonal antibody approach is the antibody. An antibody is a protein produced by a cell called a lymphocyte in

Cytokines and Obesity

The central role played by cytokines in the regulation and function of the immune system may have benefits other than the treatment of arthritis. A cytokine called interleukin-7, which is critical in the maintenance of immune cells, can also prevent obesity in a genetically engineered mouse (where a gene has been altered or replaced) that has a hypothalamus—a part of the brain associated with appetite—that does not work properly. Normally, the mice overeat and gain weight. However, injections of the cytokine produce mice of normal weight. Scientists think that the cytokine binds to the hypothalamus, somehow correcting the appetite-associated defect. Someday, weight-loss plans may include cytokine supplementation.

response to a foreign protein (an antigen). A certain type of lymphocyte produces a certain type of antibody. Since there can be many versions of lymphocytes, a huge variety of antibodies can be generated.

Lymphocytes do not stay alive indefinitely when grown outside the body, making it difficult to produce a lot of antibody for drugs. The discovery of monoclonal antibodies has made it possible to produce specific antibodies in large amounts.

Monoclonal antibodies were developed in 1974 by César Milstein (1927–2002) and Georges Köhler (1946–1995). The scientists discovered that antibody-producing cells called lymphocytes could be combined with cells obtained from tumors. Tumor cells are characterized by their ability to grow indefinitely. The resulting fusion between the lymphocytes and tumor cells produced cells that continuously made a particular type of antibody. By using different lymphocytes, Milstein and Köhler generated many types of antibody-producing cells that lived almost indefinitely. For this discovery the scientists shared part of the 1984 Nobel Prize in Physiology or Medicine.

Monoclonal antibodies to cytokine and various receptors important in arthritis have been developed and tested. Because the basis of the strategy is the recombination of two types of cells (the lymphocytes and the tumor cells), it is referred to as recombination therapy. The results have been encouraging. Assessment of the drugs in animals that develop conditions similar to human arthritis, and in clinical trials that actually test the drug in humans have indicated that the drugs are beneficial and, at least so far, acceptably safe. (There is always a risk from drug therapy, but if the risk is very small and the side effects are not too dangerous, then the use of the drug can be permitted.)

Words to Know

Antibody: A molecule created by the immune system in response to the presence of an antigen (a foreign substance or particle). It marks foreign microorganisms in the body for destruction by other immune cells.

Antigen: A molecule, usually a protein, that the body identifies as foreign and toward which it directs an immune response.

Arthritis: Inflammation of the joints.

Cytokine: Molecules produced by cells to control reactions between other cells.

Immune system: A system in the human body that fights off foreign substances, cells, and tissues in an effort to protect a person from disease.

Lymphocyte: A cell that functions as part of the lymphatic and immune systems by attacking specific invading substances.

Monoclonal antibody: Antibodies produced from a single cell line that are used in medical testing and, increasingly, in the treatment of some cancers.

Current Issues

Despite the optimism of the clinical trial data, issues need to be resolved before such recombinant therapy is routinely used in the treatment of arthritis.

One current issue concerns the long term effects of treatment. Whether the treatments prevent joint damage over time is less clear, for example. This is expected, but still needs to be shown. Also, it must be shown that the treatment itself does not cause any damage when used for a long time.

Another current issue is the potential benefit of the deliberate introduction of receptors into a patient. The reasoning here is that receptors that are floating in solution will bind the cytokine before it can bind to a surface-bound receptor and trigger the problematic immune responses. Much research is still needed to show that this strategy is effective and safe.

■■■

For More Information

Johns Hopkins University. "Rheumatoid Arthritis Treatments." <http://www.hopkins-arthritis.som.jhmi.edu/rheumatoid/rheum_treat.html> (accessed June 30, 2006).

Klooster, Aaron R., and Suzanne M. Bernier. "Tumor Necrosis Factor Alpha and Epidermal Growth Factor Act Additively to Inhibit Gene Expression by Chondrocyte." *Arthritis Research Therapy* 7 (2005): R127–R138.

Maini, R.N., and P.C. Taylor. "Anti-cytokine Therapy for Rheumatoid Arthritis." *Annual Review of Medicine* 51 (2000): 207–229.

Morand, Eric F., Michelle Leech, and Jürgen Berhagen. ''MIF: A New Cytokine Link Between Rheumatoid Arthritis and Atherosclerosis.'' *Nature Reviews Drug Discovery* 5 (2006): 399–410.

Shlotzhauer, Tammi L., James L. McGuire, and Carol M. Ziminski. *Living with Rheumatoid Arthritis*. Baltimroe, MD: Johns Hopkins University Press, 2003.

Van den Berg, Wim, and Pierre Miossec, eds. *Cytokines and Joint Injury (Progress in Inflammation Research)*. New York: Birkhäuser, 2004.

[*See Also* **Vol. 1, Corticosteroids.**]

■ ■ ■

Aspirin

Description

Aspirin is a drug used to treat pain and fever. It is called an anti-inflammatory drug because it also helps reduce swelling (inflammation) following injury.

Aspirin has been sold for more than one hundred years. It is used more than any other pain reliever in the world and is one of the least expensive treatments for arthritis (a disease of the joints usually found in older adults that can make movement painful). Aspirin is also the main ingredient in many combination drugs. According to aspirin makers, Americans take more than eighty billion tablets of aspirin a year.

In addition to being a painkiller, aspirin is a potential life saver. In recent years, scientists have shown that some people who take aspirin during a heart attack have a better chance of surviving. Aspirin is the only over-the-counter painkiller approved for the prevention of some types of heart disease and stroke (the blockage or rupture of a blood vessel in the brain) when taken regularly in small amounts. It is important to talk with a physician before using aspirin to prevent a heart attack or stroke because aspirin can increase chances of internal bleeding (the leaking of blood from blood vessels into spaces in the body) if not used properly.

Scientific Foundations

How aspirin actually worked remained a mystery for a long time. In the 1980s, British scientist John R. Vane (1927–2004) showed how aspirin stops the body from making a chemical called prostaglandin. Prostaglandin, among other functions, can cause tight muscles and contract blood vessels. This sometimes leads to pain and swelling. Prostaglandins are found in swollen tissues and

A bottle of Bayer aspirin from around 1912, when it became the first mass-produced medication to be sold in tablet form. *AP/Wide World Photos.*

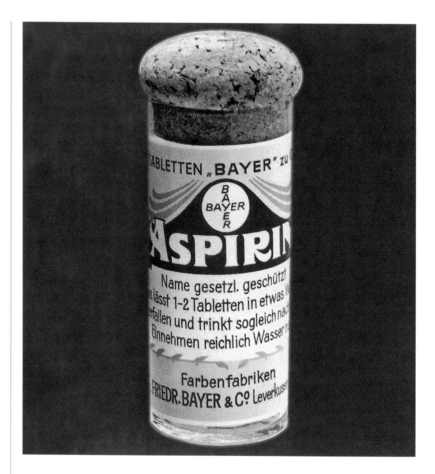

also in platelets, the part of blood that causes clotting. Blocking this chemical creates an analgesic (pain-relieving) and an anticoagulant (blood-thinning) effect. Vane received the 1982 Nobel Prize in Medicine or Physiology for his discovery.

In 1948, a California doctor named Lawrence Craven noticed that men who took aspirin appeared to have fewer heart attacks. He wrote several articles recommending an aspirin a day for men over forty years old, but few people paid attention to his work. Forty years later, the United States Food and Drug Administration (FDA) approved aspirin for reducing the risk of heart attack and some strokes. In the 1990s, the FDA said that taking aspirin during a heart attack could help save a life.

Development

Thousands of years ago the ancient Romans found that chewing the leaves and bark of the willow tree helped people feel better. In the fourth century BCE, the Greek philosopher and physician

Aspirin Is Not For Everyone

As with all drugs, aspirin should be used with caution. Children who have high fevers, chicken pox, or flu should not be given aspirin without the advice of a doctor because it can cause a rare, but serious illness called Reye's syndrome. Pregnant women should not take aspirin in the last three months of their pregnancy unless a doctor approves it. Large doses of aspirin can cause breathing problems, damage the liver, and result in death, especially in young people.

Aspirin can slow the clotting of blood (the action that stops bleeding and forms a scab following a cut). People who take medicines called anticoagulants (medicines taken to reduce blood clotting) should not take aspirin.

People who have had stomach problems should not take aspirin without their doctor's approval because it can irritate the lining of the stomach. Some drug makers sell aspirin covered with a special coating that can reduce stomach pain.

Hippocrates wrote about a white powder taken from the willow tree. The powder helped cure headaches and other aches and pains.

In the early nineteenth century, scientists learned that a chemical called salicin was found in the bark of the willow tree. Salicin is the active ingredient—the chemical responsible for making the medicine work.

Aspirin was originally made from a form of salicin called salicylic acid. This type of aspirin sometimes caused stomachaches, stomach bleeding, and left a bad taste in the mouth.

In 1897 Felix Hoffman (1868–1946), a chemist at Friedrich Bayer & Company in Germany, mixed salicylic acid with some other chemicals. He found a combination developed by French chemist Charles Frederic Gerhardt (1816–1856), made it stable (unchanging and easy to accurately reproduce) and gave it his father, who had arthritis. It relieved the arthritis pain. Hoffman's artificial version of aspirin was called acetylsalicylic acid. This became the first mass-produced drug in history. Nearly 50,000 tons of acetylsalicylic acid is produced every year all over the world for use in various forms and drugs.

In 1899, Friedrich Bayer & Company gave physicians aspirin to give to their patients. Until 1915 people needed a physician's prescription to buy aspirin. The first aspirin came in powder form. Tablets came a year later. Aspirin quickly became the world's leading drug.

By the end of World War I (1915–18), Friedrich Bayer & Company lost the exclusive right to aspirin's formula. Other com-

Words to Know

Analgesic: A compound that relieves pain without loss of consciousness.

Anticoagulant: A subtance that prevents blood from clotting.

Inflammation: A complex series of events associated with injury or disease that, when combined, serve to isolate, dilute, or destroy the agent responsible and the injured tissue.

Prostaglandin: A fatty acid in the stomach that protects it from ulcerating.

panies quickly copied the formula and sold similar products. A United States court ruled that aspirin was a common (generic) name, which meant that the word could be used by anyone.

Current Issues

Researchers are studying whether aspirin can help prevent certain types of cancer. Possible uses include decreasing breast cancer and cancer of the pancreas rates in women and preventing colon cancer from returning after surgery. Researchers with the National Cancer Institute are investigating whether an aspirin-like drug may be a useful addition to drugs treating cancer of the ovaries (female reproductive organs).

Aspirin's role in fighting serious infections is also under investigation. For example, researchers have shown that aspirin reduces the ability of certain germs to cause sepsis, a blood infection that is often responsible for deaths of persons hospitalized in intensive care units.

■ ■ ■

For More Information

The Aspirin Foundation. "Welcome to the Aspirin Foundation of America." <http://www.aspirin.org> (accessed on March 10, 2006).

Bayer. "Aspirin: Medicine of Your Life." <http://www.aspirin.com> (accessed on March 10, 2006).

Jeffreys, Diarmuid. *Aspirin: The Remarkable Story of a Wonder Drug.* New York: Bloomsbury, 2005.

[See Also **Vol. 1, Painkillers.**]

■■■

Biochip

Description

A biochip is a device that has some of the features of a computer chip but, instead of doing calculations, it uses living cells (or molecules from living cells) to greatly speed up certain laboratory tests. A typical biochip is a glass or plastic chip or tile a few inches on a side. It has hundreds or even tens of thousands of microscopic droplets of material stuck to its surface like gum on a sidewalk. A computer looks at the chip using a camera. Information from a biochip can be used to learn about the differences between genes, cells, or drugs. It can also be used to study many other questions about cells. Biochips are also called microarrays, where *micro* means "small" and an array is any regular grid, such as a chessboard. The droplets on a biochip are laid down in a checkerboard pattern. A square chip five inches (thirteen centimeters) on a side may have 40,000 or more spots on its surface.

The most common kind of biochip is the DNA microarray, also called a gene chip or DNA chip. Deoxyribonucleic acid (DNA) is the long, coded molecule used by all living things to pass on traits to offspring. DNA also tells each cell how to make all the molecules it needs to live, like a cookbook containing many recipes. The DNA of almost every living thing is at least slightly different from that of every other.

In one type of DNA chip, genes—short pieces of DNA that code for single molecules—are placed on the chip. Since even large molecules are too small to see with the naked eye, millions of copies of each gene can be placed on a tiny spot on the chip.

Scientific Foundations

There are several kinds of DNA chip. This is a simplified explanation of how one kind of DNA chip works. In a DNA chip,

A biochip device designed for medical applications.
© AFP/Corbis.

each separate spot (also called a probe) contains one type of defective gene. To find out if a person has any of these defective genes in their own DNA, DNA is taken from the person's cells. Copies of the person's DNA are made, and these copies are labeled, meaning that they include a chemical that glows when ultraviolet light (which is invisible to the eye) shines on it. Small drops of liquid containing labeled copies of the person's DNA are then added to the spots on the biochip.

A normal DNA molecule is shaped like a ladder, but the DNA copies being mixed on the biochip are one-sided copies, like a ladder that has been sawed in half lengthwise, cutting every rung in half. When two pieces of one-sided DNA that have matching rungs (or bases, as they are called) meet, they lock or zip together. When this happens, the two pieces of DNA are said to hybridize. If the patient's genes match any of the defective genes that have been put on the biochip, they will attach to (hybridize with) those defective genes.

The chip is then washed to remove any of the person's DNA that has not found a match on the chip. Finally, the chip is placed in ultraviolet light, and a camera records any spots that glow. These are spots where the labeled copies of the person's DNA have matched up with DNA on the chip.

Examining a patient's DNA for defects is called genetic screening. By using a biochip, genetic screening can be done very quickly—all the tests can be done at once, rather than doing hundreds or even thousands of separate tests.

Genetic screening is only one way of using biochips. Another important use for biochips is to study how genes are used by living cells. Each gene tells the cell how to make a certain protein molecule. Cells read the recipe given by the gene by first making another molecule, mRNA, which copies the information in the gene. The mRNA can then go to a place in a cell that will build the molecule that the gene codes for. The more mRNA a cell has for a gene at a particular time, the more it is said to be "expressing" that gene—that is, the more of that particular molecule it is making. Gene expression changes all the time for thousands of genes in every cell.

In the laboratory, scientists can make DNA molecules from the mRNA found in a cell. This matching DNA is called cDNA (complementary DNA). If a biochip has all the genes of an organism dotted on its surface, then cDNA made from the mRNA in a cell can attach to (hybridize with) the genes on the chip. The more a gene is being expressed in the cell, the more cDNA for that gene there will be, and the more that cDNA will stick to the matching genes on the biochip. Spots with more labeled cDNA will glow more brightly under ultraviolet light. In this way, scientists can literally take a snapshot of how the genes in a cell are being expressed at any one time—how much the cell is making, at that moment, of thousands of different substances. This is extremely useful in trying to understand how cancer cells grow and in many other medical problems.

Development

The development of biochips began in the 1990s, when scientists' knowledge of genetics (the science of DNA) and computers made biochips practical. To make a biochip, one must have a way of depositing thousands of microscopic droplets on a surface exactly where they need to go. Ways of handling, multiplying, and reading pieces of DNA are necessary to create biochips, and these techniques were not invented until the 1960s and 1970s.

Early Warning System

Thanks to jet airplanes and global trade in everything from raspberries to beef, viruses can spread more quickly across the world than ever before. Almost every day, the news carries reports of viruses—from the human immunodeficiency virus (HIV, the virus that causes AIDS) to influenza viruses. But it is not always easy to tell which virus is which. They are very small, far smaller than a single cell, and many of them look alike. So British scientists are building a biochip to act as an early-warning system for viruses. They will place pieces of DNA from known viruses on the chip, and add DNA from a virus to be identified. The DNA from the unknown virus will attach to matching DNA on the chip (if any is there). This can quickly show which virus the sample contains.

In 1988, a new company, Affymetrix, decided to combine the methods used to make computer chips with new DNA technologies. Affymetrix's first biochip, a DNA microarray, went on sale in 1996. Today, at least six different companies make a wide variety of biochips.

Current Issues

Biochips are being used today to do DNA screening and to study gene expression in cancer cells, as well as for many other purposes. In 2005, the U.S. Food and Drug Administration approved a biochip test system called the AmpliChip Cytochrome P450 Genotyping Test, made by Roche Molecular Systems, Inc. Cytochrome P450 genes affect how the liver breaks down some drugs. Every person has slightly different P450 genes. The AmpliChip contains different versions of the P450 genes on its surface. DNA from a patient is then added to the chip to see which kinds of P450 genes the patient happens to have. Which P450 genes they have affects how quickly their body breaks down some drugs, including drugs used for depression (sadness that will not go away) and cancer. Patients whose bodies can break down a drug more quickly may need larger drug doses.

Biochips are having an effect on the study of genes almost as great as the effect computer chips had on computing a few decades ago.

■ ■ ■

For More Information

Hall, Julie. "The Microarray Revolution." *Harvard Science Review* (Winter 2002): 82–85.

Schena, Mark. *Microarray Biochip Technology*. Natick, MA: Eaton Pub., 2000.

Words to Know

Acquired immune deficiency syndrome (AIDS): An epidemic disease caused by an infection with the human immunodeficiency virus (HIV).

Deoxyribonucleic acid (DNA): The double-helix shaped molecule that serves as the carrier of genetic information for humans and most organisms.

Expression (of gene): In cell biology, to make a protein according to the recipe in a DNA molecule. A gene that is used to make a protein is said to be expressed.

Genetic screening: Examination of a person's genes to see if they contain any defects.

Human immunodeficiency virus (HIV): The virus that causes AIDS (acquired human immunodeficiency syndrome); HIV stands for human immunodeficiency virus.

Microarray: A regular grid of spots containing biological molecules or living cells on the surface of a biochip.

ScienceDaily. ''DNA Biochip May Lead To Fast Genetic Screening, More Effective Drugs.'' October 19, 2001. <http://www.sciencedaily.com/releases/2001/10/011029073416.htm> (accessed June 3, 2006).

[*See Also* **Vol. 3, Biodetectors; Vol. 1, Bioinformatics; Vol. 3, DNA Computing; Vol. 1, Genetic Testing, Medical.**]

■■■

Bioethics

Description

Ethics are the rules or principles of right and wrong. The word is also used to mean careful, reasoned thinking (philosophy) about right and wrong. "Bio" is Greek for "life," so the word "bioethics" means the philosophy of right and wrong in matters involving living things.

There are several types of bioethics. The most common type is medical ethics, or the study of what choices are wrong or right in the practice of medicine. This type of bioethics dates back to the Hippocratic oath in ancient Greece. This oath says that a doctor promises to do no harm to patients and to behave rightly in other ways. A shortened version of the Hippocratic oath is still taken by people graduating from medical schools around the world. Today, however, medical ethics is more complicated than ever before, because biotechnology has made many new choices possible. For example, is it wrong to change human genetic material in order to cure inherited diseases? What about to make children taller or lighter-skinned? There is deep disagreement in society over these questions and many others like them.

Scientific Foundations

Science explains facts—what exists, or what may happen if certain choices are made. Science does not tell whether the choices we make about facts are right or not. Although philosophers argue about where the sense of right and wrong comes from—whether it is an insight into eternal truth, an illusion, or something else—most scientists, doctors, and philosophers agree that science cannot answer ethical, moral, or religious questions. For example, biology can describe every microscopic detail of a two-day-old human

embryo, but it cannot settle the argument about whether an early-stage human embryo is a full-fledged "person" with legal rights.

Protestor supporting stem cell research in hopes that cures for diseases like her daughter's juvenile diabetes can be found. *Getty Images.*

Development

The Hippocratic Oath was probably written by the Greek physician Hippocrates (pronounced hip-OCK-rah-tees) or one of his students about 2,400 years ago. Several other codes of medical behavior were written in the following centuries. World War II (1939–1945) triggered much thought about medical ethics because of the actions of the Nazi regime, which ruled Germany from 1933 to 1945. Nazi beliefs combined politics, claims about biology, and violence. The Nazis killed medical patients they thought unworthy of life, considered Germans a "master race," sterilized tens of thousands of people whom they thought should not have children, and justified killing Jews and Gypsies on the grounds that those groups were biologically inferior. Doctors were involved in the mass killings at Auschwitz and the other extermination camps run by the Nazis. Nazi doctors also performed experiments on

Considering Deliberate Extinction

Smallpox is a disease that has killed millions of people throughout human history. Smallpox vaccine (a medicine that prevents people from getting smallpox) first became available in the nineteenth century, yet smallpox is thought to have killed several hundred million people in the twentieth century. The United Nations' World Health Organization began a campaign to eradicate (eliminate) smallpox in 1967. By the late 1970s, the goal had been accomplished; the last natural case of smallpox occurred in 1977. However, samples of smallpox virus, the tiny organism that causes the disease, remained in laboratories. In 1978, a photographer was killed by smallpox being handled in a laboratory. Today, the only known stocks of smallpox are held by the Russian government and by the U.S. Centers for Disease Control. The World Health Organization is considering destroying these last known stocks so that smallpox can never threaten human lives again. Others say that to deliberately drive any species to extinction, even a species of virus, would be wrong.

human beings. After the war, doctors, scientists, and others realized that a new way of thinking about the morality of medical behavior was necessary in light of what the Nazis had done.

After World War II, in the United States and elsewhere, however, medical experiments continued to be done on people without their knowledge. Some prisoners and black men were allowed by researchers to suffer diseases after treatments were discovered in order to see what would happen if they were not treated. In 1979, a U.S.-government appointed group issued the famous Belmont Report, which laid down a new framework of rules for medical ethics that is used to this day.

At about the same time, modern genetics, including genetic engineering, was beginning to raise a host of new bioethical questions. These continue to be discussed, becoming more numerous and complicated as genetic technology rapidly presents us with more choices.

Current Issues

Current issues in bioethics include abortion (early termination of a pregnancy), assisted suicide, genetic engineering of plants and animals, possible genetic engineering of human beings, human cloning (making genetic copies of tissues or organisms), animal rights, extreme life support (keeping sick and injured people who

Words to Know

Smallpox: A deadly viral disease that was eradicated in the 1970s. Today the virus only exists in closely-guarded samples held by the American and Russian governments.

Vaccine: A product that produces immunity by inducing the body to form antibodies against a particular agent. Usually made from dead or weakened bacteria or viruses, vaccines cause an immune system response that makes the person immune to (safe from) a certain disease.

Virus: A very simple microorganism, much smaller than bacteria, that enters and multiples within cells. Viruses often exchange or transfer their genetic material (DNA or RNA) to cells and can cause diseases such as chickenpox, hepatitis, measles, and mumps.

have no hope of recovery alive artificially, stem cell research (research into cells that are undifferentiated, that have the potential to develop into other cells), the participation of psychologists in torture or harsh interrogation, contraception (preventing pregnancy), and many more.

■ ■ ■

For More Information

Bioethics.net. "Bioethics for Beginners." <http://www.bioethics.net/articles.php?viewCat=3> (accessed August 31, 2006).

Holland, Stephen. *Bioethics: A Philosophical Introduction*. Cambridge, UK: Polity Press, 2003.

Kuhse, Helga, and Peter Singer. *Bioethics: An Anthology*. Malden, MA: Blackwell Pub., 2006.

Loyola University, Chicago. "American Journal of Bioethics." <http://bioethics.net/> (accessed August 31, 2006).

[See Also **Vol. 3, Animal Research and Testing; Vol. 1, Human Cloning; Vol. 1, Genetic Discrimination; Vol. 2, Genetically Modified Organisms; Vol. 2, Terminator Technology.**]

Bioinformatics

Description

Bioinformatics refers to the storage and analysis of biological information using computers. Once scientists were able to isolate and sequence a particular organism's genetic sequence, there arose a need to store and analyze the information. With bioinformatics, scientists can compare data from the genetic material of a variety of living things, from tiny bacteria to large organisms, such as humans.

Bioinformatics has a number of uses. Collecting and analyzing data from people in different parts of the world gives scientists insight into how humans have evolved over time. Medical researchers can study genetic diseases and try to find effective treatments. Law enforcement officials keep large databases of genetic information obtained from criminals or collected at crime scenes. The information from these databases can be used to identify a victim or perpetrator of a crime.

Computer databases are at the heart of bioinformatics. Once information is stored in an organized way, mathematical formulas called algorithms can be written as part of the software that is used to analyze the data. Algorithms permit searches to be carried out to reveal regions of the genetic material that are similar to one another. In addition, algorithms have been constructed that can search and compare different databases. This was an important development, since different databases are not always compatible with one another.

Scientific Foundations

The genetic material of a cell is stored in the form of molecules of deoxyribonucleic acid (DNA) and ribonucleic acid (RNA), most often in the cell's nucleus. Vast amounts of information can be generated from determining the sequences of an organism's DNA and RNA. Chromo-

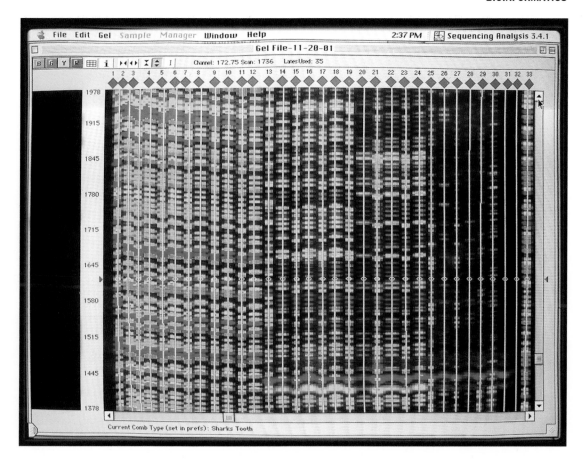

Computer image of DNA from an automated DNA sequencing machine. Once DNA sequences are stored on computers, they can be analyzed using the techniques of bioinformatics. *T. Bannor/ Custom Medical Stock Photo.*

somes are pieces of DNA that pass on traits to offspring. Chromosomes are made of thousands of genes. Each gene is a tiny section of DNA that tells a cell how to do one particular job. Genes tell cells how to produce a certain protein, which are molecules that carry out all the functions of cells.

At the beginning of the 1980s, genetic material could be sequenced, but the process was long and tedious. Then, the sequencing of DNA was automated, which greatly increased the speed of sequencing. By 1989, the first genome sequence of an entire organism, a bacterium called *Haemophilus influenzae*, was published. The following year, the Human Genome Project was begun. The goal of the project—to sequence the complete collection of genes found in a single set of human chromosomes—was achieved in 2001. Since then, the realm of bioinformatics has grown to include the analysis of protein structure, information

Bioinformatics and Privacy

Bioinformatics is valuable tool in basic science, medicine, and law enforcement. However, there is also a concern that the databanks of information on people's genetic make-up could be tampered with or used maliciously. The bioinformatic databases that are maintained by law enforcement agencies, such as the Federal Bureau of Investigation (FBI), have many safeguards and levels of user authorization in place to restrict their use. Nonetheless, computer databases are vulnerable to corruption, and so constant vigilance is necessary to protect the data. The use of bioinformatics by organizations such as insurance companies is also a concern. Disclosure of medically relevant information is allowed in the insurance industry. Critics are worried that health or life insurance might be denied based on a person's DNA profile.

concerning the function of genes and proteins, information on metabolism (the chemical reactions that take place in an organism) and other cell pathways, and data from medical studies.

Development

The need for database-analysis tools became urgent as more and more DNA sequences were unraveled. By the time the Human Genome Project finished its work, the amount of genetic information was enormous, and databases had been created in the United States (GenBank), Europe (EMBL), and elsewhere (DNA Database of Japan) to hold the data and analyze the DNA sequences. In addition, new tools were available to analyze the activity of an organism's genetic material at a given point in time. Chief among these latter techniques are microarrays.

A microarray, or biochip, is an arrangement of genetic material on a solid base, usually glass, plastic, or tile. It can analyze samples of DNA from one chosen subject at a time. The microarray's genetic material acts as a genetic test, and can bind to the sample DNA to reveal certain characteristics about the subject.

One microarray can reveal the activity of hundreds of genes at one time. Thus, tremendous amounts of information can be quickly compiled just for one microorganism. Without the analytical tools of bioinformatics, the information collected from microarrays and in large-scale studies such as the Human Genome Project could not be deciphered and, for all practical purposes, would be useless.

Words to Know

DNA: A double-helix shaped molecule inside cells that carries the genetic information.

DNA sequence: The sequence of base pairs in a DNA molecule.

Gene: A discrete unit of inheritance, represented by a portion of DNA located on a chromosome. The gene is a code for the production of a specific kind of protein or RNA molecule, and therefore for a specific inherited characteristic.

Genome: A complete set of the DNA for a species.

Human Genome Project: The joint project for designed to decode the entire human genome (hereditary information).

Microarray: A regular grid of spots containing biological molecules or living cells on the surface of a biochip.

Protein: Complex molecules that cells use to form most of the structures and control chemical reactions within a cell.

Current Issues

Since the completion of the sequencing of the human genome in 2001, bioinformatic examination of the data has begun. There is a tremendous amount of work to do to, first, identify all of the estimated 30,000 genes contained within the genome; to determine the proteins coded for by the genes; and, ultimately, to determine the structure and function of the proteins.

It is hoped that this level of understanding of the human genome will lead to strategies to correct defects that arise during the construction of proteins that are the basis of many diseases, such as sickle cell anemia, cystic fibrosis, and Alzheimer's disease.

Not only that, the use of microarrays that contain the genes associated with certain diseases and disorders can enable physicians to screen a patient's DNA for defects, a process called genetic screening. By using a microarray, genetic screening can be done very quickly; all the tests can be done at once, rather than doing hundreds or thousands of separate tests.

Bioinformatics has also become an important law enforcement tool. Analysis of DNA collected at the scene of a crime can provide valuable information on the identity of the culprit or victim. A sample of blood, hair, or semen from a crime scene can be quickly and very accurately linked (or not) with a suspect. Newly introduced DNA evidence has also exonerated many prisoners who were imprisoned for crimes they did not commit.

For More Information

Baxevanis, Andreas D., and B. F. Francis Ouellette, eds. *Bioinformatics: A Practical Guide to the Analysis of Genes and Proteins*. 3rd ed. San Francisco: Benjamin Cummings, 2006.

Campbell, A. Malcolm, and Laurie J. Heyer. *Discovering Genomics, Proteomics and Bioinformatics*. 2nd ed. Cold Spring Harbor, NY: Cold Spring Harbor Laboratory Press, 2001.

Claverie, Jean-Michel, and Cedric Notredame. *Bioinformatics for Dummies*. Indianapolis, IN: For Dummies/John Wiley, 2003.

Mount, David W. *Bioinformatics: Sequence and Genome Analysis*. Cold Spring Harbor, NY: Cold Spring Harbor Laboratory Press, 2001.

[*See Also* **Vol. 1, Biochip; Vol. 1, DNA Sequencing; Vol. 1, Gene Banks.**]

■ ■ ■

Blood-Clotting Factors

Description

Clotting, also called coagulation, is what happens when liquid blood turns into a solid (clot). This is life-saving when it stops bleeding from a wound. Blood-clotting factors are substances in the blood that help coagulation happen. There are eleven major clotting factors, numbered using Roman numerals from I to XIII (1 to 13—the numbers III and VI are not used, for historical reasons). There are some unnumbered clotting factors as well, such as von Willebrand factor.

The body's response to bleeding has four basic steps. The first is vascular constriction, which is the muscular tightening or squeezing of the injured blood vessels to reduce the flow of blood. The second is the formation of a temporary plug or clot by platelets, which are small cells in the blood that stick to the fibers in tissue exposed by a wound. The formation of a platelet plug or clot triggers the third step, which is the formation of a longer-lasting clot by a stringy material called fibrin. The fourth step is the removal of the fibrin clot during healing. This is done by a substance in the blood called plasmin.

The third step, the formation of the long-lasting fibrin clot, is the most complicated. It involves a series or cascade of reactions involving the blood-clotting factors. Each blood-clotting factor affects the action of the next factor, like dominoes falling in a row. This series of events is called the clotting cascade. Because some factors later in the clotting cascade also affect the action of factors earlier in the cascade, the cascade is actually more like a network of dominoes falling in a complex pattern that loops back on itself. This article does not discuss the details of the clotting cascade.

How blood clots. When a blood vessel is cut, platelets are activated, which starts a chain of events that produces fibrin and results in the formation of a clot. *Illustration by GGS Inc.*

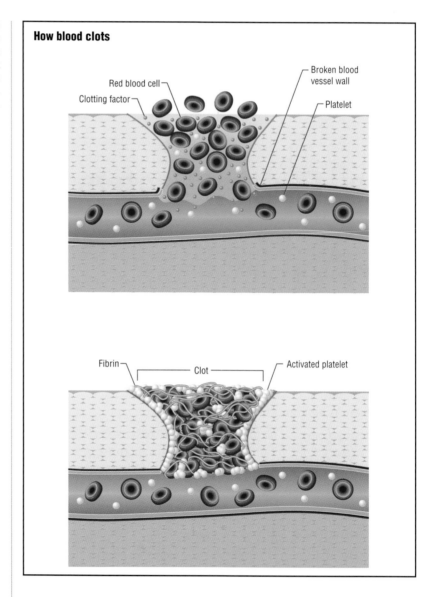

How blood clots

Scientific Foundations

Clotting factors are proteins, a type of large molecule (cluster of atoms) made by cells. Proteins are made by cells by stringing together chains of smaller molecules called amino acids. The order in which a cell chains together amino acids to make a particular protein is set by a recipe or list of instructions in a DNA molecule. DNA (deoxyribonucleic acid) is a long molecule shaped like a twisted tape or ladder; the rungs of this chemical ladder act like letters in a coded message. Three chemical "rungs" in a DNA

Clotting in Court

In 2005, a court case was heard in Pennsylvania, *Kitzmiller versus Dover Area School District*. The case was brought because the Dover board of education had said that high-school biology students must hear an official statement that the theory of evolution is flawed and that students should know about an alternative theory called intelligent design (ID). ID says that life is too complex to be explained naturally. During the trial, a molecular biologist named Michael Behe cited the blood-clotting cascade as evidence for ID because it is, he said, "irreducibly complex"—must have all its parts to work. Other scientists who spoke in court disagreed. The judge sided with scientists who argued against ID, and then ruled against the school district's anti-evolution statement.

molecule specify one amino acid in the recipe for building a protein. DNA is found in almost all cells, with a few exceptions such as platelets and red blood cells, and contains codes for thousands of different proteins. When DNA is damaged or defective, a protein will be made incorrectly or perhaps not at all.

The short sections of DNA (genes) that code for the blood-clotting factors VIII, IX, and XI (eight, nine, and eleven) are damaged in some people. This means that their blood does not clot properly, and it is hard for them to stop bleeding. They may even bleed to death from a small wound. This disorder is called hemophilia (pronounced hee-mo-FEEL-ee-ah), and people who have it are called hemophiliacs.

Development

Scientists did not fully understand blood clotting until the late twentieth century. The function of platelets was identified in 1882. Various blood factors were discovered starting in the early 1900s and continuing through 1963. The use of Roman numerals to name the factors was agreed upon in 1955. Factor XIII was that last to be discovered, in 1963. The ways in which the clotting factors affect each other took many years longer to unravel.

Current Issues

Today, genetic engineering of bacteria is used to make factors VIII and IX to give to hemophiliacs so that their blood will clot normally. These manufactured factors are called "recombinant" factors because genes from human beings are recombined with the genes in non-human cells in order to produce cells that will produce the factors.

Words to Know

Clotting: The solidification of blood in response to a wound: coagulation.

Coagulation: The solidifying or clotting of blood. Beneficial when used by the body to seal a wound; harmful if it occurs inside blood vessels.

Fibrin: A protein that functions in the blood-clotting mechanism; forms mesh-like threads that trap red blood cells.

Hemophilia: A genetic disorder in which one or more clotting factors are not released by the platelets; causes severe bleeding from even minor cuts and bruises.

Platelet: A piece of a cell that contains clotting factors.

Vascular constriction: The muscular contraction or narrowing of blood vessels in respond to injury.

To make a recombinant clotting factor, the gene in human DNA that tells cells how to make that factor is isolated. Then it is inserted into cells from hamster kidneys or ovaries (female sex organs). These cells are grown in culture (in laboratory dishes) in large numbers. The cells make the clotting factor according to the human DNA recipe that has been given to them. The factor is separated from the cell culture and purified.

Factor VIII is unstable—that is, it does not last long in storage or in the body. Research is under way to find ways of making recombinant factor VIII that is more stable. They are also seeking ways to make it more cheaply and to change it so that it does not trigger the immune systems of some hemophiliacs.

■ ■ ■

For More Information

Brewer, D. B. "Max Schultze (1865), G. Bizzozero (1882) and the Discovery of the Platelet." *British Journal of Haematology* 133 (2006): 251–258.

Canadian Hemophilia Society. "Genetically Engineered Factor Concentrates." 1999. <http://www.hemophilia.ca/en/3.5.2.php> (accessed September 6, 2006).

Colman, Robert W., ed. *Hemostasis and Thrombosis: Basic Principles and Clinical Practice.* Philadelphia: Lippincott, 1994.

[*See Also* **Vol. 1, Insulin, Recombinant Human; Vol. 2, Recombinant DNA technology.**]

■ ■ ■

Blood Transfusions

Description

A blood transfusion is a medical procedure in which blood or parts of blood are put into a person's body. A tiny tube is placed into a vein, and the new (transfused) blood flows through it. A blood transfusion can take several hours, depending on how much blood a patient needs. Transfusions are usually given when an injury, accident, sickness, or surgery causes a person to lose too much blood. People who receive cancer-killing drugs (chemotherapy) or who have certain blood diseases may need ongoing blood transfusions.

The blood used for transfusions comes from people who volunteer to donate their blood. Each year more than eight million people volunteer to give blood. Some people donate their own blood before surgery. A transfusion that uses a person's own donated blood is called an autologous blood transfusion. If a transfusion uses blood donated from someone other than the patient, it is called an allogeneic transfusion.

Scientific Foundations

Blood is grouped into four different types: A, B, AB, and O. Physicians try to match the blood in a transfusion to the patient's specific blood type. It is very important that the type of blood used in the transfusion works with the patient's own blood type. Dangerous side effects can occur if a person gets the wrong type of blood. People with AB blood can safely receive any other type of blood. These people are called universal recipients. Type O blood is considered safe for anyone, and is often used in emergencies. People who have type O blood are called universal donors.

Shelves of donated blood at a blood bank. © *Martin Schutt/dpa/Corbis.*

Blood can be broken down into many parts. The three parts of blood most often used for transfusions are red blood cells, plasma (a yellow, watery liquid that holds cells), and platelets (sticky cells that form clots to help stop bleeding). A transfusion may use only one of these parts, or it may be a whole blood transfusion using all of them.

Development

The earliest blood transfusion took place in the mid-1600s, a few years after English physician William Harvey (1578–1657) discovered how blood flowed through the body. In 1665, English physician Richard Lower (1631–1691) discovered that giving dogs blood from other dogs helped keep them alive.

More than a hundred years later, American physician Philip Syng Physick (1768–1837) completed the first human-to-human blood transfusion, but he never published the details of his work. British obstetrician James Blundell (1791–1878) is usually credited

Monitoring Blood Banks

In 1947, the American Association of Blood Banks (AABB) was formed to give the public and physicians more information about blood donation. In 1953, the group set up a national clearinghouse that supervised the exchange of blood between blood banks.

Today the central clearinghouse is called the National Blood Exchange. In 1957, the AABB formed a committee to create and monitor rules for blood banking. The first rule book, *Standards for a Blood Transfusion Service*, was published a year later in 1958.

with reporting the first human blood transfusion. In 1818, Dr. Blundell gave blood to a patient who was bleeding heavily after giving birth, using blood from her husband. Over the next several years, Dr. Blundell did ten more blood transfusions, and five of them helped his patients.

Various transfusion experiments occurred throughout the late 1880s. One physician tried to use germ-killing chemicals (antiseptics) to prevent transfusion-related infections. Others looked for a substitute for blood, and gave transfusions using milk or salt water (saline). These experimental blood transfusions caused many deaths.

Blood transfusions became much safer in 1900, when Austrian physician Karl Landsteiner (1868–1943) discovered that not all blood was the same. He grouped blood into three groups: types A, B, and C. (Type C was later renamed type O.) Dr. Landsteiner's research won him the Nobel Prize for Medicine or Physiology in 1930. Blood type AB was discovered two years later by researchers Alfred von Decastello (1872–) and Adriano Sturli (1873–1964).

In the early 1900s, researchers found ways to store donated blood for several days after collection. The first official blood bank was started in 1932 in a hospital in Leningrad, Russia. Five years later, Bernard Fantus set up the first United States hospital blood bank at Cook County Hospital in Chicago, Illinois. In 1940, the United States government established a nationwide blood collection program with the American Red Cross. By the end of World War II in 1945, the American Red Cross had collected thirteen million units of blood.

As transfusions became more popular, scientists wondered if certain diseases could spread through the blood. In 1943, American physician Paul Bruce Beeson (1908–) found that a person had caught

Words to Know

Acquired immune deficiency syndrome (AIDS): An epidemic disease caused by an infection with the human immunodeficiency virus (HIV).

Autologous blood transfusion: A transfusion a patient's own blood.

Hemophilia: A genetic disorder in which one or more clotting factors are not released by the platelets; causes severe bleeding from even minor cuts and bruises.

Hepatitis: General inflammation of the liver; may be caused by viral infection or by excessive alcohol consumption.

Human immunodeficiency virus (HIV): The virus that causes AIDS (acquired human immunodeficiency syndrome), an epidemic disease.

Plasma: The liquid part of the blood. Contains clotting elements.

Platelets: Irregularly shaped disks found in the blood of mammals that aid in clotting the blood.

hepatitis (infection of the liver) through a blood transfusion. In 1984, the human immunodeficiency virus (HIV) was discovered to cause acquired immune deficiency syndrome (AIDS), an incurable disease that affects the body's defense system. In 2002, researchers learned that West Nile virus could spread through transfusions. West Nile virus is caught through a mosquito bite. It can cause flu–like symptoms and, in severe cases, brain swelling (encephalitis). All these discoveries initiated the implementation of new tests to screen blood for disease-causing viruses.

Current Issues

A major concern regarding blood transfusion is whether the recipient will catch a disease from the donated blood. Advanced screening tests have dramatically reduced this risk. People who wish to donate blood must pass a strict screening exam. Only healthy people over age seventeen are allowed to give blood. The donated blood is then put through a number of different screening tests to check for diseases, bacteria, and other dangerous substances. Modern surgeries use fewer blood transfusions than operations performed several years ago, and there are new drugs to reduce the need for ongoing transfusions.

The most common transfusion reaction is a life-threatening event called a hemolytic transfusion reaction. This reaction occurs if the patient is given the wrong type of blood, and it causes the body to kill red blood cells. Hemolytic transfusion reactions are the most common causes of transfusion-related deaths.

In some cases, a blood transfusion may cause the body's defense system to continually produce a large number of inflammation-causing substances. This can lead to organ failure.

Blood is a valuable substance. Despite the number of blood donors, blood shortages often occur. Blood banks need a large supply of blood, so there is plenty on hand if a large number of people become sick at once time.

■ ■ ■

For More Information

American Association of Blood Banks. <http://www.aabb.org/content> (accessed on April 17, 2006).

American Red Cross. <http://www.redcross.org/> (accessed on April 17, 2006).

Blood Transfusions: Knowing Your Options. <http://www.bloodtransfusion.com/> (accessed on April 15 2006).

[*See Also* **Vol. 1, Blood-Clotting Factors.**]

Bone Marrow Transplant

Description

Bone marrow is the spongy tissue inside bones. The marrow contains special cells called stem cells. Stem cells make three kinds of blood cells: white blood cells to fight infection, red blood cells to carry oxygen, and platelets to help the blood clot (stop bleeding). A bone marrow transplant replaces damaged bone marrow with healthy marrow that can produce blood cells.

Bone marrow transplants are often used as medical treatments for people who have cancer. Some cancers treated with a bone marrow transplant are leukemia (a cancer that begins in the bone marrow), lymphoma (a cancer of the immune system cells), and multiple myeloma (a cancer that begins in white blood cells).

Cancer occurs when cells divide too quickly. These cells can, over time, damage organs. To treat cancer, doctors use anticancer drugs called chemotherapy, or high-energy rays called radiation. These treatments destroy cells that divide too quickly. Bone marrow cells divide quickly, so they can also be destroyed by these treatments. Without bone marrow, the body cannot make enough blood cells to fight infection, carry oxygen to tissues, and help blood clot.

Scientific Foundations

There are three types of bone marrow transplants:

- Syngeneic—When a person receives bone marrow from his or her identical twin.
- Allogeneic—When a person receives bone marrow from a parent, brother or sister, or from an unrelated donor.

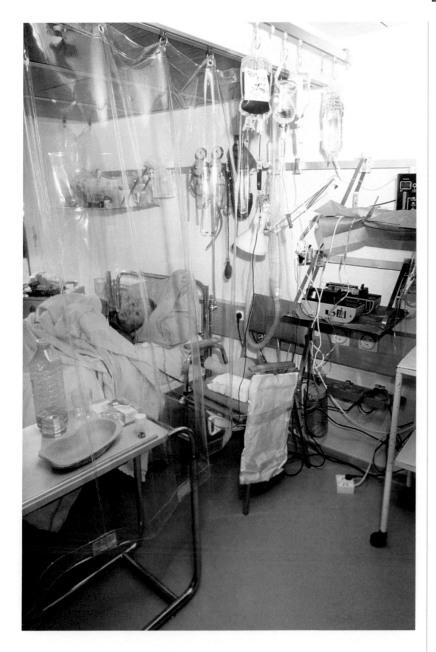

Sterile hospital room of a patient who had a bone marrow transplant. Transplant recipients are extremely vulnerable to infection following the surgery. © *Custom Medical Stock Photo, Inc.*

- Autologous—When a person receives his or her own bone marrow. The bone marrow is collected before the person has chemotherapy or radiation. It is frozen until the person is finished with treatment.

Bone marrow is removed from the donor through a process called harvesting. The donor gets medicine called anesthesia that

Donating Bone Marrow

Healthy individuals between the ages of eighteen and sixty can join the National Marrow Donor Program (NMDP). The NMDP maintains a list of donors and resources necessary to help doctors match them with patients who need a bone marrow transplant.

Two different types of bone marrow donations are collected. The first is a marrow donation that removes marrow from the donor's hip bone. This is a surgi-cal procedure. The second type of dona-tion collects peripheral (circulating) blood cells (PBSC). This procedure involves inserting a needle into the donor's arm and removing their blood, passing it through a machine that takes out the PBSC and returns the remaining blood back into the donor's other arm. In both types of collection, the donor's marrow and blood supply usually return to normal in a few weeks.

prevents him or her from feeling any pain. Bone marrow is removed from the donor's bone through a needle. Doctors usually take the bone marrow from the donor's hip bone.

To transplant the bone marrow, the doctor first removes the damaged bone marrow from the patient. Then, the doctor puts a needle into the patient's vein to put the new bone marrow into the person's blood. The healthy bone marrow travels to the holes inside the bones. Once there, it will start making white blood cells, red blood cells, and platelets. It can take as long as a year or two for the new bone marrow to be able to fully produce new blood cells.

Development

In the 1950s, scientists began to notice that the chemotherapy and radiation used to treat patients with cancer damaged bone marrow. Scientists thought it might be possible to treat this damage by giving the patients healthy bone marrow from another person.

The first human bone marrow transplants were done in France during the 1950s. The patients had been exposed to high levels of radiation. The bone marrow transplants did not work because the patients' bodies rejected the foreign bone marrow.

Successful bone marrow transplants were not possible until 1958, when a French doctor named Jean Dausset made an important dis-covery about the human immune system. He described substances in the body called human leukocyte antigens (HLA). Dausset found that the immune system uses HLAs to identify cells that belong in the body and stop the immune system from attacking them.

Words to Know

Allogeneic: Of the same species.

Anesthesia: Inducing sleep so that an individual can undergo surgery or remain unconscious until a crucial and painful period of a surgical procedure has passed.

Autologous: A transfusion or transplant of a patient's own blood, bone marrow or tissue.

Bone marrow: A spongy tissue located in the hollow centers of certain bones, such as the skull and hip bones. Bone marrow is the site of blood cell generation.

Chemotherapy: The use of chemicals to kill dangerous cells in order to treat diseases, infections, and other disorders such as cancer.

Human leukocyte antigens (HLA): A type of antigen present on white blood cells; divided into several distinct classes; each individual has one of these distinct classes present on their white blood cells.

Leukemia: A cancer of the blood-producing cells in bone marrow.

Lymphoma: A cancer of the blood cells that are part of the active immune system.

Platelets: Irregularly shaped disks found in the blood of mammals that aid in clotting the blood.

Radiation: Energy in the form of waves, or particles.

Red blood cells: Hemoglobin-containing blood cell that transports oxygen from the lungs to tissues. In the tissues, the red blood cells exchange their oxygen for carbon dioxide, which is brought back to the lungs to be exhaled.

Rejection: An event that occurs when the body'ss defense (immune) system attacks a transplanted organ.

White blood cells: Leukocytes. Cells that help fight infection and disease.

Doctors now take a blood sample from the donor and the recipient to check whether the their HLA antigens match before doing a bone marrow transplant. This reduces the chance that the recipient's body will reject the new bone marrow. An identical twin or close relative is most likely to be a close match.

Initially, doctors could only perform bone marrow transplants on identical twins because twins are the closest genetic match. The first successful bone marrow transplant not done on identical twins was in 1968. A child with a severe immune system disease received bone marrow from his sister.

Doctor Edward Donnall Thomas of the Fred Hutchison Cancer Research Center in Seattle, Washington, helped develop the bone marrow transplant as a treatment for leukemia. He was the first to successfully transplant bone marrow from one unrelated person to another. Thomas won the Nobel Prize in 1990 for his work.

In 1984, Congress passed the National Organ Transplant Act. It helped set up a national list, called a registry, of donors. This registry has helped people who need a bone marrow transplant find a well-matched donor.

Current Issues

One problem doctors need to overcome when doing bone marrow transplants is graft-versus-host disease (GVHD). This happens when white blood cells in the donor's marrow see the cells inside the recipient's body as foreign and attack them. GVHD can damage the patient's liver, intestines, and skin. Sometimes, doctors give the patient drugs to suppress, or hold back, the immune system before the bone marrow transplant to prevent GVHD.

A new transplant method uses a smaller amount of bone marrow from the donor. It is called the mini-transplant. The patient is given lower doses of radiation and chemotherapy to destroy only some of their bone marrow. Cells from both the donor and the patient work together in the patient's body to destroy the cancer.

■ ■ ■

For More Information

National Cancer Institute. "Bone Marrow Transplantation and Peripheral Blood Stem Cell Transplantation: Questions and Answers." <http://www.cancer.gov/cancertopics/factsheet/Therapy/bone-marrow-transplant> (accessed on March 27, 2006).

National Marrow Donor Program. "History of Marrow and Blood Cell Transplants."<http://www.marrow.org/NMDP/history_of_transplants.html> (accessed on March 27, 2006).

Stewart, Susan K. *Bone Marrow Transplants: A Book of Basics*. Illinois: Bmt Newsletter, 1995.

[See Also **Vol. 1, Anti-Rejection Drugs; Vol. 1, Cancer Drugs; Vol. 1, Chemotherapy Drugs.**]

Bone Substitutes

Description

Bone substitutes are materials that mimic or imitate the natural composition of bone. They are used in the medical repair of an injury or defect in bone. The bone substitute must be similar in structure and function to natural bone, so that the introduced material will not break down within the body.

Injuries, such as a broken bone that does not fully heal or bone loss due to cancer, can require surgical intervention. In many cases, natural bone can be taken from another site in the patient's body or from the skeleton of a cadaver (dead body) and reused at the site of the problem. These procedures are called autografting (AW-toe-graft-ing) and allografting (AL-o-graft-ing), respectively. However, these options may not always be available. Then, in approximately one percent of cases, an artificial bone substitute can be used.

Scientific Foundations

Bone substitutes can be made of metal, plastic, gypsum, calcium sulfate, collagen (the most prevalent protein in bone), and ceramics (a nonmetallic material such as clay that has been heat-treated to make it very hard and resistant to corrosion). While these provide suitable material, they can be brittle and prone to breakage, are unable to grow if the rest of the skeleton increases in size, and cannot change their shape if excess force is applied to them.

Because of these disadvantages, a field of science called bone tissue engineering came into being. Scientists working in this field try to blend biology and engineering principles to create living substitutes for natural bone. Cells that are the precursor to bone

Scientist preparing a liquid form of bioactive glass. This specialized material is used as a substrate, a kind of miniature scaffolding for growing human bone cells. *James King-Holmes/Photo Researchers Inc.*

are taken from the patient or obtained from another source. These cells are mixed with molecules that function in bone formation. The mixture is added to a three-dimensional support. Examples of support material include mixtures of metals, such as titanium alloy and chromium-cobalt. Some supports degrade over time, as the bone forms around it. Ultimately, the new bone is implanted into the patient.

The subsequent incorporation of the implanted bone into the adjacent bones is aided by some of the traditional bone substitutes. The best example is collagen, which enhances the fusion of the graft with existing bone.

The creation of bone substitutes used in dental implants has been aided by biologic modifiers—substances that change the activity of cells involved in forming the substitute material. One modifier is calcium carbonate, which is obtained from coral. Indeed, the structure of coral is similar to the structure of bone, with open regions interspersed in the web-like interconnections. Another modifier is the non-carbon material recovered from cattle bones. Other modifiers are synthetic (artificial); examples include

The Coming Explosion in Bone Replacement Surgery

As the people in developed countries like the United States, Japan, and France, get older, bone and joint problems are increasing, according to the World Health Organization (WHO). WHO, with the support of the United Nations, has declared 2000-2010 as the Bone and Joint Decade. Currently, bone-related joint diseases account for about 50 percent of all long-term health concerns in people over sixty-five years of age, and 40 percent of women above fifty years of age suffer a bone fracture. Currently, there are approximately 2.2 million bone transplants performed every year. As the population continues to age, the prevalence of bone-related problems will increase, along with the costs of treating them.

glass-like materials and a compound called methylmethacrylate (METH-ill-meth-ACK-rill-ate). Methylmethacrylate is particularly useful as a bridging compound between two regions of bone, serving to connect the regions together. Other modifiers exist and new ones continue to be developed.

Development

Medical researchers are attempting to better understand the process of bone formation, which is complex and influenced by a variety of genetic and external environmental factors. The aim is to speed up the formation of bone on the supporting material and to ensure that the developing bone continues to be well-supplied with blood. Currently, maintaining a blood supply is a problem.

One area of this type of research involves trying to create bone in laboratory conditions using stem cells. Stem cells are cells found in the bone marrow and other locations in the bodies of embryos and adults that have the potential to form any kind of tissue. (Bone marrow is soft tissue inside bones where blood cells are made.) If successful, this approach could allow large quantities of bone to be made and available for the thousands of bone repair surgeries performed every year in the United States.

New bone substitute materials also are being developed. The aim is to minimize the body's immune response to the implanted material and so lessen the possibility of rejection. (Rejection happens when the immune reaction is so strong that the new tissues or materials must be removed.) One example of these new materials is a paste made of bone morphogenetic proteins—glycoproteins

Words to Know

Bone: The major component that makes up the human skeleton. Bone produces blood cells and functions as a storage site for elements such as calcium and phosphorus.

Calcium: An essential macro mineral necessary for bone formation and other metabolic functions.

Collagen: A type of protein that comprises connective tissue; infiltrates the liver in cirrhosis.

Graft: A transplanted tissue.

Joint: A place of movement where bones meet.

Lipid: A family of biochemical compounds that are oily, fatty, or waxy and cannot dissolve in water.

Protein: Complex molecules that cells use to form most of the structures and control chemical reactions within a cell.

Stem cell: An unspecialized cell that can divide to form other types of specialized cells in the body. Stem cells give rise to cells that have specialized form and function such as nerve or muscle cells.

(GLI-ko-PRO-teenz) that naturally function in bone formation. When surgically implanted, the paste can help heal a broken bone.

Current Issues

A major issue concerning modern-day bone substitutes is the creation of substitutes that essentially mimic real bone. One approach seeks to create the substitute outside the body, and then implant the engineered bone inside the body. Another approach tries to bring about the construction of new bone inside the body by supplying genes that are essential in the process. Certain viruses are useful to introduce genes into other cells; this ability could be used to deliver genes that are crucial to bone formation to the site of injury. Genes may also be delivered inside a lipid vesicle—a sphere whose exterior is made of lipid. Fusion of the lipid vesicle (VES-ik-ul) with the lipid of a host cell causes the genes inside the vesicle to be released and, hopefully, to be incorporated into the cells' genetic material. Lipids are organic compounds, like fats and oils, that can't be dissolved in water.

■ ■ ■

For More Information

Carnegie Mellon University. "The Need for Bone Substitutes." <http://www.btec.cmu.edu/reFramed/tutorial/mainLayoutTutorial.html> (accessed July 3, 2006).

Gunzberg, R., ed., et al. *The Use of Bone Substitutes in Spine Surgery: A State of the Art Review*. New York: Springer, 2001.

Laurencin, Cato T., ed. *Bone Graft Substitutes*. West Conshohocken, PA: ASTM International, 2003.

Nather, Aziz, ed. *Bone Grafts and Bone Substitutes: Basic Science and Clinical Applications*. Hackensack, NJ: World Scientific Publishing Company, 2005.

Parikh, S. N. "Bone Graft Substitutes: Past, Present, Future." *Journal of Postgraduate Medicine* 48 (2002): 142–148.

U.S. Bone and Joint Decade Homepage. <http://www.usbjd.org/> (accessed July 3, 2006).

[*See Also* **Vol. 1, Bone Marrow Transplant; Vol. 1, Collagen Replacement; Vol. 1, Insulin, Recombinant Human; Vol. 1, Skin Substitutes.**]

■■■

Botox

Description

Botox® is a pure form of the botulism toxin called *Clostridium botulinum* type A. Physicians use it in very small amounts to relax muscle contractions for neurological disorders, such as cerebral palsy, and other disorders with muscle contractions (in which muscles tighten uncontrollably). Originally, it was used for the treatment of crossed eyes.

As a product of Allergan, Inc., it is a cosmetic procedure that has grown in popularity. Cosmetic surgeons inject it under the skin and into muscles to temporarily reduce facial wrinkles. It is used to remove frown lines of the nose and forehead, and wrinkles around the eyes and mouth. Patients typically see results within a week, although longer response times may occur for smaller injections. The injections can be repeated when the effect wears off, usually between three to twelve months. Dosages are kept low because repeat users usually build up an immunity to Botox®. Side affects, such as allergic reactions, are rare. Some patients may see some bruising around the injected area. The most common side effect is a headache.

Scientific Foundations

The *C. botulinum* toxin is a poisonous bacterium (a one-celled living thing that sometimes causes disease). It can cause paralysis and death when eaten in contaminated food. However, *C. botulinum* can also heal people when used in a purified form by controlling muscle contractions.

The bacteria and spores (forms of the bacteria that can grow into new bacteria) of *C. botulinum* are found in soils of farmlands and forests and sediments of streams, lakes, and coastal waters. The

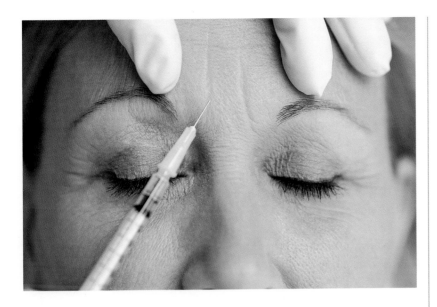

Woman receiving a cosmetic Botox® treatment for facial wrinkles. © *Rick Gomez/ Corbis.*

spores are also found on fruits and vegetables and in shellfish. The bacteria and spores cannot hurt humans. It is when they grow that the toxin is produced, which is the substance that harms people. There are seven varieties of *C. botulinum*, designated by the letters A, B, C, D, E, F, and G. Types A, B, E, and F cause human botulism, while types C and D cause animal botulism. Type G is found in soil primarily in Argentina but has not yet caused botulism.

Development

In 1989, the U.S. Food and Drug Administration (FDA) approved a pure form of the botulism toxin as a medicine called Botox®. It treated two types of muscle problems with the eyes. The toxin weakened the muscle but did not affect surrounding muscles. Since that time, Botox® has been used to treat bad muscle posture and tension, muscle spasms of the neck and shoulder, uncontrollable blinking of the eyes, clenching of the jaw muscles, bladder muscle contractions, and nerve disorders.

The American Society for Aesthetic Plastic Surgery reported that 1.6 million treatments of Botox® were given in 2001, an increase of 46 percent over 2000. On April 15, 2002, the FDA approved *C. botulinum* toxin type A for the temporary relief of frown lines between the eyebrows after a scientific study showed that test subjects that used Botox® had wrinkles reduce or disappear within thirty days.

Botox® Parties

The use of Botox® has become so popular that people are hosting Botox® parties all over the United States. They are often modeled after Tupperware® parties. At these parties, food and drinks are served while men and women gather together to buy products relating to Botox®. Activities also include doctors providing injections of Botox®. The parties help introduce people to Botox® and provide new patients to doctors. Some people say they feel more at ease to receive Botox® when friends are around. However, some doctors do not agree with Botox® parties because they feel such procedures should be performed in regulated environments such as medical facilities.

Additional information about Botox® can be found at the web sites of the American Academy of Dermatology (http://www.aad.org/), the American Society for Dermatologic Surgery (http://www.asds-net.org/), and the American Society for Aesthetic Plastic Surgery (http://www.surgery.org/).

Current Issues

The use of Botox® concerned many people because it is one of the most poisonous materials known. When it was first introduced in the United States, many people did not like the idea of being injected in the face with poison. However, it also gained support from large numbers of users because it was an easy procedure with quick results. It is also relatively inexpensive when compared to cosmetic surgeries.

Scientific studies show that 0.000001 milligram per one kilogram of body weight will cause death in people half the time. However, according to the Food and Drug Administration, its safety record is very good.

Botox® can leak into nearby areas causing temporary weakness of muscles. Around the eye, for example, the problem can cause difficulty in lifting the eyelids or double vision. People who use Botox® may develop allergic reactions or immunity to it. Injections in the same area may cause the muscle to weaken, what is called dimpling. Botox® has been used for many years so its long-term effects are well known. Some patients may develop difficulty breathing, swallowing, or talking. Pregnant women should not take Botox® because the risks to the fetus are not known.

Problems have occurred when unqualified people inject Botox® incorrectly into patients. Many times Botox® has been injected in salons, gyms, motel rooms, and other unsanitary areas that may

Words to Know

Bacterium: A single-celled microorganism that can cause disease (singular of bacteria).

Toxin: A poison that is produced by a living organism.

not be safe. The FDA recommends that all Botox® treatments be taken in a sterile environment from a physician who is certified in facial cosmetics.

■ ■ ■

For More Information

Advanced Art of Cosmetic Surgery. "Botox Injections for Wrinkles." <http://www.advanced-art.com/Botox.htm> (accessed July 22, 2006).

Brin, M. F., M. Hallett, and J. Jankovic, eds. *Scientific and Therapeutic Aspects of Botulinum Toxin.* Philadelphia, PA: Lippincott, 2002.

Kane, Michael. *The Botox Book.* New York: St. Martin's Press, 2002.

United States Food and Drug Administration. "FDA Approves Botox to Treat Frown Lines." April 15, 2002. <http://www.fda.gov/bbs/topics/ANSWERS/2002/ANS01147.html> (accessed July 22, 2006).

[See Also **Vol. 1, Collagen Replacement; Vol. 3, Cosmetics; Vol. 3, Government Regulations.**]

■■■

Cancer Drugs

Description

Anticancer drugs, also called chemotherapy drugs, are divided into several groups based on how they affect a cancer cell. Strictly speaking, cancer treatment is based on either stopping the division of the cancer cell or killing the cancer cell.

Cancer is the second leading cause of death in the United States. Academic institutes and pharmaceutical companies continue to conduct extensive research on the causes and treatments of various types of cancer.

Scientific Foundations

Cancer develops when the cells of an organ or tissue grow out of control. Normal cells grow, divide and then die. Cancer cells, instead of dying, out-live normal cells and continue to divide abnormally.

Cancer cells develop due to damage in the genetic material, or deoxyribonucleic acid (DNA), in cells. When DNA becomes damaged, normal cells repair it; however, in cancer cells, this mechanism of repair is somehow disrupted. Cancer can be inherited or it can be caused by something in the environment, like smoke, toxins, or sunlight (more specifically ultraviolet [UV] rays).

Most cancer cells eventually will become a tumor (a mass of abnormal cell growth) and can either be defined as malignant (cancerous) or benign (non-cancerous). An exception to this is leukemia; this cancer involves blood cells and circulates through the blood. When cancer cells travel to other parts of the body (metastasizes), the cancer can be life threatening.

Cancer drugs

How monoclonal antibodies are made

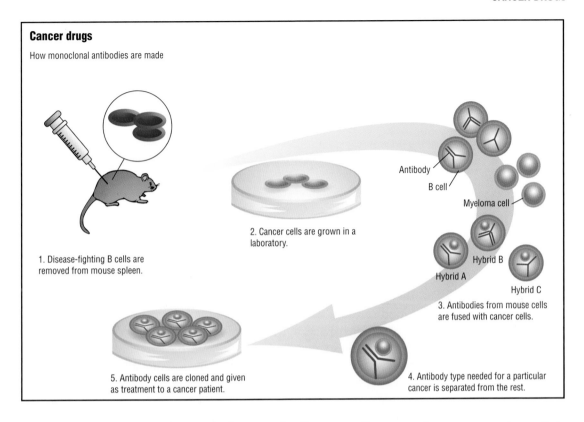

1. Disease-fighting B cells are removed from mouse spleen.

2. Cancer cells are grown in a laboratory.

Antibody
B cell
Myeloma cell

Hybrid B
Hybrid A
Hybrid C

3. Antibodies from mouse cells are fused with cancer cells.

4. Antibody type needed for a particular cancer is separated from the rest.

5. Antibody cells are cloned and given as treatment to a cancer patient.

Anticancer drugs interfere with the growth of tumor cells, eventually causing their death. Common chemotherapy drugs used in various cancers include doxorubicin (Adriamycin) in breast cancer, often administered with cyclophosphamide (Cytoxan); paclitaxel (Taxol) in lung cancer; and fluorouracil (5-FU) in colon cancer. Some are given only as injections. Others, such as imatinib (Gleevec) for leukemia are taken by mouth in tablet or liquid form.

Most chemotherapy drugs fall within one of two classes, cycle-specific drugs and non-cycle specific drugs. Cycle-specific drugs act only at specific times in the duplication of a cell, while non-cycle specific drugs act any time within the cell cycle. The drugs are often given in combination in order to achieve the maximum number of opportunities to disrupt cancerous cell growth during the cell cycle.

Traditional chemotherapy has a wide-ranging effect. Although it kills cancer cells, it can also affect surrounding normal cells, particularly those that have a tendency to divide quickly, such as cells in the stomach lining, or the hair follicles (where the hair grows). This is what produces unpleasant side effects such as

How cancer drugs called monoclonal antibodies are created for a particular patient. *Illustration by GGS Inc.*

Beans and Leaves

It is hard to pinpoint when the first cancer drug was used, as many native peoples have historically used herbs to treat some forms of cancer. Scientists now know that some herbs, tea, and bugs contain natural products that specifically target cancer cells. For example, the plant product cholchicine, isolated from the autumn crocus flower, was one of the first of plant products shown to reduce tumors in laboratory mice.

nausea and hair loss. These side effects are treatable, and are reversible after completing the course of chemotherapy.

Approximately 400 million new white blood cells are formed in the body every hour. Found mainly in the bone marrow, they are the main defense against infection. During cancer treatment, white blood cells are destroyed at a rate the body cannot replace and this is why bone marrow transplants are sometimes used after chemotherapy. Blood stem cell transplants have revolutionized cancer therapy by replacing bone marrow transplants after chemotherapy. This means patients can undergo higher doses of chemotherapy with a greater possibility of recovery.

Drugs known as monoclonal antibodies are also available to treat some types of cancer. Monoclonal antibodies attack cancer cells in much the same way that the body's immune system attacks invading organisms. These drugs have find particular receptors on the surface of cancer cells, and block or destroy the receptor sites, thus interfering with processes, such as cell growth, that are vital to the tumor's survival.

Development

The first practical anticancer drug was discovered accidentally. It was noticed that sulfur mustard gas, a toxin used as a weapon in World War I (1914–18) caused myelosuppression (bone marrow suppression). Although this gas was not used in World War II (1939–45), a considerable stock of mustard gas was stored in the Mediterranean area. An accident in the Italian port of Bari involving the leakage of one of the canisters restarted interest in the myelosuppressive effects of nitrogen mustard, leading to clinical trials in lymphoma patients. Nitrogen mustard was found to react chemically with DNA and damage it. After scientists learned to understand the structure of DNA, this gave rise to understanding

Words to Know

Benign: A growth that does not spread to other parts of the body. Recovery is favorable with treatment.

Chemotherapy: Use of powerful drugs to kill cancer cells in the human body.

Deoxyribonucleic acid (DNA): The double-helix shaped molecule that serves as the carrier of genetic information for humans and most organisms.

Metastasize: The spread of cancer from one part of the body to another.

Stem cell: An unspecialized cell that can divide to form other types of specialized cells in the body. Stem cells give rise to cells that have specialized form and function such as nerve or muscle cells.

Tumor: An uncontrolled growth of tissue, either benign (noncancerous) or malignant (cancerous).

how substances can inhibit DNA from reproducing. These include various thymine and purine forms. These agents initially dominated the development of cancer drugs.

Current Issues

There are many exciting developments in cancer therapy. At the moment, doctors know about a number of genes (called oncogenes) that predispose someone towards developing cancer. (A gene is a piece of DNA that tells cells how to do a particular job.) The understanding of the complete gene map of cancer will allow doctors to spot early those who are likely to develop the condition. Another exciting development in cancer therapy involves the understanding of the pathways that lead to resistance to certain therapies. By rationally combining therapies, it is possible to reverse the resistance to therapy in some patients. In other patients, it is possible to look for certain biomarkers (distinctive biological conditions) that increase the likelihood of success of therapy. Thus we are approaching an era where individualized medicine can be a reality.

Angiogenesis, or blood vessel growth, is also on the cutting edge of cancer therapy. Tumors encourage blood vessel growth (angiogenesis) by secreting substances called growth factors. Growth factors can encourage small blood vessels (capillaries) to grow and feed into the tumor, thus allowing the transfer of nutrients necessary for the growth of the tumors. Angiogenesis is a mechanism that transitions a small harmless cluster of cells to a large tumor. Angiogenesis is also required for the spread or migration of a tumor. Single cancer cells can break away from an established solid tumor, enter the blood vessel, and be carried to a distant site, where they can implant and begin the growth of a secondary tumor. New drugs that prohibit angiogenesis are currently under-going testing in humans, and are promising new therapies.

Monoclonal antibodies are drugs that have been researched since the 1980s. Antibodies are substances that animal bodies naturally use to attack foreign cells. Antibodies that target a patient's particular type of cancer cells can be created in the laboratory and used as a cancer treatment. Although there is much potential in the research, only a few drugs had become available as of 2006.

■ ■ ■

For More Information

American Cancer Society. "What are the different types of Chemotherapy drugs?" May 4, 2005. <http://www.cancer.org/docroot/ETO/content/ETO_1_4X_What_Are_The_Different_Types_Of_Chemotherapy_Drugs.asp?sitearea=ETO> (accessed August 10, 2006).

Baguley and Kerr. *Anticancer Development.* New York: Academic Press, 2001.

[*See Also* **Vol. 1, Bone Marrow Transplant; Vol. 1, Chemotherapy Drugs; Vol. 1, Genetic Testing, Medical; Vol. 1, Germline Gene Therapy; Vol. 1, Stem Cell Lines.**]

Chemotherapy Drugs

Description

The word "chemotherapy" usually means the use of strong medicines to treat cancer. Cancer is a disease caused by the body's own cells. Most cells reproduce by dividing in two and then re-growing, but cancer cells are cells that have changed so that they do not stop dividing. They may form colonies that grow until vital organs are destroyed, killing the patient.

There are several ways of treating cancer. All seek to kill cancer cells without harming cells in the rest of the body. Radiation, surgery, and chemotherapy are the three most common treatments for cancer. Chemotherapy is used against almost all cancers. There are dozens of anti-cancer chemotherapy drugs in use.

Scientific Foundations

All cells, including cancer cells, contain DNA (deoxyribonucleic acid), a long, twisted, tape-like molecule that contains information the cells needs to function and reproduce. During reproduction, a cell must first make a copy of its own DNA. It then splits in two, giving one copy to one of its descendants and the other copy to the other descendant. To copy its DNA and divide, a cell must go through a series of stages or phases called the cell cycle. Most chemotherapy drugs are designed to interfere with some phase of the cell cycle and prevent cancer cells from reproducing.

According to the system of grouping used by the American Cancer Society, there are seven main types of chemotherapy drugs:

Alkylating agents. These chemicals attach to DNA strands and make them unable to untangle themselves and split down the middle, a necessary step in DNA copying. If this process goes

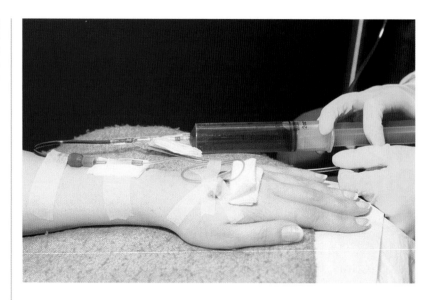

Chemotherapy drug being injected into the arm of a cancer patient. *Custom Medical Stock Photo. Reproduced by permission.*

wrong, a cell will usually kill itself. Although most normal healthy body cells also need to divide, cancer cells usually divide more often, and so can be killed by lower concentrations of alkylating agents than the rest of the body.

Anti-metabolites. These chemicals interfere with attempts by the cell to build new DNA. They resemble one of the chemicals used to build DNA but cannot be so used, and so waste the efforts of the cell trying to build DNA.

Anthracyclines. These chemicals insert themselves directly into double-sided strands of RNA and DNA, distorting them and preventing them from being duplicated.

Corticosteroid hormones. These hormones reduce cancer growth, stimulate appetite, and ease skin rashes caused by other cancer drugs. Since these substances also occur naturally in the body, they are sometimes not counted as chemotherapy drugs.

Mitotic inhibitors. These drugs, derived from plants, prevent the cell from dividing after it has duplicated its DNA.

Nitrosoureas. These substances are similar to alkylating agents. They interfere with the action of substances that repair DNA. Because these drugs can cross into brain cells, they are often used to treat brain tumors.

Topoisomerase inhibitors. Topoisomerases are substances that help the DNA maintain its proper shape. (It is not randomly tangled.) By inhibiting topoisomerases—preventing them from working—these

Clinical Trials

For a new medicine to be legal for use on patients, it must be proven effective by scientific testing. But how can a new medicine, such as a chemotherapy drug, be proven effective in the first place without using it on patients? The answer is the clinical trial. This is a controlled experiment in which the new drug or treatment is used on a small number of volunteers. There are three sizes of clinical trial, called phases: Phase I uses about 50 people, Phase II about 200, and Phase III several thousand. If the drug proves safe and effective in each phase, it goes on to the next. After Phase III, it is approved for general use. There are many clinical trials in progress, and patients may ask to be included, hoping to be early users of an effective new treatment. For example, on September 7, 2006, the National Cancer Institute's clinical trials website (www.nci. nih.gov/clinicaltrials) listed 3,622 clinical trials in progress for different cancer treatments.

drugs disrupt DNA shape and interfere with copying of DNA in cell reproduction.

Development

Strangely, the first chemotherapy drug was a chemical warfare agent. Scientists noticed that the deadly chemical called mustard gas (a sulfur compound not related to table mustard) tended to kill cells of the body's lymphatic system (part of the immune system). Some cancers—lymphomas—are cancers of lymphatic cells. In the mid 1940s, scientists tried treating lymphomas in mice with mustard gas. They found that they could shrink the cancers (temporarily) without killing the mice. The first step toward chemotherapy had been taken.

In the 1950s and 1960s, research into many other kinds of anticancer chemical continued. Combination therapy—using more than one chemotherapy drug at once, to interfere with cancer cells in several different ways at the same time—was first tried in 1965. Today, combination therapy is standard for both cancer and AIDS.

In the 1980s, research into the substances called monoclonal antibodies began. Antibodies are small molecules that stick to specific targets. Other cells in the immune system then attack whatever the antibodies have stuck to. Antibodies can be made that will stick to the cancer cells in a patient's body but not to other cells. This causes the patient's own immune system to attack the cancer cells. Although this method of fighting cancer has been intensively researched since the 1980s, as of 2006 only a few were yet in regular use for certain cancers. For example, one type of monoclonal

Words to Know

Clinical trial: A government-approved experiment using human volunteers to see if a new drug or other treatment for a disease is safe and effective.

Combination therapy: The use of more than one drug at the same time in treating a disease. Combination therapy is standard in both AIDS and cancer.

Monoclonal antibodies: Antibodies produced from a single cell line that are used in medical testing and, increasingly, in the treatment of some cancers.

antibody, called trastuzumab, has been approved for treating breast-cancer patients whose cancer cells are of a certain type.

Current Issues

Chemotherapy drugs seek to kill cancer cells. But since cancer cells are body cells that have gone awry, they are not very different from healthy cells. Drugs that kill cancer cells therefore also tend to injure other cells. In short, chemotherapy makes people sick. It interferes with the immune system, which opens the patient to infections. Many chemotherapy drugs cause nausea and vomiting. Other side effects include damage to the liver, kidneys, and heart; diarrhea or constipation; bleeding; and dulled mental activity. These side effects not only make patients miserable, but limit how much of the anti-cancer drug they can take without dying. Researchers are always looking for new chemotherapy drugs that are more effective against cancer while causing fewer side effects.

■ ■ ■

For More Information

Fischer, David S., et al. *The Cancer Chemotherapy Handbook*. Philadelphia: Mosby, 2006.

Imai, Kohzoh and Akinori Takaoka. "Comparing Antibody and Small-Molecule Therapies for Cancer." *Nature*. 6 (2006): 714–727.

National Cancer Institute. "Understanding Chemotherapy." <http://www.cancer.gov/cancertopics/chemotherapy-and-you/page2> (accessed September 7, 2006).

[See Also **Vol. 1, Cancer Drugs; Vol. 3, Government Regulations; Vol. 1, Pharmacogenetics.**]

Cloning, Human

Description

To clone a human is to create a person with the exact same deoxyribonucleic acid (DNA—the molecule inside a cell that contains its genetic information) as another person. A clone is made using a woman's egg that has had its genetic material removed and a cell from another adult.

The difference between a clone and someone born naturally to two parents is their genes. People who are born naturally have genes from both their mother and father. A cloned person only has genes from the person who donated the cell.

Scientific Foundations

In nature, a sperm from a man fertilizes an egg from a woman. The sperm carries one set of genes from the man, and the egg carries another set of genes from the woman. The genes are kept in tightly coiled structures called chromosomes, which are contained in the nucleus of the sperm and egg. The nucleus is the part of the cell that directs most of its functions. The fertilized egg begins to divide to form an embryo (a human being in the earliest stages of development). The embryo contains two complete sets of chromosomes: one from the father and one from the mother.

Sometimes a fertilized egg can naturally divide into two separate embryos. Each embryo is exactly same as the other genetically. They are called identical twins. Scientists can also create identical twins in a lab by separating an early embryo into two individual cells. After each cell has divided and grown, they are implanted into a woman's uterus (the organ in a woman's body that holds the growing fetus). This is a kind of basic cloning.

Demonstrator in Korea protesting the practice of cloning human cells at a medical school in Seoul, South Korea. *AP/Wide World Photos.*

Scientists can clone a person in a lab using an egg that has had its genetic material removed and an adult cell. They have to use an electric shock to get the egg and cell to divide and form an embryo.

Hello Dolly

In 1997, scientists at the Roslin Institute in Scotland announced that they had cloned a sheep named Dolly. To make Dolly, the scientists put a cell taken from the udder (a milk-releasing gland) of a six-year-old female sheep into an egg taken from another sheep. They first removed the nucleus, which contains the genetic material, from the egg. Then they used an electric shock to get the cells to divide.

The scientists had to try 277 times before Dolly was born. Dolly was an identical copy of the female sheep that donated the cell.

Dolly caused great debate around the world. Many people were afraid her birth would lead to the practice of human cloning. Since her birth, scientists cloned goats, cows, sheep, cats, and many other animals. But they still had not cloned a human being.

Development

Scientists have been able to clone a living creature since the 1950s. The first animal to be cloned was a tadpole. In 1997, scientists cloned the first mammal—a sheep named Dolly.

Cloning humans is much more controversial than cloning animals. In 2001, scientists from a Massachusetts company called Advanced Cell Technology produced cloned embryos. In 2002, a religious group called the Raelins said they had cloned a human, but it turned out to be a hoax.

Somatic cell nuclear transfer (SCNT) is a method scientists use to make a human clone. A somatic cell is any type of cell in the body that is not a sperm or egg cell. (These are called germ cells.) It contains a complete set of chromosomes in its nucleus. In SCNT, scientists first remove the nucleus from an adult somatic cell. They then insert it into an egg that has had its own nucleus removed. Without its nucleus, the egg does not have its own genetic material. All of the genetic material comes from the somatic cell.

Scientists then use a small electric shock to get the cells to divide. The cells keep dividing and growing until they form an embryo. That embryo is implanted in a woman's uterus. If the process is a success, the embryo would grow into a human being.

If a person were cloned, he or she would look very much like the cell donor, but they would not be identical. Even though the DNA is removed from the egg that is used to make the clone, there is still some genetic material left in the egg's mitochondria (the

Words to Know

Chromosome: A thread-shaped structure that carries genetic information in cells.

DNA: A double-helix shaped molecule inside cells that carries the genetic information.

Embryo: A stage in development after fertilization.

Ethical: Having to do with morality, or what is perceived as being the right thing to do.

Mitochondria: An organelle that specializes in ATP formation, the "powerhouse" of the cell.

Somatic cell: Cells that are part of the body but are not in the germline (able to pass their DNA on to future generations). Any type of cell in the body that is not a sperm or egg cell.

Tumor: An uncontrolled growth of tissue, either benign (noncancerous) or malignant (cancerous).

Uterus: Organ in female mammals in which the embryo and fetus grow to maturity.

structures in cells that provide energy for the cells). A cloned person would receive a small amount of DNA from the egg donor.

Current Issues

There is still a question as to whether governments and scientists will allow human cloning. Some countries want to ban the practice. In 2005, the United Nations called for a total ban on all types of human cloning. United States President George W. Bush also sought a total human cloning ban. Many doctors and scientists believe that it is not ethical (having to do with morals, or what people believe is right) to clone a human being. They believe it is playing with nature in a way that humans do not have the right to do.

The science of cloning is still far from perfected. More than ninety percent of all cloning attempts fail. Cloned animals have had many health problems. They have a higher risk of infection and tumors (abnormal growths of tissue that may be cancer) and several died very young. There is a chance that cloned humans would also have many health problems, and that most would not even survive.

Some scientists are pushing to continue with therapeutic cloning, however. In therapeutic cloning, only an embryo is cloned. It is destroyed before it can grow into a full human being. The goal of therapeutic cloning is to get stem cells. These cells can grow into every type of cell and tissue in the body. They can be used to treat disease or to grow new organs for people whose organs have been damaged.

For More Information

"Cloning Fact Sheet." *Human Genome Project*. February 20, 2006. <http://www.ornl.gov/sci/techresources/Human_Genome/elsi/cloning.shtml> (accessed April 22, 2006).

"Cloning in Focus." *Genetic Science Learning Center*. http://gslc.genetics.utah.edu/units/cloning (accessed April 23, 2006).

"Creating a Cloned Sheep Named Dolly." *National Institutes of Health*. http://science-education.nih.gov/nihHTML/ose/snapshots/multimedia/ritn/dolly/index.html (accessed April 23, 2006).

"History of Human Genetic and Reproductive Technologies." *Center for Genetics and Society*. July 21, 2004. http://genetics-and-society.org/technologies/history.html (accessed April 23, 2006).

[*See Also* **Vol. 2, Animal Cloning; Vol. 1, Bioethics; Vol. 1, Germline Gene Therapy; Vol. 3, Government Regulations; Vol. 1, Nuclear Transfer; Vol. 1, Stem Cells, Embryonic; Vol. 1, Therapeutic Cloning.**]

Collagen Replacement

Description

Collagen (KAHL-uh-jen) is a protein that makes up the bulk of connective tissue. (Proteins are the primary components of living cells.) This tissue helps protect and support organs, and holds body parts together. Examples of connective tissue include cartilage, ligaments, and tendons. Collagen is also a component of bones and teeth.

Collagen has a critical role in the body. For example, it helps maintain the strength of blood vessels, which is important since blood moves through the vessel under pressure from the pumping heart. Collagen's importance is reflected by the abundance of this protein in the mammals. Approximately 40 percent of the total protein in humans is collagen.

In the skin, the collagen and keratin found in the dermal layer (the inner layer of skin) are responsible for skin's strength and elasticity. As humans age, collagen tends to degrade. The reduced skin strength can lead to the formation of the skin folds called wrinkles. People seeking to restore their youthful skin tone can choose to have a cosmetic treatment in which collagen is re-introduced into the skin by injection with a needle.

Scientific Foundations

The shape of collagen is consistent with its support function.

Typically, collagen is long and appears as an arrangement of parallel fibers that form a spiral. A collagen fiber is formed when three strands of linked amino acids wind together to produce a triple helix (HEE-liks) or spiral. (Amino acids are the building blocks of proteins.) Adjacent spirals associate with each other to produce a structure that is similar to linked strands of rope. This

Scientist using a machine that crushes bones from cows. The crushed bones will be used to make a collagen replacement gel. © *Roger Ressmeyer/Corbis.*

structure creates a strong and inflexible molecule that is ideal for resisting forces that would deform proteins of different shapes.

Collagen differs from other proteins with respect to the amino acids it contains and their arrangement. Almost one-third of a collagen molecule is the amino acid glycine (GLI-ceen). A significant

Collagen Safety

Collagen obtained from the skin of cattle is a popular replacement for human skin tissue. It is called bovine collagen. Bovine and human collagens are very similar in amino acid composition and three-dimensional structure. However, the regions near the ends of the collagen strands do differ, which can cause an allergic reaction when bovine collagen is introduced into the human body. To minimize this risk, cattle are raised under clean conditions to reduce their risk of infection, and the end regions of the collagen are removed during the purification process. As a result, allergic reactions are now quite rare.

amount of the amino acid proline (PRO-leen) also is present is each collagen molecule. Collagen also contains hydroxyproline (HIGH-droxie-PRO-leen) and hydroxylysine (HIGH-droxie-LIE-seen), amino acids not common in other proteins. These last two amino acids are modified after being produced by the addition of a hydroxy (OH) group.

These amino acid modifications require the presence of vitamin C. People who don't get enough vitamin C in their diets often have malformed collagen and defective connective tissue. The disease scurvy is an example of the results of vitamin C-related collagen malformation.

Development

Collagen means "glue producer." The term arose from the age-old practice of boiling skin and other body parts of animals to create glue. Collagen-based glues were used in Egypt thousands of years ago, and helped form the bows of Native Americans over 1,000 years ago. The discovery of archeological specimens that still contain deposits of collagen-based glues attests to the longevity of collagen.

In addition, collagen's resilience is useful in the treatment of burns and in cosmetic procedures. Collagen replacement therapy can restore a youthful appearance to the skin. However, some people can develop an allergic reaction to the introduced collagen. In one cosmetic procedure, collagen is injected at the desired sites to eliminate skin lines and wrinkles. Because the collagen degrades over time, repeated injections are required to maintain the skin tone. In another procedure, collagen can be implanted in the dermal layer of the skin.

Aside from its importance to the body, collagen has been exploited commercially. For example, in a liquid, collagen strands will tend to separate from one another to form gelatin. When

Words to Know

Collagen: A type of protein that makes up connective tissue.

Cosmetic: Preparation or procedure intended for beautifying the body.

Protein: Complex molecules that cells use to form most of the structures

and control chemical reactions within a cell.

Skin: The largest organ of the body that provides a protective covering for internal structures and helps regulate body temperature.

flavored and sweetened, it can be served as a dessert. Collagen does not contain many of the amino acids that are essential for human health, and so has little nutritional value.

Current Issues

The support, strength, and adhesive properties of collagen have been known for a long time. These aspects are as important now as they were centuries ago. What has changed in recent times is the cosmetic use of collagen. This has spurred efforts to maximize collagen purity, since an allergic reaction to the introduction of collagen is an undesirable side effect of its use. Medical uses of modified collagen for drug delivery and in tissue engineering are being investigated.

■ ■ ■

For More Information

Brandt, Fredric. Age-Less: The Definitive Guide to Botox, Collagen, Lasers, Peels, and Other Solutions for Flawless Skin. New York: William Morrow, 2002.

Johns Hopkins University. "Modified Collagen Could Yield Important Medical Applications." August 2005. <https://hopkinsnet.jhu.edu/servlet/page?_pageid=2037&_dad=portal30p&_schema=PORTAL30P > (accessed August 2, 2006).

Trentham, David E., et al. "Treatment of Rheumatoid Arthritis Using Undenatured Type II Collagen." Original Internist 9 (2002): 12–16.

[See Also **Vol. 1, Bone Substitutes; Vol. 1, Botox; Vol. 3, Cosmetics; Vol. 1, Skin Substitutes.**]

■■■

Corticosteroids

Description

Corticosteroids are a class of hormones. Hormones are chemicals produced by one body tissue and then transported somewhere else in the body, where they cause a response. For this reason, hormones are sometimes called "chemical messengers." Corticosteroids are produced in the adrenal glands, which sit on top of the kidneys. These hormones are responsible for a variety of physical responses. Corticosteroids reduce inflammation, the body's response to injury or disease that causes swelling and pain. They are involved in the immune response (in which the body fights off foreign substances, like germs) and the stress response. Corticosteroids also regulate metabolism (how the body breaks down food) and levels of salts in the blood.

Two of the most important types of corticosteroid hormones are cortisol and aldosterone. Cortisol controls the breakdown of carbohydrate, fat, and protein in foods and has an anti-inflammatory effect (reducing pain and swelling). Aldosterone controls the body's water and salt balance, primarily by increasing sodium levels in the kidneys. (The kidneys filter wastes out of the blood and create urine.)

Scientific Foundations

The adrenal glands are two small glands, each sitting on the top of a kidney. These glands have two parts: an outer layer called the cortex and an inner region called the medulla. The adrenal cortex releases hormones directly into the blood. Once in the blood stream, these hormones travel to their target cells. The target cells have a special receptor that binds (attaches) to the specific hormone. This ensures that each hormone only communicates with specific cells

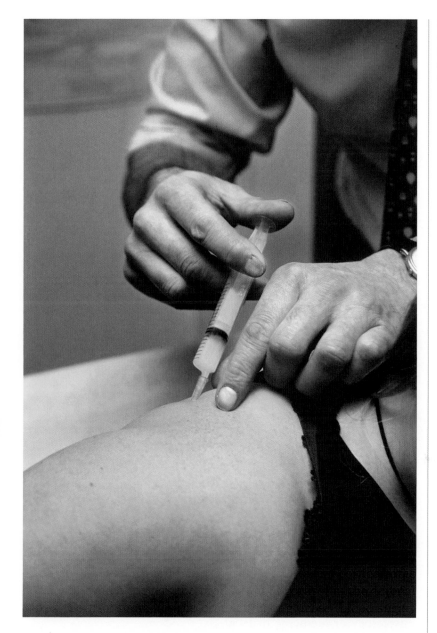

Doctor giving a patient a cortisone shot to treat a shoulder injury. *Antonia Reeve/Photo Researchers, Inc.*

that possess a receptor for that hormone. Once the hormone is bound to the target cell, it triggers a response.

For example, when the body becomes stressed, the pituitary gland at the base of the brain releases ACTH (adenocorticotropic hormone), which triggers the production of cortisol in the adrenal cortex. Cortisol promotes the production of glucose (blood sugar) from nutrients in the liver, thus providing fuel for cells when the body is under stress. When the stressful situation ends, adrenal hormone production returns to normal. The adrenal glands usually produce about 20 milligrams of cortisol per day, mostly in the morning, but they can produce five times that much when needed.

The control of corticosteroid production from the adrenal glands has interested scientists for quite some time. A disease resulting from a lack of circulating corticosteroids was known as early as the mid-nineteenth century. This disease—characterized by weakness, tiredness, and weight loss—is now called Addison's disease. Since early in the twentieth century, it was known that too much cortisol leads to Cushing's syndrome. The symptoms of this disease include obesity, thinning bones, high blood pressure, depression, a round or moon-shaped face, and a hump at the base of the neck.

Today, synthetic (human-made) corticosteroids are used in medicine to imitate or boost naturally occurring steroids. They are available in a variety of forms: inhalants, lotions, pills, and injections.

Development

In 1948, American chemist Edward Calvin Kendall (1886–1972) and American physician Philip Showalter Hench (1896–1965) discovered a compound that had anti-inflammatory activity and reversed the symptoms of rheumatoid arthritis (a disease that causes painful joints). This compound, which they named cortisone, was a form of corticosteroid.

Their patient, a middle-aged woman with rheumatoid arthritis (RA), was suffering from severe pain and joint swelling. She was given a series of experimental cortisone injections over several weeks. When the treatment was finished, her symptoms had seemed to disappear. For their contribution to medicine—specifically, their discoveries relating to the hormones of the adrenal cortex—Hench and Kendall, along with Polish-born Swiss chemist Tadeus Reichstein (1897–1996), were awarded the Nobel Prize in Physiology or Medicine in 1950.

In the 1950s, an American chemist synthesized cortisone, but its production involved a very expensive and lengthy procedure. By the end of the 1950s, a process was developed that made cortisone more easily in large quantities. Although corticosteroids were effective in treating various ailments involving inflammation, the reason why they worked was unknown. With further research, this was discovered in the 1980s.

Yams and Hormones

In the 1930s, the cost of progesterone, a hormone used to make corticosteroids, was seven times as expensive as gold. In 1941, American chemist Russell Marker (1902–1995) of Pennsylvania State University found that he could extract a chemical called diosgenin from a Mexican wild yam, and diosgenin could be converted to progesterone in a much less expensive way. The conversion of diosgenin to progesterone is known as the marker degradation. Its discovery led to the mass production of steroidal hormones, including cortisone.

Current Issues

At first, corticosteroids were thought to be a miracle drug because they worked quickly and powerfully for many conditions. Since then, many lives have been saved with corticosteroid treatment. But, as the years passed, it became clear that these powerful drugs also produced unwanted side effects. The most common side effects are weight gain, high blood pressure, thinning of the bones, increased risk of having diabetes (a disease in which the body cannot process blood sugars), increased risk of infection, poor sleep, and eye problems. The risk and severity of side effects increases with increasing doses of the drug.

Doctors have discovered that the risks of these drugs can be reduced when the drugs are used carefully. Patients are treated with the lowest effective dose, and occasionally the treatment is discontinued for a period of time. When a person experiences an acute flare-up, the dosage is increased. In addition, patients are sometimes given local injections of the drug rather than exposing the entire body to the drug's effects.

Corticosteroids are used often as a first line of defense against inflammation and may be used with other therapies. If corticosteroids are given in a large enough dose, the inflammation caused by arthritis or an autoimmune disease disappears. (An auto-immune disease is one in which the body attacks its own tissues.) However, recent research shows that, in most cases, low doses of corticosteroids alone may be enough to reduce inflammation. Today, non-steroidal anti-inflammatory drugs, or NSAIDs, are most commonly used to treat patients with rheumatoid arthritis (RA). Low-dose corticosteroid treatment of RA, although effective, is controversial because of its adverse side effects.

Words to Know

Adrenal glands: Two glands located next to the kidneys. The adrenal glands produce the hormones epinephrine and norepinephrine and the corticosteroid hormones.

Cortisol: A hormone involved with reducing the damaging nature of stress.

Cushing syndrome: A disorder in which too much of the adrenal hormone, cortisol, is produced; it may be caused by a pituitary or adrenal gland tumor.

Hormone: A chemical substance produced by the body. Hormones are created by one organ of the body but they usually carry out functions in other organs or parts of the body.

Progesterone: Hormone secreted by the female reproductive organs, used in birth control medicine.

For More Information

Alberts, Bruce, et al. *Molecular Biology of the Cell*. New York: Garland Science, 2002.

Journal of Young Investigators. "Yams of Fortune: The (Uncontrolled) Birth of Oral Contraceptives." <http://www.jyi.org/volumes/volume6/issue7/features/redig.html> (accessed August 2, 2006).

Shampo, Marc A., and Robert A. Kyle. "Edward C. Kendall—Nobel Laureate." *Mayo Clinic Proceedings* 76 (2001): 1188. This article is also available online at <http://www.mayoclinicproceedings.com/inside.asp?AID=1342&UID=> (accessed August 2, 2006).

[*See Also* **Vol. 3, Amino Acids, Commercial Use; Vol. 1, Arthritis drugs; Vol. 1, Painkillers.**]

■ ■ ■

C-Reactive Protein

Description

C-reactive protein is a large, complex molecule (cluster of atoms). It is made by the human body as part of its inflammation response. Inflammation is the redness, heat, swelling, and pain that happen in response to an injury or an infection. A sore throat, the swelling of a bug bite, and the hot feeling of sunburned skin are all signs of inflammation.

Inflammation can happen inside the body for no apparent reason. Low-grade or slight inflammation of the arteries—the blood vessels that take oxygen-rich blood from the lungs to the rest of the body—can contribute to atherosclerosis. Atherosclerosis (ATH-a-row-skla-RO-sis) is the building up of a fatty lining inside the arteries. If the lining gets too thick, blood cannot get past, and tissues downstream from the blockage can die. If the arteries supplying the heart (the coronary arteries) are blocked, the heart can be injured or stopped. This is called a heart attack. If a heart attack affects enough of the heart, the person dies. Blockage of an artery in the brain kills off part of the brain, and may damage a person's mind or kill them if there is enough damage. Blockage of blood flow to part of the brain is called a stroke or brain attack.

People with low-grade inflammation inside their bodies are more likely to have heart attacks or strokes. It is not known what causes low-grade inflammation of this kind. However, in recent years scientists have found that several proteins are increased in the blood of people who have low-grade inflammation. One of these is C-reactive protein.

Scientific Foundations

There is always some C-reactive protein in a person's blood. People who have higher levels than normal, however, are more likely

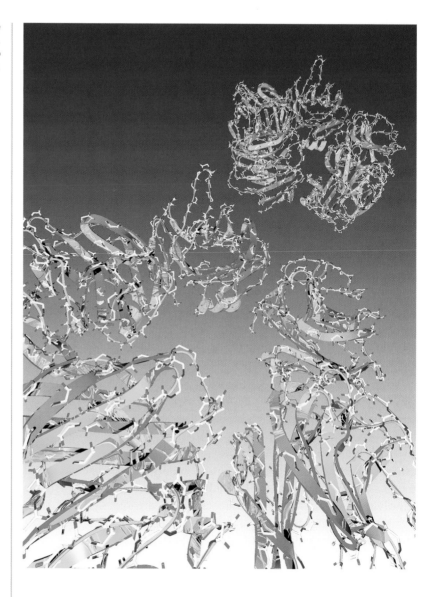

Computer model of the C-reactive protein structure. *Alfred Pasieka/Photo Researchers, Inc.*

to get diabetes, high blood pressure, heart attacks, and stroke. (Together, high blood pressure, heart attacks, and stroke are called cardiovascular disease.) A person having less than 1 milligram of C-reactive protein per liter of blood (1 mg/L) is at low risk for cardiovascular disease. A person with 1 to 3 mg/L has average risk. If a person has more than 3 mg/L, they have high risk. Smoking, lack of exercise, and being overweight increase C-reactive protein in the blood.

Don't Just Measure, Target

As of 2006, a $20 test for measuring C-reactive protein in the blood was being used by many doctors. In that year, one group of researchers suggested that inflammation actually makes tissue death worse in heart attacks and strokes. Since inflammation depends partly on C-reactive protein, these doctors suggested that chemicals that inhibited C-reactive protein—that is, which prevented it from working—might reduce the damage from heart attacks and strokes. They showed that this approach did work in mice. Further research must be done before the method is tried in humans.

Development

The name "C-reactive protein" was given to this protein because when it was first discovered in 1930, it was found to react (that is, combine chemically) with the C polysaccharide (pol-ee-SAK-a-ride) of the bacteria *Streptococcus pneumoniae*, the germ that causes strep throat. Some bacteria coat themselves with molecules called polysaccharides to ward off the immune system. Because it reacted with the C polysaccharide, the newly discovered protein was called C-reactive.

Although the link between inflammation and C-reactive protein has been known since 1930, it was not until the early 2000s that measurements of C-reactive protein levels in the blood began to be used as tests of risk for heart attack and stroke. Guidelines for using C-reactive protein testing were issued in January 2003 by the American Heart Association and the U.S. federal government's Centers for Disease Control.

Current Issues

Although much evidence shows that C-reactive protein can be used to predict risk of cardiovascular disease, not all scientists agree. As recently as February 2006, several researchers challenged the claim that C-reactive protein (and other molecular markers of inflammation) play a role in actually making disease happen, or that measuring them enables doctors to predict disease risk any better than other tests.

■ ■ ■

For More Information

American Heart Association. "Inflammation, Heart Disease and Stroke: The Role of C-Reactive Protein." September 6, 2006. <http://www.american-heart.org/presenter.jhtml?identifier=4648> (accessed September 6, 2006).

Words to Know

Atherosclerosis: Abnormal narrowing of the arteries of the body that generally originates from the buildup of fatty plaque on the artery wall.

C-reactive protein: A protein which is released during inflammation. Used as a measure of risk for heart attack and stroke.

Heart attack: Blockage of an artery bringing blood to part of the heart. May injure or kill part or all of the heart.

Inflammation: A complex series of events associated with injury or disease that, when combined, serve to isolate, dilute, or destroy the agent responsible and the injured tissue.

Polysaccharide: A molecule composed of many glucose subunits arranged in a chain.

Stroke: Blockage of an artery bringing blood to part of the brain. May injure or kill part or all of the brain.

Gordon, Lowe. "The Association Between Elevated Levels of Inflammation Biomarkers and Coronary Artery Disease and Death." *Journal of the Canadian Medical Association* 17.

Kushner, Irving, John E. Volanakis, and Henry Gewurz. *C-Reactive Protein and the Plasma Protein Response to Tissue Injury*. New York: New York Academy of Sciences, 1982.

Pepys, Mark B., et al. "Targeting C-Reactive Protein for the Treatment of Cardiovascular Disease." *Nature* 440 (2006): 1217–1221.

■■■

Cryonics

Description

Cryonics is an experimental method in which a person's body is frozen and stored immediately after death. The practice is done in the hopes that the person can one day be brought back to life when a cure for what caused their death is found.

Cryonics means "freezing of corpse." A corpse is a dead body. The dead body is kept at an extremely low temperature (below –200 degrees Fahrenheit [–129 degrees Celcius]). A body that is frozen in this manner is said to be in cryonic suspension.

Scientific Foundations

Cryonics is based, in part, on scientific reports that show that body cells can remain alive even if they are not actively working. A 1986 journal report found that large animals that were kept at freezing (32 degrees Fahrenheit [0 degrees Celsius]) after having a heart attack could be brought back to life three hours later. People in favor of cryonics point to events where humans have lived after being in icy waters for long periods of time.

Supporters also say that modern-day cryonics procedures can be used to keep the structure of the brain intact. They believe that the survival of body structure, not the ability to function, determines whether a person lives or dies. Many cryonics supporters also think that, in the future, physicians will have new tools that allow them to target and treat the individual molecules that cause disease (this is called nanomedicine).

Development

The idea surrounding cryonics dates back to 1964, when physics teacher Robert Ettinger (1918–) published a book called

Stainless steel casket used by cryonics company Trans Time, Inc., which uses liquid nitrogen to freeze people shortly after death and then store them at very low temperatures. © *Michael Macor/San Francisco Chronicle/Corbis.*

The Prospect of Immortality. Ettinger proposed that a human body could be frozen and later brought back to life when medical technology was more sophisticated. He also noted that liquid nitrogen could be used to store bodies for hundreds of years. Three years later on January 12, 1967, seventy-three-year-old James Bedford became the first person to be frozen using the cryonics method. Bedford chose the procedure with the dream that scientists would one day find a cure for the cancer that killed him. As of 2006, his body was said to be in good condition at a cryonics facility in Scottsdale, Arizona.

Cryonics companies began to open all over the United States. The expensive cost of storing a frozen body caused many to go out of business within a few years. Only a few full-service cryonics facilities are still open. In 2004, the Alcor Life Extension Foundation said it had more than fifty-nine bodies in cryonic suspension.

The first step in the cryonics process is to remove all the water from body cells and replace it with a mix of chemicals that keep

Cryonics in Popular Media

The potential benefits and problems related to cryogenics have often been the topic of movies, books, and television shows. Examples include:

- The 1992 film, *Forever Young* starring Mel Gibson

- The 1997 film, *Austin Powers: Inter-national Man of Mystery* starring Mike Myers

- The 1998 national bestseller, *The First Immortal*, by James Halperin published in 1998

- Television episodes of shows such as *Star Trek: The Next Generation* and *Boston Legal*.

the body from forming ice crystals during freezing. (The water is removed because water expands when frozen. This would cause body parts to break.) The body is then put on ice until it cools down to –202 degrees Fahrenheit (–130 degrees Celsius). The final step is the placement of the body into a metal tank that contains very cold liquid nitrogen.

Among the most famous people ever frozen is American baseball player Ted Williams (1918–2002). Williams's son and daughter had his body frozen at a cryonics facility. Their half-sister sued them for doing this. She insisted that Williams wanted to be cremated instead. The lawsuit was eventually dropped. Williams' body remains in a cryonics facility in the United States.

Current issues

Cryonics is controversial. There is currently no way to reverse the cryonics process so that a person comes back to life. No human adult has ever been brought back to life after deep freezing. Those against the practice say cryonics companies make a promise on which they cannot deliver. Cryonicists (those who support cryonics) disagree. They believe that by the mid twenty-first century, reliable methods to reverse the freezing process and heal any freeze-damaged cells will be developed.

Keeping a body stored in a cryonics center can cost hundreds of thousands of dollars. Before the person dies, they usually must join a cryonics center and pay a yearly membership fee. Many critics say cryonics organizations are robbing people out of a lot of money.

The other debate involves the term "dead." Bodies that are frozen using cryonics are said to be legally but not totally dead,

Words to Know

Cryonicists: Scientists who study cry- onics, the science of storing or preserving organisms (or parts of organisms) at very low temperatures.

Cryonic suspension: Storing or preserv- ing organisms (or parts of organisms) at very low temperatures.

and biologically alive. Cryonicists want to perform the freezing process immediately after a person dies, so that all the cells of the body remain technically alive. But the law states that cryonics can only be done on a person who has been pronounced legally dead by an authorized health care provider. The heart must stop in order to be considered legally dead. By the time the body arrives at a cryonics center, many hours may have passed, and cells stop working. This reduces the chance that a person who is frozen can be successfully brought back to life.

■ ■ ■

For More Information

Alcor Life Extension Foundation. Cryonics at Alcor. <http://www.alcor.org/> (accessed on April 17, 2006).

American Cryonics Society. Welcome Page. <http://americancryonics .org/> (accessed on April 17, 2006).

Cryonics Institute. Welcome Page. <http://www.cryonics.org/> (accessed on April 18 2006).

Ettinger, Robert C. W. *The Prospect of Immortality*. Scientific Book Club, 1965.

[*See Also* **Vol. 1, Bioethics; Vol. 2, Biopreservation.**]

Cystic Fibrosis Drugs

Description

Cystic fibrosis is a hereditary disease that affects primarily the lungs, sweat glands, digestive system. It is caused by defects in a gene involved in mucus (phlegm) production in the lungs and intestinal tract. (A gene tells cells how to do a particular job.) The disease is most common in Caucasians. Up to 10 percent of Caucasians—millions of people in the United States alone—possess this defective gene. Over 1,000 known mutations of the gene cause mild to life-threatening forms of cystic fibrosis.

In cystic fibrosis, the defective gene results in the accumulation of mucus that is much thicker and stickier than is normally the case. In the lungs, the mucus makes breathing more difficult, and it becomes an ideal location for the growth of bacteria, particularly *Pseudomonas aeruginosa*. When a person with cystic fibrosis gets a bacterial infection in the lungs, it can persist for years because the bacteria are difficult to kill once they are buried in the mucus. As the body's immune system tries to fight the infection, the progressive immune-related damage to the lungs can ultimately be lethal.

In the digestive system, the pancreas secretes enzymes into the stomach that the body needs to digest food. Enzymes are chemicals that make possible the hundreds of chemical reactions that happen every day in the body. When a person has cystic fibrosis, the mucus that the pancreas makes is very thick. It blocks the openings in the pancreas, and the enzymes cannot get to the stomach. As a result, food is not digested as it passes through the stomach.

While no cure exists for cystic fibrosis, a number of drugs are commonly used to try to reduce the number of lung infections, as

Woman receiving treatment with Alpha 1, a drug for cystic fibrosis produced from transgenic sheep. © *Karen Kasmauski/Corbis.*

well as improve the person's quality of life. The wide variety of mutations responsible for cystic fibrosis produces a many different of symptoms. Thus, the drug regimen for cystic fibrosis patients is tailored to the individual.

Scientific Foundations

Cystic fibrosis is a genetic disease, meaning that those who suffer from the disease have inherited a genetic defect from their parents' DNA (deoxyribonucleic acid, their genetic material). Cystic fibrosis is an autosomal recessive disease. This means if two parents both carry the defective gene, their child has a one-in-four chance of developing cystic fibrosis. The parents do not have to have the disease themselves; they are called carriers. They can carry the faulty gene without being sick.

As the genetics of cystic fibrosis were unraveled, the nature and mechanics of the disease have become clearer. This has allowed the drugs to be prescribed that more effectively treat the disease. Cystic fibrosis drugs are aimed at reducing lung infections, making breathing more comfortable, and ensuring that nutrition is adequate.

A Viral Cure for Cystic Fibrosis?

Adenoviruses are small infectious agents that can cause upper respiratory and other infections in humans. They also are known to be a good vehicle for transporting genes inside cells, including, hopefully, the defective lung cells of people with cystic fibrosis. Using an adeno-virus, a properly functioning gene could be introduced into these lung cells, and the patient's cells then would be able to produce a properly functioning channel protein. A trial of this treatment with cystic fibrosis patients has shown encouraging improved lung function.

Development

Antibiotics (drugs that fight infections caused by bacteria) can be very useful in treating the lung infections associated with cystic fibrosis. Generally, the first antibiotic prescribed is a drug that has been in use for some time. The idea is that if this antibiotic doesn't work, then more potent antibiotics remain to be tried. Antibiotic therapy is not always successful, since the bacteria are embedded in both the thick mucus and in a sugary substance that they produce after they attach to the lung cells. These embedded bacterial populations, which are called biofilms, are very resistant to drug treatment.

Bacteria can also develop a resistance to antibiotics, since the drug may not be able to penetrate the mucus in a concentration that is high enough to kill all the bacteria. Those bacteria that survive exposure to the antibiotic may change in ways that allow them to resist that antibiotic if it is prescribed again. For this reason, the antibiotics given to a person with cystic fibrosis may need to be shifted over time.

Other cystic fibrosis drugs target the reduced breathing capacity of the mucus-clogged lungs. The airways to the lungs can become constricted. The inhalation of drugs that are classed as bronchodilators (brong-ko-die-LATE-urs) can help increase the amount of air that enters the lungs by causing the small air passages in the lungs to expand. Another treatment supplies an enzyme called dornase. This enzyme recognizes and cleaves sites in the mucus, which makes the mucus thinner. The thinner mucus can be coughed up more easily, providing some short-term comfort and, when combined with antibiotic therapy, increasing the effectiveness of the antibiotics. Drugs that increase the volume of the mucus are also useful, since they effectively reduce its thickness.

Words to Know

Antibiotic: A compound produced by a microorganism that kills other microorganisms or retards their growth. Genes for antibiotic resistance are used as markers to indicate that successful gene transfer has occurred.

Bronchodilators: Drugs, either inhaled or taken orally, that dilate lung airway by relaxing the chest muscles.

Cystic fibrosis: A fatal disease in which a single defective gene prevents the body from making a protein, cystic fibrosis transmembrane conductance regulator.

Enzyme: A protein that helps control the rate or speed of chemical reactions in the cell.

RNA: Ribonucleic acid. Used by most cells to copy protein recipes from DNA; in retroviruses, RNA is the primary genetic material.

Inhalation of corticosteroids (kor-ti-ko-STAIR-oids) and non-steroidal anti-inflammatory drugs, such as ibuprofen, can slow the lung damage associated with cystic fibrosis, probably because they reduce the inflammation associated with the immune response such as inflammation. Much of the lung damage that occurs in cystic fibrosis is due to the reaction of immune complexes with the lung tissue.

Finally, treatment directed at proper nutrition includes providing pancreatic enzymes, which replace enzymes that are abnormal or missing completely. In addition, people with cystic fibrosis often take dietary supplements, including vitamins A, D, E, and K.

Current Issues

Researchers continue to develop and test drugs that slow the course of cystic fibrosis and its associated lung damage. Research is also being done to find ways of preventing the disease or reversing its effects.

RNA interference may be a promising strategy. RNA is short for ribonucleic acid. RNA interference blocks the process of translation—when an RNA species is used as a blueprint for the manufacture of a protein. Scientists have successfully restored the function of the defective channel in cystic fibrosis lung cells by blocking the activity of a particular protein. While the research is a long way from being ready to use in patients, scientists hope that RNA interference may someday cure cystic fibrosis.

For now, the knowledge of the genetic causes of cystic fibrosis is being used to better identify those people who carry one of these defective genes. In the United States, this service—called genetic screening or genetic testing—is offered to couples who have a family history of the disease and to other prospective parents who wish to be tested.

■ ■ ■

For More Information

Kepron, Wayne. *Cystic Fibrosis: Everything You Need to Know*. Richmond Hill, Canada: Firefly Books, 2004.

Kirn, Timothy F. "Antibiotics Still Key to Survival in Cystic Fibrosis." *Pediatric News* 39 (2005): 12–14.

March of Dimes. "Cystic Fibrosis." April 2002. <http://www.marchofdimes.com/professionals/681_1213.asp> (accessed July 4, 2006).

National Institutes of Health. "Cystic Fibrosis." May 5, 2006. <http://www.nlm.nih.gov/medlineplus/ency/article/000107.htm> (accessed July 4, 2006).

Orenstein, David Michael. *Cystic Fibrosis: A Guide for Patient and Family*. Philadelphia, PA: Lippincott Williams & Wilkins, 2003.

[See Also **Vol. 2, Genetic Engineering; Vol. 1, Vaccines.**]

■■■

Designer Genes

Description

Genes are the traits children inherit from their parents. Genes give a child his mother's eyes, or her father's dimples. Genes are segments of DNA (deoxyribonucleic acid, an organism's heriditary material). Genes contain instructions for the production of chemicals called proteins that direct the functions of the different cells in the body. Through the new technology of genetic engineering, it is theoretically possible to manipulate the genes of humans in a way that people can choose what kind of characteristics they would want a child to have. Genetic materials that are manipulated in this way are sometimes called designer genes.

Scientific Foundations

Scientists already use genetic engineering techniques to place another organism's DNA into a plant or animal, in order to achieve a number of desired traits. This is done to make agricultural crops stronger and more disease-resistant. Scientists also can genetically alter animals to make them bigger and to give their meat more nutrients for people to eat.

The next step is changing human genes. Doctors can use genes to select some traits a child will have. They can test an embryo in the lab to make sure it does not have a genetic mutation (a damaged or missing gene). Genetic mutations cause diseases such as Tay Sachs (a disease that causes a fatty substance to build up in nerve cells of the brain) and cystic fibrosis (a disease that causes a sticky substance to form in the lungs, making it hard for the person to breathe). By choosing an embryo without these mutations, doctors can make sure the baby will not have the genetic disease. Genetic diseases such as Tay Sachs are determined by just one gene. Scientists may soon be able to test to see whether a person might develop diseases such as heart disease or cancer. These diseases are determined by several genes.

Doctors can choose the sex of the baby by looking at the embryo's chromosomes (structures in the cells that carry the genes). If they implant an embryo in the mother with the XX chromosomes, the baby will be a girl. If they implant an embryo with the XY chromosomes, the baby will be a boy.

The next step is to actually change or add genes in the embryo so that the child has certain traits. There are two ways to change human genes. The first is used in people who have a faulty gene that causes them to have a genetic disease such as cystic fibrosis. Doctors inject the person with the correct gene, which is usually carried into the person's body on a virus. The idea is that the normal gene will replace the person's faulty gene.

The other way to create designer genes is to remove a cell from a fertilized embryo. Scientists add, remove, or change some of the genes in that cell. They put the genetically modified cell into a woman's egg that has had its nucleus (the part of the cell that contains DNA) removed. If the embryo grows into a child, the changed genes tell the child's body to produce certain proteins that affect a certain trait. That child develops the traits that those genes determine, and pass those traits on to his or her children.

Development

In 1953, American researcher James Watson and British researcher Francis Crick announced that they had "found the secret of life." The pair of scientists had identified the structure of DNA, the container of all hereditary information needed to make human beings. In the 1960s, scientists identified the codes for all the major amino acids, the building blocks of the proteins that tell the human body how to work.

The first time scientists were able to make a "test-tube" baby in a lab was in 1978. Doctors took an egg from the baby's mother and merged it with sperm from the father in a lab, then re-implanted it into the mother to grow. This is called in-vitro fertilization.

In 2001, the first genetically engineered babies were born. The fifteen mothers who participated had genetic defects that they might have passed to their babies. A fertility clinic in New Jersey took an egg from each of the women, combined it with their partner's sperm, and added part of an egg donated by another woman to prevent the babies from having the defect. At least two of the babies who were born had genes from all three parents.

Designer Baby Saves Sibling

In 2000, a Colorado couple created a test-tube baby to save the life of their six-year-old daughter, Molly, who had a bone marrow disease called Fanconi anemia. Molly needed a bone marrow transplant (a treatment in which she would receive new cells to replace her damaged bone marrow cells) in order to survive. Her parents used a procedure that tests the mother's egg and the father's sperm in a laboratory to make sure they did not contain the gene for Fanconi anemia. Scientists then combined the best egg and sperm to create an embryo that contained the exact kind of cells Molly needed for her transplant.

When Molly's baby brother, Adam, was born, doctors collected cells from his umbilical cord to use in the transplant. These cells, called stem cells, were able to successfully make healthy new bone marrow cells that saved Molly's life.

A major breakthrough for designer genes came in 2003. In that year, researchers at the Human Genome Project announced they had sequenced the entire 20,000–25,000 genes in human DNA. They discovered the instructions for making a human being. Their discovery helps scientists find and change genes in an embryo to prevent disease or create certain traits.

Current Issues

Designer genes have the potential to one day prevent health problems such as cancer and blindness, or change the way people look or act. Some people think the practice is morally wrong. They do not believe parents should have the right to engineer their child to be as tall as a basketball star, or as brilliant as Albert Einstein. They picture a world in which parents can mix and match a child, choosing everything from their eye color to their abilities. They fear rich people will be able to buy themselves the best and brightest children.

Many people are afraid designer genes could lead to the practice of eugenics—creating only perfect children to improve the human race. Or, they worry that the practice will create superhuman people with bizarre traits. They imagine people strong enough to lift cars, or people with vision sharp enough to see in the dark. Even more worrisome to some is that these new designer genes could be passed down from generation to generation.

Words to Know

Chromosome: A thread-shaped structure that carries genetic information in cells.

Cystic fibrosis: A fatal disease in which a single defective gene prevents the body from making a protein, cystic fibrosis transmembrane conductance regulator.

Deoxyribonucleic acid (DNA): The double-helix shaped molecule that serves as the carrier of genetic information for humans and most organisms.

Embryo: An organism (human being, other animals, and plants) in its earliest stage of development.

Eugenics: A social movement in which the population of a society, country, or the world is to be improved by controlling the passing on of hereditary information through selective breeding.

Genes: Pieces of DNA that carry instructions for traits and diseases.

Genetic mutation: A change in the genes caused by a change in the base sequence.

Nucleus: The part of the cell that contains most of its genetic material, including chromosomes and DNA.

Protein: Complex molecules that cells use to form most of the structures and control chemical reactions within a cell.

For More Information

Deneen, Sally. "Designer People." *E Magazine.* http://www.emagazine.com/view/?112> May/June 20032005 (accessed April 5, 2006).

McKibben, Bill. "Designer Genes." *Orion Magazine* <http://www.oriononline.org/pages/om/03–3om/McKibben.html> (accessed April 7, 2006).

Wickelgren, Ingrid. "Designer genes: Will DNA Technology Let Parents Design Their Kids?(Life)." *Current Science, a Weekly Reader publication* (December 3, 2004): 10–15.

Wright, Robert. "James Watson & Francis Crick." *The Time 100.* <http://www.time.com/time/time100/scientist/profile/watsoncrick.html> March 29, 1999 (accessed April 7, 2006).

[See Also **Vol. 1, Bioethics; Vol. 1, Frozen Egg Technology; Vol. 1, Gene Therapy; Vol. 1, In-Vitro Fertilization.**]

■■■

Dialysis

Description

In many animals, as the blood circulates, it collects waste products from the body's cells. Normally, these wastes are filtered from the blood by a pair of organs called the kidneys. The kidneys pass the wastes on in fluid called urine, which then leaves the body. Kidneys can become damaged from disease or injury and stop working. When a person's kidneys fail, partly or completely, there are only two ways to keep that person from dying. The first is a kidney transplant. In a kidney transplant, a kidney is taken from the body of a living person (a volunteer) or from a person who has died recently. Kidney transplants can only work if the body chemistry of the donor (the person from whom the kidney is coming) is similar enough to the body chemistry of the recipient (the person getting the kidney). There is a long waiting list for kidneys, and most people with kidney failure cannot count on getting a transplant.

The second treatment is dialysis (pronounced die-AL-ah-sis, from the Greek word for "separation"). Dialysis is the artificial removal of waste chemicals from the blood. In order to stay alive, a person without working kidneys must undergo dialysis every few days. There are two kinds of dialysis, hemodialysis and peritoneal dialysis.

The prefix "hemo-" means blood, so hemodialysis means "separation of the blood." In hemodialysis, wastes are separated from the blood using a machine. Three times a week, dialysis patients must spent three to five hours hooked up to a hemodialysis machine. Blood leaves the body slowly through a needle and tube, is filtered by the dialyzer machine using a thin membrane, and is returned to the body through another needle.

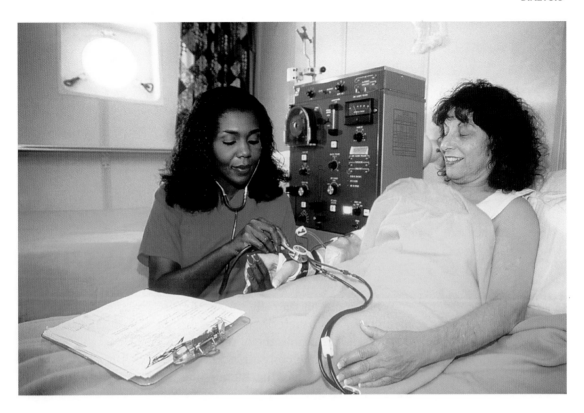

Woman receiving hemodialysis treatment on a cruise ship. © *Jeff Greenberg/Visuals Unlimited.*

Another kind of dialysis is peritoneal dialysis. The peritoneum is a thin sack of tissue that contains most of the organs of the gut, including the liver and intestines. In peritoneal dialysis, a tube is used to fill this sack with a cleaning fluid called dialysis solution. The fluid enters through a permanent opening in the side of the body. The peritoneum acts like the membrane in a mechanical dialyzer, allowing poisons to move from the blood into the fluid. After thirty minutes or so, the fluid is drained.

Scientific Foundations

In hemodialysis, separation of wastes takes place in a device called a dialyzer or artificial kidney. The dialyzer makes blood flow on one side of thin membrane or sheet of material and a solution of salt and water on the other side. The membrane is semipermeable (pronounced SEM-ee-PUR-mee-ah-bul), meaning that some molecules (clusters of atoms) can pass through it and others cannot. A semipermeable membrane can be thought of as being punctured by millions of tiny holes that are large enough to let smaller molecules pass but not large molecules or blood cells.

Livers, Too

For over 40 years dialysis has been regularly used to replace the function of the kidneys. However, the kidney is not the only organ that removes toxins from the blood; the liver does, too. While kidneys (and artificial kidneys) remove poisons that can be dissolved in water, livers perform a more difficult trick: they remove substances that are chemically bound to a blood protein called albumin. It is more difficult to imitate this function mechanically than to imitate the filtering action of a kidney. Today there are several kinds of liver dialysis machines, but their stage of development is about where the kidney dialysis machine was in the 1950s, before the invention of the Scribner Shunt: liver dialysis can help keep people with liver failure alive until an organ is available for transplant, but it cannot keep a person alive indefinitely.

Waste molecules are free to pass back and forth through the membrane. Since there are fewer waste molecules on the water side of the semipermeable membrane, more molecules will pass, on average, from the blood side to the water side. A few of these will pass back again into the blood, but they are outnumbered by molecules passing from the blood to the water. This process of movement from high concentration (in this case, the blood side) to low concentration (the water side) is called diffusion. A dialyzer removes waste products from the blood by diffusion.

Development

Early dialysis machines were not good enough to keep people alive who had no kidney function. The first dialyzer or artificial kidney was built in 1943 by a Dutch doctor, Willem Kolff (1911–). Kolff moved to the United States in the late 1940s and continued his research. In the 1950s, he produced improved models.

In 1963, Dr. Belding Scribner (1921–2003) had the idea of feeding blood from a patient's artery through a dialyzer through Teflon plastic tubes, then back into the patient through a vein, in a continuous loop. This invention, the Scribner Shunt, made it possible to perform modern dialysis. In 1962, Scribner opened the world's first dialysis clinic, where people living otherwise ordinary lives would come regularly to have their blood cleansed.

Peritoneal dialysis first became a practical treatment for kidney failure in the 1980s.

Words to Know

Dialysis: The mechanical filtering of blood to replace the functioning of kidneys or liver.

Diffusion: Random movement of molecules which leads to a net movement of molecules from a region of high concentration to a region of low concentration.

Hemodialysis: A method of mechanically cleansing the blood outside of the body, used when an individual is in relative or complete kidney failure, in order to remove various substances which would normally be cleared by the kidneys.

Peritoneal dialysis: An alternative to hemodialysis in cases of kidney failure. Instead of pumping blood out of the body, dialysis fluid is drained into and out of the abdomen to absorb toxins.

Current Issues

Dialysis is not a perfect replacement for a natural kidney. There are several medical problems that often trouble people who are depending on dialysis. These include weakening of the bones, which afflicts 90 percent of all dialysis patients; itching; inability to sleep; and amyloidosis, which is pain in the joints caused by the buildup of proteins that living kidneys can remove but dialyzers cannot.

■ ■ ■

For More Information

Fine, Richard N. *Dialysis Therapy*. Philadelphia: Hanley & Belfus, 2002.

Henrich, William L. *Principles and Practice of Dialysis*. Philadelphia: Lippincott Williams & Wilkins, 2004.

National Institutes of Health. "Treatment Methods for Kidney Failure: Hemodialysis." September, 2003. <http://kidney.niddk.nih.gov/kudiseases/pubs/hemodialysis/> (accessed September 6, 2006).

[See Also **Vol. 1, Organ Transplants.**]

■ ■ ■

DNA Fingerprinting

Description

Deoxyribonucleic acid (DNA) is the genetic material inside every cell in the human body. It is made up of pairs of the chemicals adenine (A), cytosine (C), guanine (G), and thymine (T). The combinations of these base pairs form a code that gives instructions to the body's cells. Every person's code is a bit different (except for identical twins). By looking for unique pieces of this code, scientists can identify a person by a strand of their hair, a drop of their blood, or other piece of their body tissue.

Fingerprints left at a crime scene have long been used by police investigators to find out whether a certain person committed the crime. DNA fingerprints can be used for the same purpose. The difference is, regular fingerprints can only be found on the tips of a person's fingers. DNA fingerprints are in every cell and tissue in the body.

DNA fingerprinting can also be used for other purposes. It can help find out if a newborn baby has an inherited disease, determine who a child's father is (paternity testing), and it can help identify a body found at an accident scene.

Scientific foundations

Picking out matching pieces of DNA is not easy, since each human being has about three billion DNA base pairs. About ninty-nine percent of a person's DNA is exactly the same as everyone else's DNA. But one percent of DNA (about three million base pairs) is unique to each person. Scientists look for those specific areas of unique DNA when trying to match a sample to a person.

To make a DNA fingerprint, scientists pull DNA from a tissue sample. The sample may be a drop of blood, a hair, or a piece of

Researcher comparing two DNA fingerprints to determine the identity of a criminal. © *Visuals Unlimited.*

skin found at the scene of a crime. They also take a DNA sample from a person who is a suspect in the crime. Then they remove the DNA from the nucleus of the cell.

An older method for DNA fingerprinting is called restriction length fragment polymorphism (RFLP). Scientists break the DNA into pieces using a special enzyme (a protein in the body that

To compare DNA fingerprints, a DNA sample is obtained from, in this case, two people, A and B. Once the DNA is analyzed and put on x ray film, it can be compared to a sample DNA fingerprint, for example, taken from a crime scene to make a match. *Illustration by GGS Inc.*

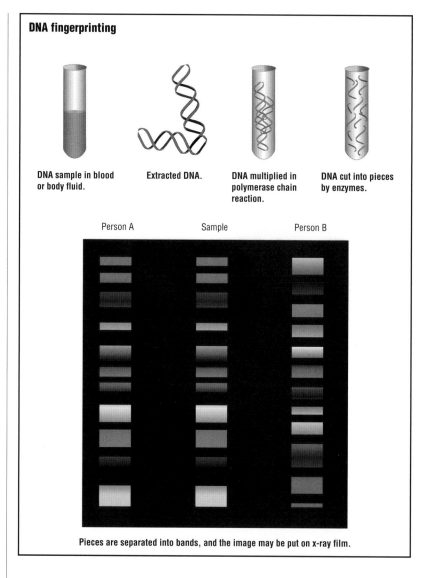

DNA fingerprinting

DNA sample in blood or body fluid.

Extracted DNA.

DNA multiplied in polymerase chain reaction.

DNA cut into pieces by enzymes.

Person A   Sample   Person B

Pieces are separated into bands, and the image may be put on x-ray film.

triggers chemical reactions). The enzyme cuts the DNA at certain sequences of bases. Each type of enzyme looks for a certain sequence to cut (for example, one enzyme might look for the pattern, GAATTC). The cut segments of DNA are separated using a special gel. Then the DNA is moved from the gel onto a type of nylon film. Radioactive (giving off high-energy rays) strands of DNA, called probes, are placed on the film. The probes only stick to certain parts of the DNA. This produces a picture pattern when seen with an x-ray machine (which uses high-energy rays to make a picture). The pattern is the person's DNA fingerprint. It looks a

Wrongly Accused

DNA not only can find someone who is guilty of a crime, it also can free a person who was falsely accused of a crime. In 1992, Guy Paul Marin of Canada was convicted of the murder of a nine-year-old girl and was put in jail. When he was convicted, DNA testing was still a new science. A few years later, it had improved. A test of Marin's DNA in 1995 showed that he had not committed the murder. He was cleared of the crime. In 1997, DNA testing also helped to free a man named Kenneth Adams from prison. He had spent eighteen years in jail for a murder that he did not commit.

lot like a supermarket bar code. Scientists compare the DNA pattern with that of a sample that they know comes from the suspect. If the DNA samples match in a few places, chances are they are from the same person.

Although RFLP is good at finding DNA matches, it can only be used when scientists have a lot of DNA from a person. A newer method, called polymerase chain reaction (PCR), works with much smaller DNA samples. It uses small sequences (about one to four base pairs) of DNA. These small sequences are sometimes called short tandem repeats (STRs). They repeat over and over again. PCR uses special enzymes to make more of the DNA sequences. When they have made enough DNA, scientists can find STRs that are unique to the person.

In the future, scientists may not have to wait to get back to the laboratory to get a DNA fingerprint. A new method called lab-on-a-chip is a small computer that would analyze DNA samples right at a crime scene.

Development

Genetic fingerprinting was invented in the early 1980s by a scientist named Alec Jeffreys at Leicester University in England. Professor Jeffreys and his assistants had been studying DNA to see how it differed from one person to another. They were trying to learn how to track hereditary diseases through families. Professor Jeffreys was using x-ray film to look at the DNA. When he pulled the film out of the developing tank, he noticed patterns in the DNA. He realized that he could use these patterns to identify people.

The first criminal was caught using DNA fingerprinting in 1987. Two years later, the method was used to help free a man who was

Words to Know

Deoxyribonucleic acid (DNA): The double-helix shaped molecule that serves as the carrier of genetic information for humans and most organisms.

Enzyme: A protein that helps control the rate or speed of chemical reactions in the cell.

Paternity: The genetic father of an offspring.

Polymerase chain reaction (PCR): Polymerase chain reaction. A method of making many copies of a short piece of DNA quickly.

Radioactive: The production of high-energy rays as a result of changes in the atomic structure of matter.

Restriction length fragment polymorphism (RFLP): A variation in the DNA sequence, identifiable by restriction enzymes.

X ray: Electromagnetic radiation of very short wavelength, and very high energy.

previously convicted of rape. The courts today look at thousands of DNA fingerprints in criminal cases.

Current issues

DNA fingerprinting is the most accurate method for identifying people to date. But because it is done by hand, there can be mistakes. For example, a hat found at a crime scene may have been worn by more than one person, so it would contain more than one person's DNA. There is a small chance that someone who is linked to a crime by DNA fingerprinting could be innocent.

To help them solve crimes, the Federal Bureau of Investigation (FBI) keeps a computer record of DNA fingerprints. It contains more than one million profiles on people and samples from crime scenes. Some people fear that this database threatens people's privacy. They think the government might be able to learn everything about a person's health from his or her DNA fingerprint and keep it in its database.

■ ■ ■

For More Information

BBC News. "Two Decades of DNA Fingerprints." http://news.bbc.co.uk/2/hi/science/nature/3636050.stm (accessed April 9, 2006).

Cline, Erin. *The Tech Museum of Innovation.* "DNA Fingerprinting —It's Everywhere!" http://www.thetech.org/genetics/news.php?id=16 (accessed April 10, 2006).

Dove, Alan. ''Molecular Cops: Forensic Genomics Harnassed for the Law.'' *Genomics and Proteomics,* June 1, 2004, pg. 23.

The Human Genome Project. ''DNA Forensics.'' http://www.ornl.gov/sci/techresources/Human_Genome/elsi/forensics.shtml (accessed April 9, 2006).

Lampton, Christopher. *DNA Fingerprinting*. London, England: Franklin Watts, 1991.

[*See Also* **Vol. 1, DNA Sequencing; Vol. 3, Fingerprint Technology; Vol. 1, Forensic DNA Testing.**]

■■■

DNA Sequencing

Description

DNA (deoxyribonucleic acid) is the molecule used by almost all living things to control the chemistry of life and to pass on traits to offspring. Messages are coded into DNA as strings of small chemical building blocks called bases. The bases act like letters in written language. Much like finding out how words are spelled by examining the order of letters composing the word, DNA sequencing is the process of finding out the order (sequence) of the bases in a DNA molecule.

Creatures of the same species have similar DNA sequences, but there are still differences between individuals. DNA differences are part of what makes people different in color, height, health, and other traits that can been seen and measured.

DNA sequencing is done using special laboratory equipment that combines DNA with other chemicals to identify a few bases at a time. Several methods for DNA sequencing have been invented.

DNA is basic to all living things, so knowledge of DNA sequences can be used in many ways. DNA sequences are useful in tracing how different species have evolved (changed over time). They are also useful in creating new medical treatments. As with most technologies, however, DNA sequencing could also be used in harmful ways. For example, people whose DNA is thought to have defects might be discriminated against.

Scientific Foundations

The DNA molecule is shaped like a ladder with millions of rungs. Each rung of the ladder is made of two chemicals called bases that lock together form a pair. There are four types of bases,

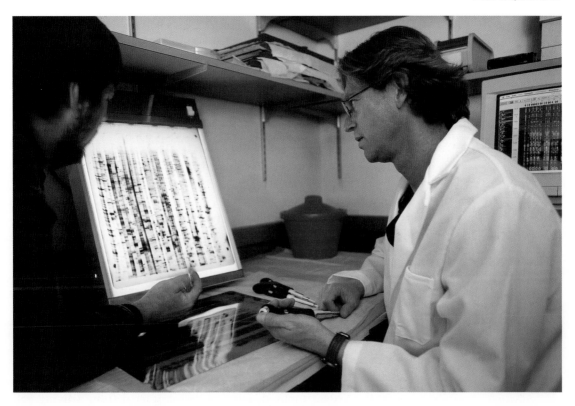

Researchers analyzing a DNA sequence. *Custom Medical Stock Photo. Reproduced by permission.*

usually abbreviated as A, G, C, and T (the first letters of the DNA bases adenine, guanine, cytosine, and thymine), that can make up the base-pair rungs of the DNA ladder. The sequence of As, Cs, Ts, and Gs running up the ladder is what DNA sequencing determines.

Each DNA molecule twists along its length like a licorice stick to form a double spiral or double helix. The double helix is then crumpled and mixed with other molecules to form a bundle called a chromosome. Chromosomes are too small to see without a powerful microscope. Apart from red blood cells, which lose their DNA, every cell in the human body contains 46 chromosomes (22 chromosome pairs and two special sex chromosomes designated as X and Y chromosomes). Females carry two X chromosomes. Males carry an X and a Y chromosome. Chromosomes are separate DNA molecules. There are about three billion base pairs in the human chromosomes in each cell.

Development

A Swiss biologist named Johann Miescher discovered the DNA molecule in the late 1800s. In 1929, Russian-American scientist

Phoebus Levine discovered that DNA contained the A, C, G, and T bases. In the 1940s, scientists began to understood that DNA is the genetic material, that is, the substance that carries the information that allows information (and traits such as eye color) to pass from parent to child. The discovery that it has a twisted-ladder or double-helix shape was finally made in 1953 by English Physicist Francis Crick and American Molecular Biologist James Watson.

The genetic code was discovered in the late 1950s. The genetic code is the way in which sequences of A, C, G, and T bases specify the structures of the large molecules called proteins, which carry out most of the body's chemical tasks. Each series of bases that specifies a protein is called a gene. The average gene is 3,000 bases long, but some genes are over two million bases long. There are about 30,000 genes in the human genome (complete set of human DNA) and about 100,000 different proteins in the human body.

To understand the genome of any species, the sequence of bases in the DNA of that species must be known. DNA sequencing is the technology that makes this knowledge possible. In 1977, two methods of sequencing DNA were developed. The one that is more widely used is the chain termination method or Sanger method, was invented by Frederick Sanger.

In the Sanger method, DNA is first extracted from a living cell and broken into fragments. Each DNA fragment is mixed with chemicals that make millions of copies of it grow in a lengthwise, base-by-base way. Four such mixtures are made. In one, another chemical causes each DNA copy to stop growing when it ends with an A base. In another, a chemical causes each DNA copy to stop growing when it ends with a C base. Two other mixtures produce DNA copies that end only in Gs and Ts. The growth-stopping chemicals are present in low enough concentrations so that growth is sometimes stopped the first time an A, C, G, or T base is reached, sometimes the second time, and so forth. The result is that fragments of all possible lengths are produced in each mixture.

The next step in the Sanger method uses the fact that longer DNA fragments are larger molecules. Using the method called gel electrophoresis, each of the four types of fragment mixtures—that containing all possible fragments ending in A, that containing all possible fragments ending in C, and likewise for G and T—are made to travel through a strip of gel or jelly that slows down larger molecules more than it slows down small ones. In this way, fragments of different lengths are separated in the gel, just as fast runners move away from slow runners on a race track.

Ninety-Six Percent Monkey

Fast DNA sequencing has recently made it practical to sequence the genomes (all the DNA) of several species of animal. A first draft of the human genome was published in 2001, of the mouse genome in 2002, of the rat genome in 2004, and of the chimpanzee genome in 2005. A final sequence for the human genome was released in 2003.

We can now compare the DNA of chimpanzees and of humans in detail. It turns out that 96 percent of chimp and human DNA is the same. Scientists have long known that chimpanzees are our closest evolutionary cousins—the two species are descended from a single ancestor species that lived about six million years ago—but by comparing DNA base by base and gene by gene, they can now begin to track exactly what it is that makes us genetically human.

All the DNA fragments ending in A are separated in one gel strip, all the sequence fragments ending in C are separated in another, and likewise for G and T. Four gel strips are produced. Each strip shows a series of spaced-out dark bands. Each band is a place where DNA fragments of a particular length have separated from all others.

If the gel strips with four bands are laid side by side, the base sequence of the original DNA can finally be read. For example, if the first dark band on any of the four strips is in the A strip, then the first base in the DNA being sequenced is an A. If the second dark band is on the C strip, then the second base is a C—and so on to the end of the sequence.

Originally, all the steps of the Sanger method had to be done by hand. In the 1990s, the process was automated so that it could be controlled by computer. This made DNA sequencing much faster. By 2003, the entire human genome had been sequenced.

Current Issues

Everyone's DNA is a little different from everyone else's. Most of these differences are harmless, but about 4,000 are known to cause diseases. DNA sequencing allows a patient's genes to be tested for disease-causing genes. If a disease-causing gene is present, doctors can watch for the beginnings of that disease, and if discovered, begin treatment early. On the other hand, this information could be also used against the patient. For instance, insurance companies might refuse to give health insurance to people who carry genes that might cause certain diseases (even if the chances are small that they will develop a particular disease), or employers might refuse to hire them.

Words to Know

Base: One of the four chemical letters in the DNA code. There are four kinds, called A, C, G, and T (short for adenine, cytosine, guanine, and thymine).

DNA: A double-helix shaped molecule inside cells that carries the genetic information.

DNA sequencing: A method of finding out the sequence of base pairs in a DNA molecule.

Gel electrophoresis: A laboratory test that separates molecules based on their size, shape, or electrical charge.

DNA sequencing is used in police work to match suspects with DNA left at crime scenes. A number of people imprisoned for crimes have been proven innocent and released because their DNA did not match DNA from crime scenes.

Another use for DNA sequencing is the prevention of drug reactions. Over 100,000 people die in the United States every year after taking certain medicines. The difference between the people who are helped by a drug and the people who are hurt is thought to be in their DNA. Scientists are trying to discover which DNA differences make which medicines risky. If a patient's DNA is sequenced, then it may be possible to identify which drugs they should not take.

DNA sequencing is also allowing scientists to trace the evolutionary family tree of life in greater detail than ever before. The theory of evolution has been confirmed by the huge amount of new information supplied by DNA sequencing.

■ ■ ■

For More Information

Gonick, Larry and Mark Wheelis. *The Cartoon Guide to Genetics*. New York: Collins, 1991.

National Institutes of Health. "New Genome Comparison Finds Chimps, Humans Very Similar at the DNA Level." August 31, 2005. <http://www.genome.gov/15515096> (accessed April 28, 2006).

Palladino, Michael. *Understanding the Human Genome Project*. Menlo Park, CA: Benjamin Cummings, 2005.

U.S. Department of Energy. "Facts About Genome Sequencing." October 27, 2004. <http://www.ornl.gov/sci/techresources/Human_Genome/faq/seqfacts.shtml> (accessed April 28, 2006).

[*See Also* **Vol. 1, DNA Fingerprinting; Vol. 1, Gene Therapy; Vol. 1, Genetic Discrimination; Vol. 1, Genetic Testing, Medical; Vol. 1, Genomics.**]

■ ■ ■

DNA Vaccines

Description

Vaccines are substances made of dead or weakened germs (such as viruses or bacteria) that help protect people against diseases. Effective vaccines change the immune system (the body's natural defense system against foreign chemicals and organisms) so it acts as if it has already developed a disease. The vaccine prepares the immune system and its antibodies (disease-fighting substances) to react quickly and effectively when threatened by the same disease in the future.

A DNA vaccine is a bit different from a regular vaccine. Instead of using the whole virus (or other disease-causing organism) to trigger an immune response, it uses just a few genes (pieces of DNA that carry instructions for traits and diseases) from that virus. The DNA provides information, or codes, that tells cells how to make proteins (substances that carry out different functions of the cells). The genes in the DNA vaccines teach the vaccinated person's immune system to respond to the virus when it sees it. It is able to protect the body against further attacks because the protein lives a long time.

Development

The first vaccine was created by British physician Edward Jenner (1749–1823) in 1789. It protected against a dangerous illness called smallpox by using the related, less-dangerous cowpox virus to build up immunity. Jenner also coined the word "vaccination" to refer to this treatment. Since then, scientists have made vaccines for polio, mumps, whooping cough, and many other serious diseases.

For two hundred years, regular vaccines were the main methods for preventing diseases. However, in 1993, researchers at Merck

Rows of DNA synthesizers, automatic and high speed machines used to make short sequences of customized DNA (DNA with specific base sequences), are used to make the artifical DNA used in some DNA vaccines. *AP Images.*

Research Laboratories in Pennsylvania made a major discovery. They injected just the genes for a flu virus protein into mouse muscles. The mouse muscle cells began producing the virus protein. That protein caused an immune response that protected the mouse from the flu. This was the beginning of DNA vaccines.

In 2005, the first DNA vaccines were approved for animals. One vaccine protects salmon from a dangerous virus. The other protects horses from the West Nile virus (a disease that can cause swelling of the brain and spinal cord). No DNA vaccines have yet been approved for human use.

At first, when DNA vaccines were experimentally given to people, they did not work well because the genes were not able to get into the human cells. In later tests, human DNA vaccines were more effective. Scientists are testing DNA vaccines for diseases such as acquired immune deficiency syndrome (AIDS—a disease that damages the immune system), cancer, smallpox, and the flu. DNA vaccines might also be used to protect against cancer, allergies, and other health problems. As of mid-2006, DNA vaccines for human use are still under development, but progress is being made toward their approval worldwide.

Research into a DNA Vaccine for HIV

As of 2006, there was no vaccine to prevent infection by the human immunodeficiency virus (HIV), the virus that causes AIDS. It is important to develop an effective and safe vaccine, since over 25 million people died from AIDS-related causes between 1981 and 2005. Consequently, scientists around the world are working intensively to develop a DNA vaccine and have tested many of these vaccines. Such vaccines are made artificially, so they do not contain any actual HIV viruses. As a result, DNA vaccines cannot infect anyone with HIV. So far, the only side effects associated with experimental HIV DNA vaccines have been minor irritation around the injection area, a low fever, and minor body aches that quickly go away. As with other experimental DNA vaccines, a future HIV vaccine should be safe, inexpensive to make, and not need refrigeration, so that it will be easy to store and give to those who need it.

Scientific Foundations

DNA vaccines are made of gold particles. The particles are coated with a small, circular piece of DNA. The particles are injected into a person's cells, usually within a muscle because muscle cells are more receptive. The vaccine then delivers the DNA into the cells.

The vaccine's DNA contains genes that code for a certain protein, called an antigen. This protein causes an immune response, just like a regular vaccine. The vaccine teaches the person's immune system to fight off the target disease.

In the future, there may be other ways to deliver a DNA vaccine. A nasal spray is one possible method. The spray would carry the vaccine into the person's lungs, where the genes would be taken into lung cells.

Current Issues

DNA vaccines have several advantages over regular vaccines:

- With a regular vaccine, the vaccine itself causes an immune response in the person who is vaccinated. As a result, the effects of regular vaccines can sometimes wear off. Some vaccines have to be given more than once to protect a person. Since DNA vaccines generate the immune response with genes functioning inside a person's own cells, they can protect a person from a disease for a lifetime.

Words to Know

Acquired immune deficiency syndrome (AIDS): An epidemic disease caused by an infection with the human immunodeficiency virus (HIV).

Antigen: A molecule, usually a protein, that the body identifies as foreign and toward which it directs an immune response.

Antibody: A molecule created by the immune system in response to the presence of an antigen (a foreign substance or particle). It marks foreign microorganisms in the body for destruction by other immune cells.

Bacteria: Microscopic organisms whose activities range from the development of disease to fermentation.

DNA: A double-helix shaped molecule inside cells that carries the genetic information.

Gene: A discrete unit of inheritance, represented by a portion of DNA located on a chromosome. The gene is a code for the production of a specific kind of protein or RNA molecule, and therefore for a specific inherited characteristic.

Immune system: A system in the human body that fights off foreign substances, cells, and tissues in an effort to protect a person from disease.

Mutation: A change in a gene's DNA. Whether a mutation is harmful is determined by the effect on the product for which the gene codes.

Pathogen: A disease causing agent, such as a bacteria, virus, fungus, etc.

Polio: A disease (poliomyelitis) caused by a virus that can result in muscle weakness, paralysis, or death.

Protein: Complex molecules that cells use to form most of the structures and control chemical reactions within a cell.

Smallpox: A deadly viral disease that was eradicated in the 1970s. Today the virus only exists in closely-guarded samples held by the American and Russian governments.

Virus: A very simple microorganism, much smaller than bacteria, that enters and multiples within cells. Viruses often exchange or transfer their genetic material (DNA or RNA) to cells and can cause diseases such as chickenpox, hepatitis, measles, and mumps.

Whooping cough: An acute infectious disease caused by *Bordetella pertussis* that causes spasms of coughing and convulsions.

- Many regular vaccines contain live, but weakened, versions of the pathogen (disease-causing organism). Some people can get sick, if their immune systems are not strong enough to fight off even the weaker version of the pathogen. DNA vaccines only contain the certain genes from the pathogen, not the whole organism. As a result, they cannot make a person sick. This makes the DNA vaccine useful for diseases such as AIDS, which are too dangerous to use as a regular vaccine.

- Regular vaccines must be given one shot at a time. To get all of his or her vaccinations, a child might have to visit the doctor many times. But, a single shot of a DNA vaccine could protect against more than one disease.

- Regular vaccines are very expensive and difficult to make. Most are grown inside chicken eggs. Making just a one-year supply of the flu vaccine, for example, takes millions of chicken eggs. It also can take more than six months to produce the vaccine. This means scientists cannot make a regular flu vaccine quickly if needed. DNA vaccines can be made much more rapidly using machines that make custom DNA (DNA with specific base sequences). This makes DNA vaccines both less expensive and faster to produce than regular vaccines.

- Regular vaccines must be kept cold, which makes them hard to carry from place to place. In addition, scientists must make new batches every year because they do not store well. DNA vaccines can be stored at many different temperatures. And they can be kept for many years without going bad.

There are some concerns about DNA vaccines. One of the biggest concerns is that the DNA from the pathogen might get into a person's genes. This could possibly cause a permanent change to the genes, called a mutation. Although tests with DNA vaccines are promising, they still have not proven effective in protecting humans.

■ ■ ■

For More Information

Access Excellence. "DNA Vaccine Outlook." December 1, 1997. <http://www.accessexcellence.org/WN/SUA11/dnavax1297.html> (accessed April 12, 2006).

Crabtree, Penni. "DNA Vaccines Approved for Animals." *San Diego Union-Tribune* (July 20, 2005).

"DNA Vaccine May Stem Spread." *USA Today Magazine* (December 2005): 14–15.

Wired News. "DNA Could Speed Flu Vaccine." October 30, 2005. <http://www.wired.com/news/medtech/0,1286,69422,00.html> (accessed April 12, 2006).

[See Also **Vol. 1, Genomics; Vol. 2, Recombinant DNA technology; Vol. 1, Vaccines.**]

■■■

Enzyme Replacement Therapy

Description

An enzyme is a chemical that plays an important role in the chemical reactions that take place inside an organism. Essentially, all the functions of the cells in our bodies are chemical reactions, and many different enzymes are essential to ensure that our cells are working properly. Enzymes are types of proteins, which are the primary components of living cells.

Enzymes are vital for many functions in the body. When an enzyme malfunctions or does not function at all, diseases can development. Examples of diseases caused by missing or malfunctioning enzymes include cystic fibrosis, Fabry disease, and Gaucher disease.

Enzyme replacement therapy is a treatment that replaces a specific nonfunctioning enzyme with a functional version of the protein. Alternately, this therapy can supply the body with a gene that will ultimately produce a functional version of the particular enzyme. A gene is a piece of DNA, or genetic material, that tells a cell how to produce a particular protein. If the correctly functioning gene is supplied through enzyme replacement therapy, it will tell a cell how to produce the enzyme needed. If the defective enzyme has caused a disease, then enzyme replacement therapy can reverse these effects. Enzyme replacement therapy is a new, experimental treatment for some diseases.

Scientific Foundations

Cystic fibrosis, Fabry disease, and Gaucher disease are all genetic disorders. This means that those who suffer from these diseases have inherited a genetic defect from one or both of their parents. Since genes tell cells how to make proteins, including

enzymes, having a faulty or missing gene (a mutation) can result in cells that do not make enough, or any, of a particular enzyme. The result can be a genetic disorder. Not all people with the same genetic disorder have the same symptoms. Sometimes there are many different mutations for a single gene, and which mutation a person has determines the type and severity of symptoms.

Replacing an absent or malfunctioning enzyme can be done by directly supplying the enzyme as a part of medical treatment for a disease. Alternately, the gene encoding the enzyme can be supplied. If the gene is successfully incorporated into the hosts' genetic material, then the inserted gene can direct cells to produce the appropriate enzyme. Enzymes may be isolated from human or animal blood or tissues, or they may be genetically engineered. Genetically engineered enzymes often cause fewer bad reactions in patients, and they can be produced in much larger quantities than can be obtained from natural sources.

Family affected by Pompe's disease, a genetic disorder for which enzyme replacement therapy is being tested. The girl and boy in front have the condition. © *Najalh Feanny/Corbis.*

Another Cost of Enzyme Replacement Therapy

Enzyme replacement therapies for relatively rare maladies, such as Gaucher disease and Fabry disease, are expensive on a per-patient basis. In countries where medical care is largely provided through tax revenues, the resources for health care are limited and must be allotted. This creates a dilemma. The allocation of funds to very expensive treatments for relatively few people could result in less money to treat diseases that affect more people. As populations age and the need for medical care increases, the debate about the accessibility to publicly funded medical care will continue to grow in urgency.

Development

One disease that can be successfully treated using enzyme replacement therapy is Gaucher disease. In this disease, there is not enough of an enzyme called glucocerebrosidase (GLOO-koh-sair-a-BROH-sa-days). This causes the accumulation of a compound called glucocerebroside (GLOO-koh-SAIR-a-broh-side) in cells. As a consequence, the compound accumulates in the liver and spleen (both organs filter blood), which become enlarged. Various organs stop working properly, and the skeletal system deteriorates.

By regularly receiving doses of a glucocerebrosidase-containing medication, these symptoms can be reversed in people who have Gaucher disease. Because the enzyme is supplied directly, the medication must throughout the person's life for the beneficial effects to be maintained.

Another disease that is treated with enzyme replacement therapy is Fabry disease. In Fabry disease, an enzyme called alpha-galactosidase (al-fa-ga-LAK-toe-sa-days) is missing, and its absence causes fats to build up in blood vessels over time. The reduced efficiency of blood flow causes the kidneys and heart to malfunction or even to stop functioning. While rare, Fabry disease is a serious health concern. The treatment of Fabry disease consists of regular infusions of an enzyme, in this case a genetically engineered form of alpha-galactosidase.

People with cystic fibrosis have mucus (phlegm) that is thicker and stickier than normal. In addition to breathing problems, patients can experience difficulty in digesting food, due to mucus that clogs the digestive system. The mucus also inhibits digestive enzymes from being able to break down food in the stomach and intestines. In the past, those with cystic fibrosis often needed to

Words to Know

Enzyme: A protein that helps control the rate or speed of chemical reactions in the cell.

Gene: A discrete unit of inheritance, represented by a portion of DNA located on a chromosome. The gene is a code for the production of a specific kind of protein or RNA molecule, and therefore for a specific inherited characteristic.

Protein: Complex molecules that cells use to form most of the structures and control chemical reactions within a cell.

Vector: A vehicle used to deliver foreign genes into another organism's DNA. Viruses are the most commonly used vectors.

adopt a different diet to compensate for this enzyme deficiency. By giving people with cystic fibrosis the enzymes that are normally produced by the pancreas, their intestinal levels of these enzymes are raised, which enables food to be digested more efficiently. For patients on enzyme replacement therapy, a normal diet is possible.

Current Issues

Despite its successes, enzyme replacement therapy is still in its infancy. Ensuring that an enzyme reaches its target and that its activity is maintained is not easy. But, with experience, the number of diseases that respond positively to the addition of a critical enzyme(s) will surely grow.

Research into gene-mediated enzyme replacement will continue, as will other types of gene therapy. If it can work well, gene-mediated enzyme replacement is a better treatment for some diseases, since it would eliminate the need to periodically supply patients with the preformed enzyme. Once a gene is inserted into a host's genetic material, the beneficial enzyme could produced by that person's body indefinitely.

Getting the gene into the body is a challenge as well. Other types of gene therapy use viruses as vectors. This means that the beneficial gene is put inside the virus, which is then injected into the body. The virus then delivers the gene to cells. The most common viral vectors are adenoviruses, which are the same kind of viruses that cause colds.

In the laboratory, gene delivery has been achieved using liposomes (LIP-a-sohmes). Liposomes are artificially created hollow spheres whose outer wall is constructed of lipid (fat) molecules. The beneficial is injected into the liposome, which is delivered into the body.

More efficiency enzyme replacement therapies also will reduce the cost of the therapy, which is currently very expensive.

■ ■ ■

For More Information

Beutler, Ernest. "Enzyme Replacement in Gaucher Disease." *PLoS Medicine* 1 (2004): e21–30.

Wilcox, W. R., et al. "Long-term Safety and Efficacy of Enzyme Replacement Therapy for Fabry Disease." *American Journal of Human Genetics* 75 (2004): 65–74.

Zoler, Mitchel L. "Enzyme Replacement Therapy Resolves Fabry Disease." *Family Practice News* 31 (2001): 7.

[*See Also* **Vol. 1, Cystic Fibrosis Drugs; Vol. 1, Designer Genes.**]

Forensic DNA Testing

Description

Deoxyribonucleic acid (DNA) is the material that contains a person's genetic information. DNA testing is used to analyze and compare DNA from two or more people. Sometimes, members of law enforcement perform DNA testing—what they sometimes call DNA profiling—on people who are victims or suspects in crimes. Police officials use DNA from blood, hair, skin, and other materials found at crime scenes to find out who is (or is not) responsible for crimes. When DNA testing is performed to solve crimes, it is called forensic DNA testing.

Forensic scientists check about thirteen different DNA regions that have been found to vary from person to person. Information is collected in a DNA profile (sometimes called a DNA fingerprint) that identifies an individual. By using these different DNA regions, scientists can decide whether two people have the same or different DNA profile.

After a person's DNA profile is determined, law-enforcement officers use computers to record the information digitally. In this way, they can use the DNA information in the future and share it with other police around the world. The courts in the United States accept forensic DNA information as evidence in paternity suits and generally accept it in criminal trials.

Scientific Foundations

DNA is a molecule that looks like a ladder that has been twisted into the shape of a winding staircase—what scientists call a double helix (HEE-liks). The rungs of this chemical ladder are small molecules or building-blocks that spell out a chemical message like a long line of letters. Cells read the DNA code like a book of

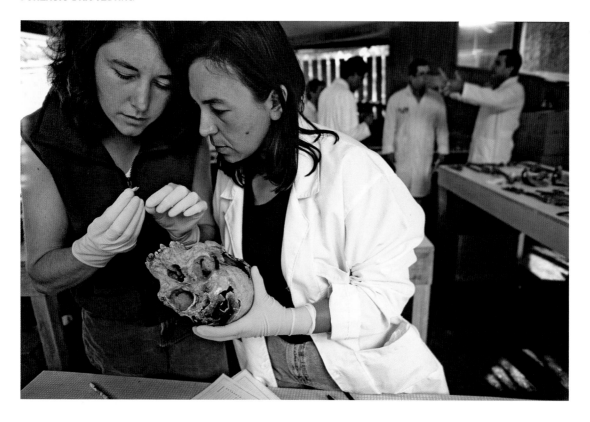

Researchers using forensic testing to identify a human rights abuse victim in Guatemala. © *Karen Kasmauski/Corbis.*

recipes, putting together many different molecules that the cell needs to live. All living organisms that contain cells have DNA. In mammals, such as humans, pieces of DNA are grouped into chromosomes, which are located in the nucleus of each cell. DNA also is the molecule used by all living cells to pass traits on to the next generation. For example, if a child has red hair, then either her mother or father (or both) passed that trait to the daughter before she was born.

Development

American biologist James Watson (1928–), English biologist Francis Crick (1916–2004), and New Zealander-English biophysicist Maurice Wilkins (1916–2004) shared the Nobel Prize in physiology or medicine in 1962 for discovering the structure of DNA. In 1985, English geneticist Sir Alec Jeffreys (1950–), while doing research at the University of Leicester, invented DNA testing. Soon after, this technique was used to solve crimes (what is called forensics). In fact, Jeffreys' technique was first used to

Super Bowl and Olympic Souvenirs

DNA technology is used in many ways, and the number of ways are increasing each year. For example, footballs used in Super Bowl competitions are marked with an invisible, permanent piece of artificial DNA. Balls, caps, jerseys, and other items used in Olympic Games are marked with natural DNA from unidentified athletes. Such sports souvenirs are marked with DNA and tested with specially designed lasers to make sure that people can recognize real souvenirs from those made by dishonest means. Unfortunately, souvenir fraud has become common in sports. By using DNA technology, such fraud can be stopped with the use of forensic DNA testing.

identify a man who murdered two English people in 1983 and 1986. The DNA of the suspect was tested and found to match DNA found at the crime scene. The suspect was later convicted of murder based partially on the DNA evidence.

Jeffreys later improved on his DNA testing technique by identifying a few characteristics (what he called minisatellites) of the DNA. By concentrating on these minisatellites, Jeffreys was able to make DNA testing more accurate. In 1995, the technique developed by Jeffreys was used to establish the National DNA Database (NDNAD) in England.

Current Issues

Only about 0.1 percent of DNA differs from person to person. From that tiny amount of difference, forensic DNA testing can result in a non-match or a match. A non-match proves without a doubt (100 percent) that the two samples came from two different people. However, when two samples are considered identical (a match), there is only a very high likelihood (well over 99.99 percent, but still not quite 100 percent) that the two samples came from the same person. In a criminal case, for example, DNA evidence can show that the odds of an accused person actually committing the crime to be one in one billion. The result does not absolutely mean that the accused person did not commit the crime. However, it does show that it is very likely that the person did not commit the crime. Many people are found guilty or innocent of crimes based on DNA evidence.

The media and members of the legal profession, such as defense lawyers, have questioned the reliability of forensic DNA testing. However, no court has ever rejected DNA evidence based on its

Words to Know

Chromosome: A thread-shaped structure that carries genetic information in cells.

Nucleus: A compartment in the cell which is enclosed by a membrane and which contains its genetic information.

Paternity: The genetic father of an offspring.

unreliability. DNA evidence has only been rejected due to errors in the testing process, such as incorrect readings by laboratory technicians. In fact, laboratory errors have been one of the biggest problems to DNA testing. Human errors are becoming less common as technicians gain more experience in reading DNA samples and as more standard tests are used throughout the world.

■ ■ ■

For More Information

Fischer, Eric A. *DNA Identification and Evidence: Application and Issues*. Huntington, NY: Novinka Books, 2001.

Hamilton, Janet. *James Watson: Solving the Mystery of DNA*. Berkeley Heights, NJ: Enslow Publishers, 2004.

Inman, Keith. *An Introduction to Forensic DNA Analysis*. Boca Raton, FL: CRC Press, 1997.

Marian Koshland Science Museum of the National Academy of Sciences. ''Putting DNA to Work.'' <http://www.koshlandscience.org/exhibitdna/index.jsp> (accessed June 30, 2006).

[See Also **Vol. 1, DNA Fingerprinting; Vol. 1, DNA Sequencing; Vol. 3, Fingerprint Technology.**]

■■■

Frozen Egg Technology

Description

The process of freezing a woman's eggs so that they can be used at a future time is a new technology. Once a woman is ready to have a baby, the eggs can be thawed and fertilized (merging sperm with an egg to form a new human being). Eggs and sperm contain the hereditary material, or DNA (deoxyribonucleic acid), of the parents. DNA is packaged in sections called genes.

In vitro fertilization is a process that combines a woman's egg with a man's sperm in a laboratory to form an embryo (a multi-celled fertilized egg). The embryo can then be implanted in the woman's uterus where it continues to develop into a baby. Doctors have been able to freeze embryos for many years. In vitro fertilization often results in too many embryos. The extra embryos may be frozen until the woman is ready to get pregnant, but many stay frozen for years because the parents do not use them. Keeping embryos frozen is controversial because some people believe embryos are human lives. Freezing only the eggs provides another option.

Scientific Foundations

In order to collect eggs from a woman, she is given specific hormones (chemicals in the body that control the actions of cells and organs) that make her ovaries produce more eggs than normal. A doctor then surgically removes the eggs from the woman's ovary using a small needle.

The eggs must be protected during the freezing process so they are not damaged. One way to do this is by adding chemicals to the eggs. The chemicals replace the water in the eggs to prevent ice

Frozen Zoo®

Frozen eggs could also play an important part in preserving endangered animals. The Frozen Zoo, affiliated with the San Diego Zoo, collects and maintains frozen eggs, sperm, embryos, DNA, and tissue samples of animals whose numbers are dwindling in the wild. Scientists hope to ensure the survival of endangered species by learning efficient techniques to assist their reproduction.

crystals from forming when the eggs are frozen. Another method is to freeze them so quickly that ice crystals do not have a chance to form.

When a woman is ready to get pregnant, doctors thaw one or more eggs using special chemicals. The eggs and sperm are combined in a lab. If they make an embryo, the doctor places it in the woman's uterus to grow.

Development

Doctors have been able to freeze and thaw sperm for many years. They have also been able to freeze embryos. But freezing eggs has taken longer because it is hard to do without damaging them.

Eggs contain a lot of water. When a human egg is frozen, ice crystals form. The ice crystals destroy the chromosomes (the structures that contain the genes) in the eggs. Researchers discovered this in the 1980s when they experimented with freezing mouse eggs. Freezing also forms a coating around the egg that is hard for the sperm to swim through.

In 1986, the first baby was born using frozen eggs with the help of a doctor in Australia. A year later, doctors in Germany also achieved pregnancies using frozen eggs. However, it was another ten years before doctors started using frozen eggs regularly.

The first American woman to have a baby using a frozen egg was in 1997. In 2004, doctors in Italy reported that they were able to fertilize 123 frozen eggs. Out of those eggs, thirteen babies were born. By the beginning of the twenty-first century, fewer than two hundred babies had been born using frozen eggs.

Eggs can be frozen for many reasons. It can preserve a woman's eggs until she is ready to have a baby. The older a woman gets, the harder it is for her to get pregnant. With age, the eggs lose quality. When a woman goes through menopause in her forties or fifties, her periods stop and her body no longer releases eggs. A woman

Words to Know

Chromosome: A thread-shaped structure that carries genetic information in cells.

DNA: A double-helix shaped molecule inside cells that carries the genetic information.

Embryo: An organism (human being, other animals, and plants) in its earliest stage of development.

Genes: Pieces of DNA that carry instructions for traits and diseases.

Hormone: A chemical substance produced by the body. Hormones are created by one organ of the body but they usually carry out functions in other organs or parts of the body.

In-vitro fertilization: Combining an egg and a sperm in the laboratory to create an embryo that is then implanted in the mother's uterus.

Ovaries: Female reproductive organs that contain unfertilized eggs.

Menopause: The time in a woman's life when the chemical environment of her body changes, resulting in decreased estrogen production (among other things) and the cessation of her menstrual period.

Uterus: Organ in female mammals in which the embryo and fetus grow to maturity.

can freeze her eggs when she is young and then use them when she is older if she is having trouble getting pregnant.

Freezing eggs can also help a woman who has cancer have a baby. A treatment for cancer called chemotherapy uses drugs to kill cancer cells. These drugs may damage the ovaries (the female sex glands that produce eggs and hormones). Without working ovaries, a woman cannot produce eggs. If a woman freezes her eggs first, she can use them to get pregnant once her cancer treatment is finished.

Women who are unable to get pregnant with their own eggs can receive donor eggs. Donor eggs can be frozen in order to move them from one city to another.

Even with advances in the science of frozen eggs, success rates remain low. By 2006, only about two out of every one hundred frozen eggs resulted in a live birth. In comparison, in vitro fertilization using non-frozen eggs produced about eight or nine babies per one hundred eggs.

Current Issues

Before they were able to freeze eggs, doctors could freeze embryos. Some people objected to the fact that embryos could remain frozen for years. Many people believe that embryos are still human life, and should not be wasted.

Freezing eggs has less controversy, but there are still issues with the process. One issue is that frozen eggs could allow much older women to have babies. Some people believe women in their fifties, sixties, or seventies are too old to have a baby.

There also may be problems with using eggs that have been frozen. Scientists are still not sure whether freezing could affect the chromosomes in the eggs because the science is relatively new. Changes to the chromosomes could potentially cause the babies to have health problems.

■ ■ ■

For More Information

"Former Tech Exec Launches Company to Freeze Women's Eggs." *Women's Health Weekly* (October 14, 2004): 150.

Haddix, Dar. "Frozen Fertility for Working Women?" *The Washington Times.* <http://www.washtimes.com/upi–breaking/20040723–075248–2068r.htm> July 23, 2004 (accessed April 15, 2006).

Kolata, Gina. "Successful Births Reported with Frozen Human Eggs." *The New York Times.* <http://query.nytimes.com/gst/fullpage.html?sec=health&res=9E05E2D7133FF934A25753C1A961958260> October 17, 1997 (accessed April 15, 2006).

Newman, Judith. "Fertility." *Discover.* <http://www.discover.com/issues/oct–05/features/fertility/> October 2005 (accessed April 15, 2006).

Philipkoski, Kristen. "Frozen Eggs Showing Promise." *Wired News.* <http://www.wired.com/news/technology/medtech/0,64916–0.html> September 13, 2004 (accessed April 15, 2006).

[*See Also* **Vol. 1, Bioethics; Vol. 1, In-Vitro Fertilization.**]

■■■

GenBank

Description

GenBank is a database run by the National Institutes of Health (NIH), part of the U.S. government. A database is a collection of information that can be seen using a computer. The GenBank database contains all stretches of decoded DNA that have been made available to the public. Anyone with a computer can look at the GenBank database for free.

GenBank is used by scientists around in the world in many ways. For example, by examining differences between the DNA of similar species, biologists who study evolution can tell how species are related. They can even tell how long ago species split apart into separate lines of descent.

Despite its name, GenBank is not a gene bank. A gene bank contains actual DNA molecules; GenBank contains only information.

Scientific Foundations

DNA (short for deoxyribonucleic acid) is the molecule that controls heredity and the manufacture of the molecules called proteins in almost all living cells. Heredity is the passing on of traits from one generation to the next.

Each DNA molecule is a long chain of atoms that resembles a twisted ladder having thousands or millions of rungs. Each rung in this chemical ladder is made of two smaller molecules locked together in the middle. Each of these smaller molecules is called a base. There are only four kinds of base in DNA, called adenine, cytosine, guanine, and thymine (A, C, G, and T for short). The order in which these four bases occur along the length of the DNA molecule is like a code. The code gives cells instructions for

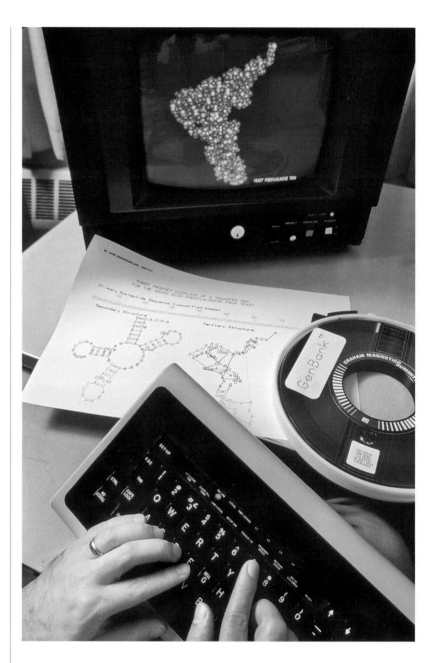

A computer terminal for GenBank, a computer database of genetic information. © *Ted Spiegel/ Corbis.*

making proteins. Cells live and reproduce by making proteins according to the recipes coded into their DNA.

Most base pairs are grouped together in strings or packages called genes. A gene is a short section of DNA that controls the manufacture of a protein in a living cell or helps control how other

100 Billion Served

GenBank works with two other DNA database projects, the European Molecular Biology Laboratory's European Bioinformatics Institute and the DNA Data Bank of Japan, to keep track of all the DNA sequences known to science. In August 2005, the three projects made a proud joint announcement: together, they had made available to the public information on 100 billion bases (letters of the genetic code). One hundred billion is about the number of nerve cells in the human brain or stars in our galaxy. The public DNA library offered by GenBank and its partners now contains over 55 million sequences from at least 200,000 different organisms. Thanks to these databases, biologists can now study the DNA of entire ecosystems (communities of living things) and study life in other complex ways that were never possible before.

genes are decoded. Genes are passed from parent to offspring in all living things. A single gene often contains thousands of base pairs. The complete set of genes of an organism is called the genome.

Much of the information in GenBank is long lists of base pairs, recorded as the letters A, C, G, and T. GenBank also lists sequence information for RNA, a molecule that is similar to DNA and is also found in almost all living cells.

A sample GenBank file, for a single gene of the common yeast *Saccharomyces cerevisiae*, can be seen online at http://www.ncbi.nlm.nih.gov/Sitemap/samplerecord.html. Part of the record looks like this:

ctaacgaaga atccattgtg tcgtattacg gacgttctca gttgtataat gcgccgttac

Development

In 1980, the NIH sponsored a meeting of scientists to talk about the need for a DNA database or "data bank" as it was then called. Based on advice from the scientists, and working with the National Cancer Institute and other official organizations, the NIH set about setting up the Genetic Sequence Data Bank or GenBank. The information in GenBank first became available to the public on October 1, 1982. Earlier that year the European Molecular Biology Laboratory's European Bioinformatics Institute, had already opened for business, becoming the world's first public DNA database.

At that time the Internet did not exist, and distribution of Gen-Bank information was mostly by means of computer-readable magnetic tapes and a yearly printout in book form. Today, access to GenBank is entirely online. A software package from the National

Words to Know

Base: One of the four chemical letters in the DNA code. There are four kinds, called A, C, G, and T (short for adenine, cytosine, guanine, and thymine).

Base pair: Two bases bonded together— either A with T, or C with G—to bridge the two spirals of a DNA molecule, much as a rung connects the two uprights of a ladder.

DNA: A double-helix shaped molecule inside cells that carries the genetic information.

Genome: A complete set of the DNA for a species.

Protein: Complex molecules that cells use to form most of the structures and control chemical reactions within a cell.

Center for Biotechnology Information (NCBI) called Entrez allows access to the information in GenBank, along with information on taxonomy (how species are related to each other), protein structure, genome mapping, and more. Scientists add data to GenBank over the Internet using other software supplied by the NCBI.

Current Issues

GenBank has become a necessary tool for many scientists. It is also, thanks to cheap DNA sequencing technologies that had become available starting in the 1990s, growing faster than ever. As of 2003, GenBank contained records of over 33 billion bases in 27 million sequences and was growing at almost a million sequences (lists of DNA bases) a month. In that year alone, more than 40 complete bacterial genomes were added to the database.

The information in GenBank concerns species; it does not contain DNA information about particular people. Therefore, there has been no public controversy about whether the NIH has a right to hold the information it has in GenBank and make that information available to the public. There is nothing personal or private about any of the information in GenBank.

■ ■ ■

For More Information

Baxevanis, Andreas D. and Ouelette, B. F. Francis, eds. *Bioinformatics: A Practical Guide to the Analysis of Genes and Proteins*. New York: Wiley-Interscience, 2001.

Benson, Dennis A., et al. "GenBank: Update." *Nucleic Acids Research*. 2004 (32):D23–D26.

Cinkosky, Michael J., et al. "Electronic Data Publishing and GenBank." *Science*. 1991 (252): 1273–1277.

National Center for Biotechnology Information, National Institutes of Health. "GenBank Overview." March 28, 2006. <http://www.ncbi.nlm.nih.gov/Genbank/index.html> (accessed August 10, 2006).

[*See Also* **Vol. 1, Bioinformatics; Vol. 1, DNA Sequencing; Vol. 1, Gene Banks; Vol. 1, Human Genome Project.**]

Gene Banks

Description

A gene bank is a collection of seeds or of DNA samples. Such collections are called gene banks because they keep either living genes or information about genes safe for later use.

The gene is the basic unit by which characters or traits are passed from parents to offspring. Each gene is a short piece of DNA that tells cells how to make a particular protein or does some other job. Each human's DNA contains about 25,000 genes. Differences between individual plants and animals are partly the result of differences between their genes. If all corn plants, for example, had exactly the same genes, they would be as much alike as human identical twins.

The two types of gene bank—seed banks and DNA banks—have different purposes. A seed bank tries to make sure that varieties of plants are not lost. Having many species and varieties (also called biodiversity) is important in agriculture for several reasons. Some plant varieties, for example, are better than others at fighting off certain diseases or pests. Others may thrive with different kinds of weather. When varieties are lost, food supplies are more easily harmed by one kind of pest or one kind of bad weather.

DNA banks contain samples of DNA, often from human beings. Police forces and governments can identify people by comparing DNA found on crime scenes with DNA in the gene bank. This method can be used to identify criminals or to acquit people falsely accused of crimes. DNA banks can also be used for medical research. Many people have genes that make them more likely to get certain diseases. By studying genes from many

These varieties of corn are maintained at the Maize Genetics Cooperation Stock Center, a seed bank. *Photo courtesy of the Agricultural Research Service, USDA.*

people, scientists can discover how which genes relate to which diseases.

There is also a British gene-bank project called Frozen Ark, which since 2004 has been collecting DNA samples from endangered animal species.

Gene Bank on the Moon

In 2006, a group called Alliance to Rescue Civilization proposed a gene bank on the Moon that would preserve samples of all Earth's useful seeds from nuclear war, asteroid impacts, or other disasters. The plan was supported by Buzz Aldrin, who in 1969 was the second man to walk on the Moon. "It's a reasonable thing to do with our space technology," Aldrin said, "sending valuable stuff to a reliable off-site location." However, seed scientists answer that merely putting seeds in a safe, whether it is on the Moon or not, cannot preserve biodiversity in the long run. There are a few cases of seeds germinating after 100 years, but most seeds start to die after only 40 years in storage. The only way to keep seed varieties going is to keep raising new seeds from old in greenhouses or fields—which would be hard to do on the Moon, especially if the goal were to save all the many thousands of Earth's crop varieties.

Scientific Foundations

Genes are sections of DNA (deoxyribonucleic acid), the molecule that controls heredity and tells cells how to make proteins. Heredity is the passing on of traits from one generation to the next. A protein is a kind of molecule that is found in all living things.

Almost all living cells contain DNA. Each DNA molecule is a long, twisted chain of atoms. Coded along the chain are instructions for making proteins. Cells live and reproduce by making proteins according to the recipes coded into their DNA.

Development

Seed banks or collections have existed for centuries, but long-term, super-dry, refrigerated storage was not possible until the twentieth century. As of 2006 there were about six million seed varieties saved in some 1,470 gene banks around the world.

A number of tissue banks—institutions that save samples of brain, blood, muscle, or the like—have been saving samples of human and animal tissue for many years. The U.S. National Pathology Repository, for example, has been collecting tissue samples since 1917. Since all tissue samples contain DNA, such repositories act as DNA banks even though that was not their original purpose. Special-purpose DNA banks are a more recent invention. The largest DNA bank in the world, the United Kingdom National Criminal Intelligence DNA Database, was set up in 1995. By 2006, the UK government had more

Words to Know

Biodiversity: Literally, "life diversity": the number of different kinds of living things. The more different kinds, the greater the biodiversity.

DNA: A double-helix shaped molecule inside cells that carries the genetic information.

Gene: A discrete unit of inheritance, represented by a portion of DNA located on a chro-

mosome. The gene is a code for the production of a specific kind of protein or RNA molecule, and therefore for a specific inherited characteristic.

Genetic discrimination: The denial of rights or privileges to people because of the nature of their DNA.

DNA samples than any country, with samples from more than a twentieth of the United Kingdom's population. Some other ambitious DNA banks, such as UK Biobank (founded 2002), had yet to gather any DNA samples as of 2005.

Current Issues

Seeds must be kept super-dry and super-cold to make them last. Even under these conditions, all seeds slowly die in storage. The only solution is to keep creating fresh seeds by raising adult plants from the old ones. This costs money, but many of the seed banks of the world are poor. In 2002, a report from Imperial College in England said that many seed banks in poor countries were losing funding or electric power due to war. Without electricity, seeds cannot be kept dry and cold; without money, staff cannot be hired to grow fresh seed. "Many critical gene bank collections are in a precarious state," said Professor Jeff Waage, head of the college's department of agricultural sciences. "If these collections are allowed to fail, then we will lose the valuable crop diversity they contain forever." At the 2002 World Summit on Sustainable Development, a United Nations-sponsored effort to raise $260 million for the world's seed banks was launched.

Human DNA banks are a different matter. There is no problem, in principle, with keeping DNA intact for hundreds of thousands of years. There is, however, disagreement over what it will be used for. Since 2004, police in England and Wales have been collecting DNA from every person arrested, even if that person later turns out to be innocent of a crime. Some DNA in the UK criminal database has been used for medical research without the permission of the original owners. Also, some people fear that information from

DNA banks might be used for genetic discrimination—treating people with unusual DNA as if they were not as good as other people.

■ ■ ■

For More Information

Cherry, Michael. "Gene-Bank Expansion Plan Launched at Earth Summit." *Nature* 419 (2002): 7.

Nazarea, Virginia. *Cultural Memory and Biodiversity*. Tucson, AZ: University of Arizona Press, 1998.

Plucknett, Donald L., et al. *Gene Banks and the World's Food*. Princeton, NJ: Princeton University Press, 1987.

Williams, Garrath. "Human Gene Banks." *Lahey Clinic Medical Ethics* Winter 2005.

[*See Also* **Vol. 1, DNA Fingerprinting; Vol. 1, Forensic DNA Testing; Vol. 1, Genetic Discrimination.**]

Gene Therapy

Description

Gene therapy is an experimental medical procedure that attempts to correct a genetic mutation (missing or changed genes) so that properly functioning genes are restored to cells. When gene therapy works, the correct instructions for building proteins (chemicals that direct and control chemical reactions in the body) are once again available to cells, and the body returns to normal or healthier function.

Scientific Foundations

Genes hold the instructions that direct both the form and function of the human body. In humans, genes are small areas in a molecule of deoxyribonucleic acid (DNA). Each gene directs the making of a protein. Proteins are present in every living thing and regulate almost all the functions in the human body. Genetic mutations can be inherited from one or both parents, or they may arise on their own, through a mistake in the reproductive process.

Genes that are mutated can send the wrong instructions to the parts of the cell that build proteins, causing the proteins that are produced to not function properly, or causing the protein to not be made at all. The result can be a disease called a genetic disorder. Because genes also control reproduction and are passed from parents to children, genetic disorders can be passed from parent to child.

There are two basic types of gene therapy, somatic therapy and germline therapy. Somatic cell gene therapy affects only non–reproductive cells. The new genes cannot be passed on to future generations. Germline gene therapy affects reproductive cells (egg

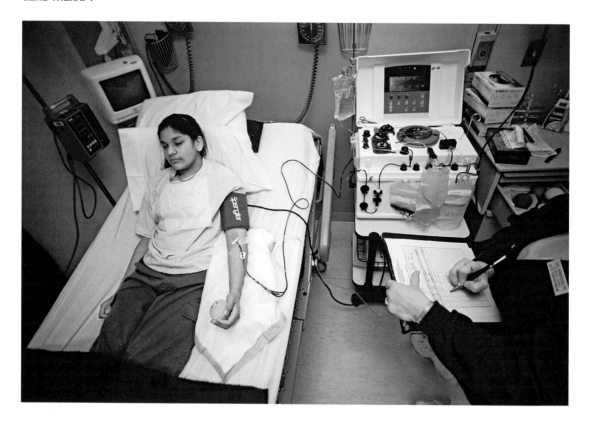

Ashanti de Silva at age thirteen. She was the first patient to receive gene therapy when she first started treatments at age four for an immune system disorder. © *Karen Kasmauski/Corbis.*

and sperm cells) so the new genes can be passed on to future generations.

The way scientists usually deliver genes into the patient's cells is by using a virus as a vector (carrier). Viruses normally carry colds and other diseases into human cells. The viruses used in gene therapy are changed to deliver normal DNA into the cell. The normal genes can then begin making the correct proteins.

Researchers are also working on a way to deliver new genes by inserting an extra, artificial chromosome into cells. Normally, humans have forty–six chromosomes (twenty–three pairs). The additional, forty–seventh chromosome would carry the new genes.

Development

Scientists first began discussing the possibility of gene therapy in the 1960s. In 1970, American doctor Stanfield Rogers at Oak Ridge National Laboratory in Tennessee tried to use gene therapy to treat two sisters who had a genetic disorder called argininemia. With this genetic disorder, the body lacks an enzyme (a type of protein) called arginase. People with this disorder can have seizures and

Retroviruses Rejected for Gene Therapy

In 2000, French researcher Alain Fischer was able to cure children of a similar kind of immune system disorder. Fischer used retroviruses as gene carriers. Retroviruses are a type of virus that uses ribonucleic acid (RNA) as its genetic material, instead of DNA. Retroviruses produce an enzyme (a protein that controls a biochemical reaction) that builds DNA upon a strand of RNA (the opposite of what normally happens in humans where RNA is made on sections of DNA). The most well known of these retro-viruses is the human immunodeficiency virus (HIV), the virus responsible for acquired immune deficiency syndrome (AIDS). Fischer inserted a retrovirus carrying the normal gene into the children's blood stem cells. Several months later, two of the children in the trial developed a disease similar to leukemia (a type of cancer that starts in the cells that make blood cells). As a result, the U.S. Food and Drug Administration (FDA) halted all gene therapy that used retroviruses in the United States.

mental impairment. Rogers tried to treat the sisters by using a virus to carry the healthy gene into their cells. In this case, the gene therapy was unsuccessful.

In 1977, scientists were able to use gene therapy techniques to deliver a gene into the cells of mammals. American doctor W. French Anderson performed one of the first studies of gene therapy in humans in 1990 on a four–year–old girl who had a rare genetic immune system disorder called severe combined immunodeficiency (SCID). The immune system fights off infections from bacteria and viruses, and the disorder made it difficult for her body to stay healthy. Anderson and his team genetically altered her white blood cells and then returned them to her body. The new white blood cells strengthened the girl's immune system and made it possible for her to survive.

Another setback to gene therapy occurred in 1999. An eighteen–year–old patient named Jesse Gelsinger was involved in a gene therapy trial for a genetic disease called ornithine transcarboxylase deficiency (OTCD). This rare disease prevents the liver from breaking down ammonia, which can build up in the body and become toxic. Gelsinger died from organ failure four days after starting treatment. Researchers believe his immune system reacted to the virus that carried the new gene into his cells.

Although gene therapy research moved slowly, it still moved forward. In 2003, the first officially licensed gene therapy was

Words to Know

Deoxyribonucleic acid (DNA): The double-helix shaped molecule that serves as the carrier of genetic information for humans and most organisms.

Gene: A discrete unit of inheritance, represented by a portion of DNA located on a chromosome. The gene is a code for the production of a specific kind of protein or RNA molecule, and therefore for a specific inherited characteristic.

Gene therapy: Treating disease by replacing nonfunctional genes or supplying genes that do function properly.

Genetic disorder: An inherited disorder.

Germline gene therapy: The introduction of genes into reproductive cells or embryos

to correct inherited genetic defects that can cause disease.

Leukemia: A cancer of the blood-producing cells in bone marrow.

Reproductive cells: Specialized cells capable of fusion in the sexual cycle; female gametes are termed egg cells; male gametes may be zoospores or sperm cells.

Retrovirus: A virus whose genetic material is RNA (ribonucleic acid), not DNA.

Somatic cell gene therapy: The introduction of genes into tissue or cells to treat a genetic related disease in an individual.

Vector: A vehicle used to deliver foreign genes into another organism's DNA. Viruses are the most commonly used vectors.

available in China. Several types of gene therapy are waiting for approval from the U.S. Food and Drug Administration.

Current Issues

The FDA has to approve all new drugs and therapies before they can be used by the public. As of early 2006, the FDA had not approved any gene therapy technique.

Although there have been a few successes, gene therapy is generally considered experimental. Scientists must overcome a few problems before the therapy can be used by patients. First, the effects of gene therapy often do not last because cells are always dividing. As cells with mutations divide, they keep making more and more faulty genes. Patients must receive some gene therapies many times in order to make sure enough of the new genes reach the targeted cells to make the right proteins.

Second, the immune system recognizes anything that enters the body as foreign. When it sees the viruses that carry the new genes, it tends to attack them. Patients may also have a reaction to the carrier virus itself. Finally, many of the biggest diseases that affect humans (such as cancer and heart disease) are caused by more than one faulty gene. Trying to fix all of those genes simultaneously is a difficult challenge.

Some controversy also surrounds gene therapies. Scientists are concerned that germline gene therapy could have unknown consequences on future generations. Some religious groups argue that altering genes is unethical, even if the goal is curing disease. Others argue that the technique is still too risky.

■ ■ ■

For More Information

American Society of Gene Therapy. "Brief History of Gene Therapy."<http://www.asgt.org/history.shtml> (accessed March 21, 2006).

Food and Drug Administration. "Fundamentals of Gene Therapy.".<http://www.fda.gov/fdac/features/2000/gene.html> (accessed March 21, 2006).

Human Genome Project. "Gene Therapy." <http://www.ornl.gov/sci/techresources/Human_Genome/medicine/genetherapy.shtl> (accessed March 21, 2006).

[*See Also* **Vol. 1, Somatic Cell Therapy; Vol. 1, Germline Gene Therapy; Vol. 1, Protein Therapies.**]

■■■

Genetic Testing, Medical

Description

Genetic testing is when doctors look at a person's DNA (genetic information) to see if they or their children are likely to have medical problems in the future.

Carrier identification. Some diseases, called genetic diseases, are passed by their parents to their children. In some cases the parents may not have the disease themselves: a person must have two copies of a defective gene (DNA segment) to get the disease, and often a person has one copy. The person with one copy is called a carrier. If both parents have the defective gene, however, then the chances are high that at least some of their children will get two copies and therefore have the disease.

Prenatal diagnosis. This is when DNA taken from a developing fetus is tested, usually to see if there is mental retardation or some other severe birth defect. Parents sometimes choose abortion if the test shows that their developing fetus is likely to be born with severe mental retardation.

Newborn screening. Newborn screening is when newborn babies are tested to see if they have genetic disorders that can be better treated if treatment starts at once. Newborn screening can test for dozens of disorders, many involving the body's ability to produce certain substances that are vital to life. If caught early, sickness and death can sometimes be prevented.

Late-onset disorders. Genetic tests are also available for diseases that affect people later in life, such as heart disease, colon cancer, certain kinds of breast cancer, and some other cancers. These tests do not prove that a person is going to have a certain disease, but a positive result means that the person is more likely than other people to get that disease.

Lab technician performing genetic tests. The tests are done three times on the same sample to minimize the chance of errors. © *Hulton/ Archive.*

Scientific Foundations

All living things, whether single-celled or made of billions of cells, use DNA (deoxyribonucleic acid) to pass on traits to their offspring. They also use DNA like a book of recipes for making all the complex molecules (clusters of atoms) called "proteins" that they need to produce during their lifetime. Since almost everybody has slightly different DNA, their bodies make slightly different proteins. This affects how they react to various drugs and foods, and whether they are more or less likely to develop certain diseases, including cancer. (What people eats, how they live, and what chemicals and radiation they are exposed to also affects their health.) In some cases, genes contain errors that can cause serious

Genetic Horoscopes

In the early 2000s, genetic testing went commercial. A number of companies offer predictive genetic testing online. Send them a sample of your DNA and they will analyze it for genetic risks, for a price. Under the heading of "nutrigenetic" testing, they will even tell you what you should eat in order to stay healthy, based on your particular genes. In 2006, the General Accounting Office, which investigates issues on behalf of the U.S. Congress, announced that it had posed as a customer for four genetic testing companies. It had posed as fourteen different customers, in fact, but had sent the companies DNA from only two people. The results should have been similar or identical when the same DNA was used, but were wildly various. Some of the tests—though not all—were, in the words of one government official, no more meaningful than "genetic horoscopes."

birth defects in children. In genetic testing, DNA is isolated from cells, and parts of the DNA are analyzed using DNA sequencing machines. Sequencing is reading the order of the chemical code-words in the DNA molecule.

Development

Before doctors could test for genes that might give trouble, they had to understand what genes are and how they work. This knowledge was gained starting in the early 1950s, when the nature of the DNA molecule was first understood. By the late 1980s, devices existed that allow doctors to sequence DNA cheaply and quickly enough to make genetic testing possible. The popularity and usefulness of genetic testing grew during the 1990s. Today it is a common procedure.

Current Issues

Scientists are beginning to understand the way that genetic differences between persons affect the way that their bodies handle drugs. Some people do better with smaller doses of certain drugs and other people with larger doses, depending, ultimately, on what exact proteins their DNA tells their cells to make. For example, one Caucasion (white) person in about 3,500 makes a version of a protein that breaks down the muscle-relaxing drug suxamethonium chloride. Because these people make a protein that does not break down the drug very well, they recover much more slowly from the drug. Testing somebody's DNA to see how they should be medicated is called pharmacogenetics. The prefix "pharma-" means

Words to Know

DNA sequencing: A method of finding out the sequence of base pairs in a DNA molecule.

Paternity testing: Genetic testing to determine the father of an offspring.

Pharmacogenetics: The study of how a person's genetic makeup affects his or her response to medications.

Protein: Complex molecules that cells use to form most of the structures and control chemical reactions within a cell.

"drugs"; genetics is the study of genes. However, there are many drugs and many genes, and a person's reaction to a single drug may depend on one gene or on many genes. Scientists will therefore have to build up a large base of experimental knowledge about which genes and which drugs matter to each other before it is useful to test everybody's DNA before giving them medicines.

■ ■ ■

For More Information

Alper, Joseph S., ed. *The Double-Edged Helix: Social Implications of Genetics in a Diverse Society*. Baltimore, MD: Johns Hopkins University Press, 2002.

American Board of Genetic Counseling. "Welcome to ABGC." March 6, 2006. <http://www.abgc.net/english/view.asp?x=1> (accessed September 8, 2006).

Evans, W. E. and H. L. McLeod. "Pharmacogenomics—Drug Disposition, Drug Targets, and Side Effects." *New England Journal of Medicine* 348 (2003): 358–349.

Russo, Gene. "Home Health Tests Are 'Genetic Horoscopes.'" *Nature* 442 (2006): 497.

Scheuerle, Angela. *Understanding Genetics: A Primer for Couples and Families*. Westport, CT: Praeger, 2005.

[See Also **Vol. 1, DNA Sequencing; Vol. 1, Genetic Discrimination.**]

■■■

Genetic Discrimination

Description

Discrimination is when people are treated unfairly because of who they are. For example, not hiring someone for a job because they have a certain skin color or religion is discrimination. Genetic discrimination is discrimination based on differences in a person's genes.

Insurance companies have sometimes denied, limited, or canceled health insurance policies for certain people because they thought that those people's genes made them more likely to get sick (in which case they would collect insurance payments). Companies have also fired or refuse to hire people with possibly defective genes because they feared the expense of having employees fall sick. In China, the law allows the government to sterilize people with genetic defects (to perform surgery on them so they cannot have children) or forbid them to marry each other.

Scientific Foundations

DNA (deoxyribonucleic acid) is the long, narrow molecule that all living things use to reproduce themselves. It is also used as a cookbook for making the large molecules called proteins that cells need during life. Genes are sections of DNA that control the how proteins are made. All living things, from bacteria to people, have genes. Each human being has about 25,000 genes. Only identical siblings (like identical twins) have exactly the same genes.

Sometimes a gene is defective or missing, causing the person to suffer from a disease. Other genes only increase their owners' chances of having some disease. For example, there are genes that make people more likely to have breast cancer or to be overweight.

China's Eugenics Law

In 1993, the Chinese government proposed a new law, the Eugenics and Health Protection Law. It spoke of "abnormal" children as a burden on society and said that China had "more than 10 million disabled persons who could have been prevented through better controls." In Gansu province, officials were already requiring supposedly defective women to be sterilized before marriage, and were seeking to sterilize 260,000 more (that is, to perform surgery on their sexual organs so that they could not have children). According to the national eugenics law, which was passed in 1994 and was still in force in 2006, "serious hereditary disease" is grounds for refusing a marriage license unless the partners agree not to have children. Genetic tests that examine DNA directly are one way of seeing if such diseases are present. As genetic testing becomes cheaper and quicker, it may be used to screen Chinese couples to see if they are to be allowed to marry—a form of genetic discrimination.

However, these genes do not guarantee that these things will happen. The outcome also depends partly on chance, diet, exercise, and other factors not controlled by genes.

Development

The idea of discriminating against some people because of inherited traits—or traits believed to be inherited—is ancient. Over two thousand years ago, Greek philosophers talked about the possibility of breeding human beings to make them better. This idea is called eugenics, a Greek word meaning "well-born."

In the early twentieth century, sixteen American states passed eugenics laws and caused thousands of people to be surgically sterilized. The Nazis, who ruled Germany from 1933 to 1945, also believed in eugenics. They pointed to the American sterilization laws as a good example and passed eugenics laws of their own. The Nazis sterilized about 2 million people whom they thought were unfit to have children. The Nazi policies of eugenics, euthanasia (killing of the sick), and genocide (killing of entire peoples) were so horrible that after World War II (1938–1945), most people in Europe and America turned against the idea of eugenics.

DNA was not mentioned by early eugenics policies because its role in heredity was not yet known. The DNA molecule was first decoded in the 1950s. In the 1990s, it became possible to quickly and cheaply decode any person's DNA using DNA sequencing machines. During

Words to Know

DNA: A double-helix shaped molecule inside cells that carries the genetic information.

DNA sequencing: A method of finding out the sequence of base pairs in a DNA molecule.

Eugenics: A social movement in which the population of a society, country, or the world is to be improved by controlling the passing on of hereditary information through selective breeding.

Gene: A discrete unit of inheritance, represented by a portion of DNA located on a chromosome. The gene is a code for the production of a specific kind of protein or RNA molecule, and therefore for a specific inherited characteristic.

Sterilization: An operation that makes a person unable to have children. Usually this is done by cutting or tying off the tubes that convey eggs or sperm to the sexual organs.

that decade, cases of employers and insurance companies discriminating against people because of their DNA began to occur. Although there have not been a great many such cases—as of 2005, they were apparently occurring at the rate of a few a week in the United States—people with hereditary disorders or risk are concerned that their genetic information might be used against them.

Current Issues

In 2000, President Bill Clinton signed an executive order stopping any part of the U.S. federal government from using genetic information in hiring or promotion decisions. In 2001, President George W. Bush announced his support for a law banning genetic discrimination by insurers and employers. In 2003, the Genetic Privacy and Nondiscrimination Act, which would ban all forms of genetic discrimination, was passed by the U.S. Senate and sent to the House of Representatives for a vote. The vote did not take place, however, and the bill was re-introduced in 2005 (109th Congress). As of August 2006 had not yet been passed, and there was still no U.S. federal law banning genetic discrimination. Some U.S. states and several European countries have already passed laws against genetic discrimination.

Some protection against genetic discrimination is given by the Health Insurance Portability and Accountability Act of 1996 (a U.S. federal law), which bans the use of personal medical information to discriminate against people in hiring and insurance. However, that act deals with diseases or disabilities that people already have, and genetic discrimination may happen to people for diseases or disabilities they do not have yet but are at risk for.

■ ■ ■

For More Information

Alper, Joseph S., et al. *The Double-Edged Helix: Social Implications of Genetics in a Diverse Society*. Baltimore, MD: Johns Hopkins University Press, 2002.

Guo, Sun-Wei. "Cultural Differences and the Eugenics Law." *American Journal of Human Genetics* 65, no. 4 (1999): 1197–1199.

Lohr, Steve. "I.B.M. to Put Genetic Data of Workers Off Limits." *The New York Times*. October 10, 2005.

National Human Genome Research Institute. "Genetic Discrimination." July, 2006. <http://www.genome.gov/10002077> (accessed August 11, 2006).

Nowlan, William. "A Rational View of Insurance and Genetic Discrimination." *Science* 197 (2002): 195–196.

Stolberg, Sheryl Gay. "Senate Sends to House a Bill on Safeguarding Genetic Privacy." *New York Times*. October 15, 2003.

Tyler, Patrick E. "Some Chinese Provinces Forcing Sterilization of Retarded Couples." *The New York Times*. August 14, 1999.

[*See Also* **Vol. 1, Bioethics; Vol. 1, DNA Fingerprinting; Vol. 1, DNA Sequencing; Vol. 1, Genetic Testing, Medical; Vol. 3, Government Regulations.**]

■■■

Genetically Modified Foods

Description

When an organism's genes (its genetic materials) are changed in a laboratory, the organism is called genetically modified or transgenic. Genetically modified foods are products that contain transgenic animals or plants as ingredients.

Genetically modifying food sources can make them bigger, stronger, and more nutritious. Changing genes in plants can protect them against disease. It can also help them survive when exposed to herbicides (chemicals used to kill weeds and plants) and insects.

There are many uses for genetically modified foods. For example, in parts of Africa, people eat large amounts of rice. Regular rice is not very nutritious, so scientists have genetically modified rice plants. These modified plants produce proteins that give their rice extra iron and vitamins. Scientists have also modified pigs to produce healthier meat and coffee plants to produce decaffeinated coffee beans, among other things.

Scientific Foundations

Genes are the basic units of heredity. They are contained within a double-stranded structure called deoxyribonucleic acid (DNA). The sequence of genes contains the instructions that tell cells how to create particular proteins. Proteins are primary components of living cells. How these proteins are produced determines what traits an animal or plant will have.

In nature, genes are passed from one generation to another. The genes of the parent determine which genes the offspring will have.

Today, scientists can add or change genes in a lab to create animals and plants with certain traits.

WHAT IS THE FDA TRYING TO FEED US?

STOP GENETICALLY ENGINEERED FOODS!

Should your refrigerator be condemned?

DA:

+ 🐟 = ?

) CAN ANSWER

Demonstrators in Chicago protesting the availability of genetically modified foods. *Photograph by Associated Press/AP.*

Development

The idea of creating plants with specific traits is ancient, but it started as a science with the studies of an Austrian monk named Gregor Mendel (1822–1884) in the 1860s. Mendel discovered how plants passed their traits from one generation to another. Botanists (scientists who study plants) used his discovery to help them breed plants to have desired traits, such as sweeter fruit or extra seeds. This selective breeding took time. Scientists had to try different combinations to see which ones worked. Animal breeding worked in almost the same way. Scientists would mate animals that had the desired traits to try to create more animals with those same traits.

Cotton, soybeans, and canola (rapeseed) are the most commonly genetically modified crops. *Graph by GGS Inc.*

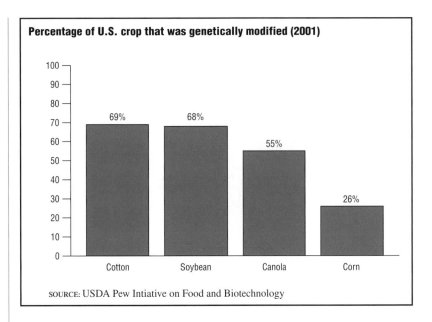

Percentage of U.S. crop that was genetically modified (2001)

- Cotton: 69%
- Soybean: 68%
- Canola: 55%
- Corn: 26%

SOURCE: USDA Pew Intiative on Food and Biotechnology

Scientists from three different research groups in Belgium and the United States were the first to make genetically modified plants. In the early 1980s they used bacteria to put a gene from one plant species into another plant species. One of the groups inserted a bean gene into a sunflower plant.

To genetically modify an animal or plant, scientists first have to find the gene that controls the trait they want to change. Then, they separate that gene and make many copies of it in a lab. Finally, they put the copied genes into animals or plants.

There are a couple ways to insert new genes in plants. The first uses a type of bacteria called *Agrobacterium* to transfer the gene. The *Agrobacterium* contains a circular piece of DNA called a plasmid. When the bacterium infects the plant, it copies its genes through the plasmid into the plant's genes. Another way to insert the gene is with a gene gun. The gun shoots tiny gold balls coated with the changed DNA into the plant's cells. Those genes then become part of the plant's DNA.

To genetically modify an animal, scientists combine its DNA and the DNA from another animal. They first cut the DNA using special enzymes (proteins that trigger chemical reactions in the body). Then they join the different animals' DNA together. A needle is used to insert the new genes into a fertilized egg or embryo (an animal in its earliest stages of development). The fertilized egg or embryo is then implanted in the mother's uterus

Combining Genes

In 1973, Herbert Boyer (1936–) of the University of California and Stanley Cohen (1935–) of Stanford University were the first scientists to combine genes from two different species in a lab. The method they discovered is called recombinant DNA technology (a method for cutting and joining together DNA from different species). It paved the way for genetically modified foods. In 1974, a German scientist named Rudolf Jaenisch inserted foreign DNA into mouse embryo cells. The mice carried the new DNA in their tissues. They were the first transgenic animals.

(the organ in a female's body in which the fetus develops). The gene becomes part of the embryo's cells. Another way to insert the gene is to use a virus or bacterium to carry the new gene into the animal's cells.

Current Issues

People who support genetically modified foods argue that they can help people who live in areas with poor growing conditions. They believe these foods can help end world hunger. Those on the other side of the debate worry about the safety of genetically modified foods. They fear that mixing genes from different species could create strange new animal and plant breeds.

Environmental groups worry that genetically altering foods could be dangerous to human health. They are not sure what effects genetically modified plants and animals might have on the people who eat them. Critics call these foods "Frankenfoods" because they have been pieced together using genes from different species.

One specific concern is that a gene might mistakenly be taken from a plant to which many people are allergic. For example, if a gene taken from a peanut were inserted into soybeans, it could cause the soybeans to produce peanut proteins. Those proteins could trigger a reaction in anyone who was allergic to peanuts. Another worry is that genetically modified plants might breed with the plants growing around them. Then the wild plants could pick up the traits from the modified plants. This cross-breeding could create problems such as weeds that herbicides cannot kill.

Words to Know

DNA: A double-helix shaped molecule inside cells that carries the genetic information.

Genetically modified food: A food product that contains a genetically modified plant or animal as an ingredient.

Transgenic: A genetically engineered animal or plant that contains genes from another species.

Virus: A very simple microorganism, much smaller than bacteria, that enters and multiples within cells. Viruses often exchange or transfer their genetic material (DNA or RNA) to cells and can cause diseases such as chickenpox, hepatitis, measles, and mumps.

For More Information

Human Genome Project. ''Genetically Modified Foods & Organisms.'' September 17, 2004. <http://www.ornl.gov/sci/techresources/Human_Genome/elsi/gmfood.shtml> (accessed April 20, 2006).

NewScientist.com. ''GM Organisms: Instant Expert.'' December 13, 2004. <http://www.newscientist.com/channel/life/gm-food> (accessed April 20, 2006).

Ruse, Michael and David Castle, editors. *Genetically Modified Foods: Debating Biotechnology*. Amherst, NY: Prometheus Books, 2002.

World Health Organization. ''20 Questions on Genetically Modified Foods.'' <http://www.who.int/foodsafety/publications/biotech/20questions/en/index.html> (accessed April 20, 2006).

[*See Also* **Vol. 2, Alfalfa, Genetically Engineered; Vol. 2, Corn, Genetically Engineered; Vol. 2, Cotton, Genetically Engineered; Vol. 2, Genetic Engineering; Vol. 2, Genetically Engineered Animals; Vol. 2, Genetically Modified Organisms; Vol. 2, Rice, Genetically Engineered; Vol. 2, Transgenic Animals; Vol. 2, Transgenic Plants.**]

■■■

Genomics

Description

The study of the sequences of genes within living things is called genomics. Genes are the basic units of heredity. Sequencing means that the structure of deoxyribonucleic acid (DNA) from a particular organism is discovered—what scientists called mapped. Specifically, genomic scientists identify and analyze the structure of genes within segments of DNA. Inside any organism, the complete set of chromosomes—or all the genetic information contained in genes—is called its genome. The set of chromosomes inside people is called the human genome.

Genomics is especially important in biology and medicine, and in industries such as agriculture and food production. Although the study of genomics is still in an early stage of development, it promises to provide valuable information for the discovery and treatment of human diseases. For example, a genomic test has been developed to diagnose breast cancer in women and to determine how likely it is that each woman will benefit from treatment to stop the cancer from growing inside her body.

Scientific Foundations

DNA is a molecule that contains the genetic code of a living thing, or the physical characteristics that are passed down to a child from his or her parents. Its structure is similar to a ladder that has been twisted into the shape of a winding staircase—what scientists call a twisted double-strand double helix (HEE-licks). All living things that contain cells have DNA. In mammals, such as humans, the pieces of DNA are grouped into structures called chromosomes (KROH-ma-sohmes), which are located in the nucleus of each cell. The genetic material

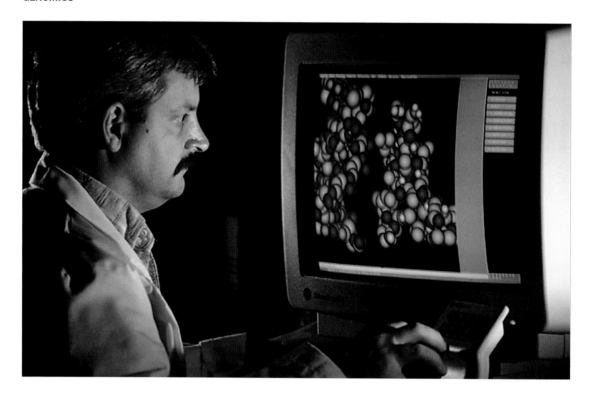

Scientist designing complex chemicals with the help of a computer. Scientists can use genomics to specially design drugs for patients based on their genes.
© *Richard Nowitz/ PHOTOTAKE NYC.*

that is needed for humans to develop and grow is contained in DNA. The hereditary characteristics that pass from one generation to the next are also contained in DNA. An example of a hereditary characteristic that is inherited from parent to child is the blonde hair of a son born to parents who both have blonde hair.

Development

Genomics developed from genetics (the study of heredity) when DNA was first sequenced in 1977 by the independent work of English biochemist Frederick Sanger (1918–) and American molecular biologists Walter Gilbert (1932–) and Allan Maxam. In 1980, the first genome was completely sequenced when a bacteriophage called Phi-X174 (a particular virus infects a bacterium) was mapped. In 1989, American physician-geneticist Francis Collins (1950–) and Chinese geneticist Lap-Chee Tsui (1950–) sequenced the first human gene.

In 1990, the Human Genome Project (HGP) began in the United States. It was a coordinated international scientific project to understand and map the human genome so that all of its genes would be identified. Other countries participating in HGP included France, Germany, Japan, and the United Kingdom. HGP members

Genomics Can Make Better Drinking Water and Potatoes

Sometimes water in remote areas, such as tropical vacation spots, is not fit to drink. It makes people sick because of contamination with tiny, one-celled organisms called protists. These organisms cause illnesses such as diarrhea and malaria. However, genomics research is investigating the genetic composition of protists with the hope of finding ways to prevent people from getting sick after drinking contaminated water.

Millions of people around the world eat potatoes every day. Potatoes provide many nutrients and are inexpensive to grow. However, potato crops are prone to a number of diseases. The 1845–1850 potato famine in Ireland is one familiar example of how a potato disease led to the deaths of millions of people and forced large numbers of people to leave Ireland and move to other countries. Genomics research is exploring ways to grow stronger and more disease-resistant potatoes without the need for chemicals.

identified about 20,000 to 25,000 genes in the nucleus of a human cell and mapped the location of these genes on the twenty-three pairs of human chromosomes. The Human Genome Project and Celera Genomics simultaneously released an initial draft of the human genome in February 2001. The HGP completed the final sequencing of the human genome (with 99 percent of the genome sequenced to a 99.99 percent accuracy) in April 2003.

Current Issues

There are two major issues that are generally in dispute related to genomics: genetic engineering and genetic information. Genetic engineering involves the deliberate changing of genetic materials in a laboratory. Changing genetic material, for example, will let doctors diagnose and treat many diseases and help scientists improve the safety of foods. It will also give scientists the ability to change the physical and psychological traits of people. If a woman has an inherited heart problem, doctors could alter her genetic material so her future children will not have this problem. Scientists could also alter such minor physical characteristics as hair color and height. Many people do not think it is ethical to change such traits by altering genetic materials.

Genetic information involves gathering and storing data related to a person's DNA. Many questions about how this information should be stored and used are being asked such as: Who should be given this information? Who should be in charge of storing the

Words to Know

Chromosome: A thread-shaped structure that carries genetic information in cells.

DNA: A double-helix shaped molecule inside cells that carries the genetic information.

Gene: A discrete unit of inheritance, represented by a portion of DNA located on a chromosome. The gene is a code for the production of a specific kind of protein or RNA molecule, and therefore for a specific inherited characteristic.

Genome: A complete set of the DNA for a species.

information? Questions about personal privacy and other ethical considerations concerning genetic information have yet to be resolved. Lawmakers, health insurance companies, medical organizations, and U.S. citizens will all take a part in answering these sensitive questions. As scientific capabilities increase, more genetic information will become available. Humans will—no doubt—face more difficult ethical and privacy questions about genomics in the future.

■ ■ ■

For More Information

Centers for Disease Control and Prevention (CDC). National Office of Public Health Genomics. <http://www.cdc.gov/genomics/> (accessed August 9, 2006).

DeSalle, Rob. *Welcome to the Genome: A User's Guide to the Genetic Past, Present, and Future.* Hoboken, NJ: Wiley-Liss, 2005.

Palladino, Michael Angelo. *Understanding the Human Genome Project.* San Francisco: Benjamin Cummings, 2002.

Smith, Gina. *The Genomics Age: How DNA Technology is Transforming the Way We Live and Who We Are.* New York: AMACOM—American Management Association, 2005.

U.S. Department of Energy Office of Science. "DOEgenomes.org." <http://doegenomes.org/> (accessed August 9, 2006).

Wade, Nicholas. *Life Script: How the Human Genome Discoveries Will Transform Medicine and Enhance Your Health.* New York: Simon & Schuster, 2001.

[*See Also* **Vol. 1, DNA Sequencing; Vol. 2, Genetic Engineering; Vol. 1, Genetically Modified Foods; Vol. 2, Genetically Modified Organisms; Vol. 1, Human Genome Project.**]

■■■

Germline Gene Therapy

Description

Gene therapy is the treatment of disease by changing an organism's genes. Many diseases are caused by defective genes, including Huntington's disease, sickle-cell anemia, and cystic fibrosis. The word "germline" refers to cells that contain genes (segments of genetic information) that can be passed on to future generations. Sperm cells, egg cells, and the small cluster of cells that makes up the human embryo soon after fertilization of an egg by a sperm are all germline cells. The cells that produce egg and sperm cells are also germline cells. The rest of the cells in the body, which cannot pass on their DNA (genetic information) to offspring, for example muscle cells or skin cells, are called somatic or body cells. Gene therapy that changes DNA in somatic cells is called somatic gene therapy, and gene therapy that changes DNA in germline cells is called germline gene therapy.

The difference between somatic and germline gene therapy is that changes made to DNA in germline gene therapy could be passed on through all future generations. Changes made to DNA in somatic gene therapy disappear when the person who has been treated dies. Germline therapy is a form of genetic engineering of human beings.

Scientific Foundations

Many genetic diseases are caused by defective genes (short sections of DNA, deoxyribonucleic acid) that keep certain substances from being made by the body's cells. For example, cystic fibrosis afflicts people who lack a working gene for making a certain protein, cystic fibrosis transmembrane conductance regulator (CFTCR for short).

On Losing One's Heads

One possible use for germline modification of embryos was proposed by a British scientist in 1997. The scientist, Jonathan Slack, announced that he had learned how to grow headless frogs by manipulating genes in the embryo. Why not, he said, grow headless human embryos and use them as a source of organs for transplant into sick people? Since the embryos would have no brains, they would not be human, he argued. They could be grown in artificial wombs outside any human body. (A prototype of such a womb was announced in 2002.) Some thought that the idea was horrible. "This sort of thinking beggars belief," said an animal ethicist at Oxford University, Andrew Linzey. Another British biology professor said he thought the idea presented "no ethical issues" and added that whether it would be done was only a question of what he called "the 'yuk' factor"—whether or not the public would be too grossed out by the idea to allow it.

Cystic fibrosis might be treated by giving a child's cells the gene they need to make CFTCR. This can be done in two ways. The first is to take cells from the patient's body, genetically engineer those cells to give them a working copy of the gene for CFTCR, and put those cells back into the body. The engineered body cells will then make the protein that the body needs. The second is to change the DNA of the parents' egg and sperm cells before the child is conceived, or to change the DNA of the first few cells (embryonic stem cells) that appear after fertilization of the egg. This second method is germline gene therapy.

Development

Gene therapy was not possible until the 1980s, when laboratory methods for changing DNA became available. Somatic gene therapy was first attempted in experiments in the 1990s. As of 2006, somatic gene therapy was still in the experimental stages, with some successes and some failures. Germline gene therapy is more difficult, although problems were being solved one by one in the early 2000s. By 2006, researchers had changed genes in mouse sperm before conception and in human embryonic stem cells. It seemed that the ability to do germline therapy could not be many years away.

Current Issues

To use the word "therapy" assumes that there will be benefit. There are many genetic diseases that might be treated with germline gene therapy. On the other hand, scientific critics point out how hard

Words to Know

Cystic fibrosis: A fatal disease in which a single defective gene prevents the body from making a protein, cystic fibrosis transmembrane conductance regulator.

Germline: Cells that can pass their DNA on to future generations, including egg and sperm cells and a few other types.

Somatic: Cells that are part of the body but are not in the germline (able to pass their DNA on to future generations) are somatic cells. Any type of cell in the body that is not a sperm or egg cell.

it is to control exactly what happens when genes are changed. In one mouse experiment, for instance, germline gene therapy cured a hereditary genetic disorder, but the later generations of mice that no longer had the original disorder had a higher rate of cancer.

Some scientists have already talked enthusiastically about changing future generations through germline manipulation so that they are better at computers, more musical, or more "emotionally stable." But this raises obvious questions about right and wrong. For example, some people might think that being "emotionally stable" means being obedient, non-rebellious, easy to control—a born slave. Who is qualified to decide what kind of emotions future generations of people should have?

However, some people—some scientists, some not—believe that the time has come for the human race to, as they put it, take charge of its own evolution. They believe that changing the nature of the human body and combining the human body with computers will increase freedom and happiness.

■ ■ ■

For More Information

Billings, P. R., R. Hubbard, and S. A. Newman. "Human Germline Gene Modification: A Dissent." *The Lancet.* 353 (1999): 1873–1875.

Blankenstein, Thomas, ed. *Gene Therapy: Principles and Applications.* Boston, MA: Verlag, 1999.

Council for Responsible Genetics. "Human Germline Manipulation." 2001. <www.gene-watch.org/educational/ germline_manipulationPP.pdf> (accessed September 4, 2006).

[See Also **Vol. 1, Bioethics; Vol. 1, Somatic Cell Therapy; Vol. 1, Gene Therapy; Vol. 1, Therapeutic Cloning.**]

■■■

HapMap Project

Description

HapMap stands for Haplotype Map. A haplotype is a pattern of genetic differences shared by some individuals of a species, but not by all. The International HapMap project is an effort by several countries to identify common human haplotypes, creating a haplotype map for several major human groups (African, European, Asian). This map will be used to find out which genetic differences increase the risk for certain diseases. Scientists hope this will help them develop new ways to prevent, diagnose, and treat disease. The HapMap will describe the common haplotypes, where they are located in the human genome (the complete set of a species' genes), and which human populations tend to have specific haplotypes.

Scientific Foundations

Genes are the chemical code-words that tell living cells which proteins to make. Slightly different genes produce slightly different proteins. Some of these differences are harmless, but others can cause disease or make an organism more susceptible to certain diseases.

Genes are passed down from one generation to the next in the deoxyribonucleic acid (DNA) contained in most cells of every living thing. In species that reproduce sexually, half the genes in each offspring are from the male parent and half are from the female. When the genes of the offspring are first put together, the genes of the two parents are broken into sections and shuffled together randomly. Some genes tend not to get separated during this shuffling process, and so these genes are inherited together down through the generations. Bundles of genes inherited together

Still Evolving

Biologists studying results of the HapMap Project found evidence that human beings have been evolving as recently as the last 5,000 to 15,000 years. That may sound like a long time, but humans with bodies and brains basically the same as our own have existed for about 200,000 years. In biological terms, 5,000 years ago is very recent.

Since the DNA samples used in the HapMap Project came from groups of African, Asian, and European descent, genetic differences between those groups can be discovered in the data produced by the project. The histor-

ical switch from a life based on hunting to one based on growing crops, which happened about 10,000 years ago, seems to have put selective pressure on many genes in different groups. The colonization of Europe by people out of Africa also caused some genes to become more common in people of European descent because the climate is so different in Europe.

Despite these group differences, scientists say that the idea of "race" has no strict biological meaning. All people are more or less related to each other.

can build up slight differences from similar bundles inherited by other groups of individuals. These slightly different bundles of genes are called haplotypes.

Development

The HapMap project could not begin until another project, the Human Genome Project, was finished. The Human Genome Project (1986–2003), mapped the twenty-four long DNA molecules (chromosomes) that transmit all physical human traits from one generation to the next. (Humans have twenty two pairs of non-sex chromosomes plus two sex chromosomes.) However, a single genetic map cannot completely describe the DNA of all human beings because the DNA of most human beings is slightly different from that of all others. Only a few people, like identical twins or triplets, have exactly the same DNA as someone else. Any other two people can have only 99.9 percent identical DNA. In 2003, when researchers completed the Human Genome Project and could map where the all the genes are in human DNA, they began to map where the slight differences in human DNA occur. This effort to map the variations in human DNA is the HapMap Project.

The HapMap Project began in 2003 and was done by university researchers and private companies in Canada, China, Japan, Nigeria, the United Kingdom, and the United States. It cost about $100 million and was paid for by government groups, including the National Institutes of Health in the United States.

Words to Know

DNA: A double-helix shaped molecule inside cells that carries the genetic information.

Gene: A discrete unit of inheritance, represented by a portion of DNA located on a chromosome. The gene is a code for the production of a specific kind of protein or RNA molecule, and therefore for a specific inherited characteristic.

Haplotype: A group of genes that are inherited together by some people.

Protein: Complex molecules that cells use to form most of the structures and control chemical reactions within a cell.

The HapMap project collected blood samples from 270 people. (Red blood cells do not contain DNA, but there are other kinds of cells in blood that do.) Ninety were from Nigeria, forty-five from Japan, forty-five from China, and ninety from the United States. Such small numbers were good enough because the goal of the project was not to record all existing haplotypes, but only the most common ones. The HapMap project greatly advanced scientific knowledge of human genetics.

The complete haplotype map was released in October 2005. In 2006, the HapMap Project was still releasing small fixes to the map.

Current Issues

The haplotype map produced by the HapMap Project does not directly help human health. Its purpose is to help researchers track down the genetic causes of various diseases. This can be done by comparing the haplotypes of people who have a certain disease, such as cancer, with the haplotypes of people who are less likely to who have the disease, or who do not have it at all. If one haplotype is more common in the people who get the disease, then it is likely that a gene somewhere in the haplotype helps cause the disease. This makes it easier to identify the disease gene. Many diseases, including cancer, heart disease, and some mental problems, are caused partly by genes and partly by what biologists call environmental factors—poisons, viruses, poor diet, painful experiences, and so on. It may take years for new disease treatments to be created from the new knowledge provided by the HapMap Project.

If some populations turn out to be more genetically susceptible to certain diseases than others, this knowledge could be used as an excuse for discrimination against them. Scientists working for the HapMap Project also point out that many people have strong beliefs about their ancestral origins or their relation to other groups, and knowledge from genetic studies like the Human Genome Project and the HapMap Project may disturb those beliefs.

■ ■ ■

For More Information

International HapMap Project. ''HapMap Homepage.'' March 30, 2006. http://www.hapmap.org (accessed April 28, 2006).

Wade, Nicholas. ''Still Evolving, Human Genes Tell New Story.'' *The New York Times*. March 7, 2006.

Watson, James D., and Andrew Berry. *DNA: The Secret of Life*. New York: Knopf, 2003.

[See Also **Vol. 1, DNA Sequencing; Vol. 1, Genetic Discrimination; Vol. 1, Genomics; Vol. 1, Human Genome Project.**]

■■■

Heart Disease Drugs

Description

In medicine, the terms heart disease or cardiac (cardiac means heart) disease are often sometimes used to refer to all diseases of the circulatory system—the heart itself, blood volume and pressure, and the veins and arteries through which blood travels. As of 2006, at least 88 drugs were being used for disorders of the heart and circulatory system. Some were centuries old, but others had been developed only in the last few years.

Heart disease drugs are divided into groups based on how they affect the body. One way of grouping them is as follows:

Blood pressure medicines. Blood circulating through the body is under pressure, like water in a faucet. If the pressure is too low, a person will feel sick and faint. If the pressure is too high, it can cause strokes (stoppage of blood flow to part the brain), kidney damage, and other problems. To raise blood pressure, doctors sometimes tell patients to eat extra salt and drinks lots of water. Lowering blood pressure often must be done using drugs. Drugs that are used to lower high blood pressure (also called hypertension) include beta blockers, angiotensin-converting enzyme (ACE) inhibitors, and diuretics (water pills), among others.

Antiarrhythmic agents. The heart can beat poorly by going too fast (tachycardia, pronounced tack-ih-CAR-dee-ah), going too slow (bradycardia, pronounced brad-ih-CAR-dee-ah), or by beating irregularly (arrhythmia, pronounced ah-RITH-mee-ah). Different drugs are used to treat these different kinds of abnormal heartbeat.

Anticoagulants. Coagulation is when blood clots or turns to a solid. This is a good thing when the skin is broken because it stops bleeding. Inside the body, however, coagulation can be deadly. If it happens in blood vessels that supply oxygen to the brain or heart,

The Effects of Aspirin

Aspirin has long been known to reduce the ability of the blood to clot or solidify. This can be a good thing, in moderation; for over twenty years, doctors have been recommending that some of their adult patients take small doses of aspirin to reduce the chances of stroke and heart attack. In 2006, however, a surprising result was found. In a study of over 90,000 adults taking a small amount of aspirin every day, it was found that aspirin decreased the number of heart attacks being suffered by men by almost a third (32 percent), but did not affect the heart-attack rate in women at all. On the other hand, aspirin decreased the number of strokes in women by 17 percent—yet did not affect the stroke rate in men. Researchers do not yet know why the genders react so differently to aspirin.

part of the brain or heart can die, which can be fatal. Anticoagulants are drugs that make the blood less likely to coagulate. One of the most popular anticoagulants is aspirin, also taken as a pain medicine. Adults who are at risk for heart attack or stroke may be advised by their doctors to take about 80 milligrams of aspirin a day (about a tenth of what one would take for headache).

Scientific Foundations

Heart drugs work on the body in many different ways. Those that affect how the heart beats, for example, do so by affecting how substances that are naturally present act in the body. For example, the nerve cells that control how hard and how fast the heart beats become more active when they are in contact with hormones such as adrenaline (a chemical that is released into the blood when a person is frightened or angry, and in lesser amounts at other times). These chemicals are sensed by molecules called beta-adrenergic receptors that stud the surface of these nerve cells. Chemicals that block the ability of the beta-adrenergic receptors to sense chemicals like adrenaline are called beta blockers. Beta blockers make the nerves less excitable, with the result that the heart beats more slowly and fully. Some other heart medications act by affecting how much of the element calcium can enter heart muscle fibers from the fluid around them. Others, such as aspirin, act by completely different means. Because the circulatory system is so complicated, there are many ways it can be medicated.

Development

The function of the heart was not known until 1616, when English doctor William Harvey (1578–1657) announced that he had discovered the nature of the circulatory system. Harvey showed that the

Words to Know

Arrhythmia: Any abnormal rhythm of the heart, which can be too rapid, too slow, or irregular in pace; one of the symptoms of anxiety disorder.

Bradycardia: Too slow a hearbeat.

Cardiac: Having to do with the heart.

Clotting: The solidification of blood in response to a wound: coagulation.

Coagulation: The solidifying or clotting of blood. Beneficial when used by the body to seal a wound; harmful if it occurs inside blood vessels.

Hypertension: High blood pressure.

Tachycardia: An elevated heart rate due to exercise or some other condition such as an anxiety attack.

heart pumps blood through the arteries and veins of the body in a closed loop—or, rather, two closed loops, one for the lungs and one for the rest of the body. With this basic understanding, modern medical treatment of the circulatory system began to evolve.

One of the earliest medications for heart conditions, which is still in use, is digitalis. Digitalis is extracted from the foxglove plant. Its use for heart problems was first described by English physician William Withering in 1785. The cardiac benefits of aspirin were first realized in the 1940s, but aspirin was not prescribed regularly for heart attack and stroke until the late 1980s and early 1990s. Most other modern heart medications are the products of research over the last few decades. New medications are always being developed.

Current Issues

Almost all medications have undesirable side effects. For example, beta blockers can cause chest pain, shortness of breath, dizziness, and disturbed sleep. Antiarrhythmic agents can actually make an irregular heart rhythm worse instead of better. They can also cause nausea, vomiting, diarrhea, low blood pressure, and headache. Aspirin can cause nausea, vomiting, diarrhea, and other problems. Research is going on all the time to create heart medications that treat diseases better while having fewer side effects. It is difficult and expensive, however, to develop a new drug, and many new drugs turn out to cause new side effects.

■ ■ ■

For More Information

American Heart Association. "Cardiac Medications At-A-Glance." 2003. <http://www.americanheart.org/presenter.jhtml?identifier=3038814> (accessed September 11, 2006).

Maximin, Anita, Lori Stevic-Rust, Lori White, and Lori White Kenyon. *Heart Therapy: Regaining Your Cardiac Health*. Oakland, CA: New Harbinger, 1998.

Torrance Memorial Medical Center. ''Cardiac Medications.'' 2003. <http://www.torrancememorial.org/carmed1.htm> (accessed September 11, 2006).

[See Also **Vol. 1, Aspirin; Vol. 1, Blood Transfusions; Vol. 1, Blood-Clotting Factors.**]

■■■

HIV/AIDS Drugs

Description

HIV is short for "human immunodeficiency virus." Viruses are tiny germs that live inside other cells and cause disease.) HIV causes the disease AIDS (short for "acquired immunodeficiency syndrome"). Immunodeficiency is a deficiency or lack in the immune system, which is the body's defense against foreign attackers that cause disease.

HIV invades cells in the immune system and forces them to make more virus. This weakens and kills the cells. When too many immune-system cells have died, other germs can attack the body easily and can cause death. HIV/AIDS drugs are medicines that slow down HIV's spread in the body. As of 2006, there was no cure for HIV. HIV/AIDS drugs could not destroy the virus completely. They did enable some people to live longer with the disease.

The AIDS virus mutates quickly. That is, its genetic material—which, unlike that of most living things, is RNA, not DNA—suffers frequent changes or mistakes (mutations) as the virus reproduces. Some of these mutations are harmful to the new generations of virus, but a few make the virus more resistant to HIV/AIDS drugs.

Because HIV can quickly evolve resistance to a single drug, anti-HIV drugs are given in mixtures of three or four. This is called combination therapy. It is harder for HIV to evolve resistance to three drugs than to one drug. If the patient does not miss many doses, it can take about 10 years for the virus to evolve resistance to the combination therapy. When resistance does evolve, doctors switch the patient to a different combination therapy.

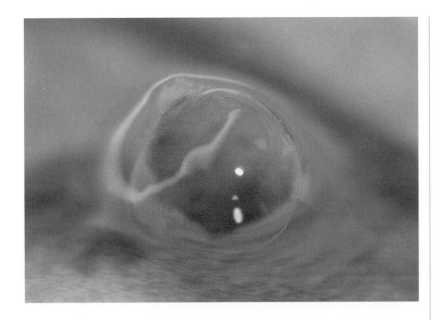

An organ-like group of cells created through genetic engineering that produces anti-HIV antibodies and CD4 receptors, another drug treatment for HIV/AIDS. © *Vo Trung Du/CORBIS SYGMA.*

As of 2006, AIDS had killed about 25 million people since 1981.

Scientific Foundations

HIV is a retrovirus. A retrovirus is a kind of virus that contains not DNA—the hereditary material of all other living things—but RNA, which cells usually use only to copy protein recipes from DNA. In order to force a cell to make new virus, HIV's RNA must first be copied into DNA. The cell is then tricked into making new copies of the virus using this DNA. Anti-HIV drugs (called anti-retrovirals) interfere with some part of this cycle. Some antiretrovirals may prevent viruses from attaching to cells, others interfere with the construction of new virus particles in the cell, and others interfere with the working of reverse transcriptase.

Development

AIDS was discovered in 1981, when a rare type of pneumonia (infection of the lungs) was found in five gay men in Los Angeles, California. (It was soon learned that most of the people with AIDS worldwide are not gay.) In 1983, the HIV virus was found to be the cause of AIDS, and in 1987 a drug called azidothymidine (AZT) was discovered that could slow down HIV's reproduction. AZT is still used against AIDS, along with some twenty other, newer drugs.

Needed: HIV Drugs for Kids

In 2005, about three million people died of AIDS, about 600,000 of them children. Many babies are born every year with HIV, and half die before the age of two. In 2005, the international aid group Doctors Without Borders said that one reason for this high rate of infant death is that drug companies do not make combination-therapy pills small enough for young children. Doctors in poor countries, where most babies with AIDS are born, must therefore chop or crush pills meant for adults. The doses children receive are not always the right size, and this helps AIDS evolve resistance to the drugs and become deadly. Doctors Without Borders called on drug companies to develop more "child-friendly" versions of combination-therapy pills.

As of 2006, there was still no proven vaccine for HIV. (A vaccine is a substance which, given to a healthy person, prevents them from being infected by a certain virus or bacteria [one-celled germs that can cause diseases].) However, as of August, 2006, nine separate studies in the United States were testing experimental HIV vaccines.

Current Issues

AIDS continues to spread quickly in Africa, where about 25 million people had the virus in 2006. The United Nations estimated in 2005 that as many as 90 million Africans might die from AIDS over the next twenty years—a tenth of the population—unless more is done to stop the spread of AIDS there. Some groups, such as Doctors Without Borders, have accused the U.S. government of blocking the use of cheaper, non-brand-name AIDS drugs and of three-in-one combination therapy pills in order to protect the profits of large drug-making companies. The U.S. government has denied the charges and points to global AIDS spending by the United States, up from $2.4 billion in 2004 to $3.2 billion in 2006. Critics responded that the amount was still small for a country as rich as the United States, which, according to its own Defense Department, was spending about $4.5 billion per month on the war in Iraq as of August, 2006. The U.S. Food and Drug Administration approved a three-in-one pill for countries receiving U.S. AIDS assistance in July 2006.

Words to Know

Retrovirus: A virus whose genetic material is RNA (ribonucleic acid), not DNA.

RNA: Ribonucleic acid. Used by most cells to copy protein recipes from DNA; in retroviruses, RNA is the primary genetic material.

Vaccine: A product that produces immunity by inducing the body to form antibodies against a particular agent. Usually made from dead or weakened bacteria or viruses, vaccines cause an immune system response that makes the person immune to (safe from) a certain disease.

Virus: A very simple microorganism, much smaller than bacteria, that enters and multiples within cells. Viruses often exchange or transfer their genetic material (DNA or RNA) to cells and can cause diseases such as chickenpox, hepatitis, measles, and mumps.

For More Information

Johns Hopkins AIDS Service. "Pocket Guide: Adult HIV/AIDS Treatment." January 2006. <http://www.hopkins-aids.edu/publications/pocketguide/pocketgd0106.pdf> (accessed September 1, 2006).

Project Inform, Carolyn B. Mitchell, Martin Delaney. *The HIV Drug Book*. New York: Pocket Books, 1998.

U.S. National Institutes of Health. "AidsInfo." August 25, 2006. <http://www.aidsinfo.nih.gov/> (accessed September 1, 2006).

■■■

Human Genome Project

Description

The Human Genome Project is a worldwide program with the goal of identifying all the genes in human DNA (deoxyribonucleic acid—an organism's hereditary material), discovering how they are arranged, and storing the information in a place where scientists could later study it. Scientists believed that the number of genes in the human body ranged from 50,000 to as many as 140,000. Researchers involved in the project also studied the genetic material in bacteria, flies, and mice.

Scientific Foundations

A genome is a genetic map, or blueprint, of an entire organism. Genome information is contained in tiny molecules of DNA, which are found in nearly every cell of an organism. DNA is packaged into sections called genes. Genes are the basic building blocks of the human body. Each gene contains instructions telling cells how to produce a particular chemical. Genes and the chemicals they code for, called proteins, help determine what a person looks like and how his or her body works. Broken (defective) or missing genes can lead to disease.

Development

In 1985, scientists started talking seriously about the idea of mapping the entire human genome. It was a complicated task, and some scientists were not sure it could be done. By outlining the order of DNA in the human body, the scientists hoped it would eventually lead to new ways to spot diseases passed down through families. In 1986, the United States Department of Energy (DOE) announced its Human Genome Initiative. The initiative pushed for the development of new tools for scientists who study living things (biologists).

Section of the human genome mapped for the Human Genome Project. The letters A, T, C, and G stand for the components of DNA, which combine to spell out the genetic code. *Raphael Gaillarde/Getty Images.*

U.S. scientists originally thought the project would take fifteen years. New tools and computer software helped scientists finish the project two years ahead of schedule. Researchers had mapped out all the genes for the human body by 2003. According to the NIH, the project revealed there were about 30,000 to 40,000 genes in the human body; this number was a lot smaller than expected. Scientists now had a map that showed their exact locations. The International Human Genome Sequencing Consortium published their findings in two scientific journals.

Identifying the number and order of genes in the human body was the first step in the Human Genome Project. The next step is to identify how each gene individually affects human life and to determine how all the parts of cells work together. This will likely take several years. Scientists do not know the function of more than half of the genes identified. It is believed that knowing how each gene works will change human health because scientists will better understand how certain diseases occur. This could lead to better medicines that target the exact cause of a disease and blood tests that tell which person has a specific gene or gene problem. Scientists have already identified genes responsible for breast cancer,

Project Participants

The United States Human Genome Project officially started in 1990. It was a team effort between the DOE and the National Institutes of Health (NIH). Researcher Ari Patrinos lead the DOE effort, and American doctor Francis Collins supervised the program at the NIH. The U.S. government gave money to support the program. Other countries soon joined the project. At least eighteen countries set up their own human genome research programs, including Australia, Brazil, Canada, China, Denmark, France, Germany, Israel, Italy, Japan, Korea, Mexico, Netherlands, Russia, Sweden, and the United Kingdom. Private companies, including U.S.-based Celera, also set up programs. The race to map out the entire human genome soon became a heated scientific competition.

deafness, diabetes, and asthma. However, it could be ten to fifteen years before new drugs based on the information from the project become available for widespread public use.

Current Issues

The Human Genome Project has raised important concerns. Some people think that cracking the code to the human body could threaten the natural course of life. People who oppose the project fear that someday people could pay to create babies with perfect genes, and that people with genetic problems may be considered to be of a lower class. Others question who should have access to a person's genetic blueprint. Many people want to keep such information private. Public genetic records could lead to genetic discrimination, in which insurers or employers would turn away a person with certain genes or gene problems (defects).

Some people are against testing for genetic diseases when there is no treatment available. Scientists have identified gene defects responsible for a number of diseases, but many of them cannot be corrected with modern medicine. Critics say that telling a person they have a genetic disorder when there is no treatment available does more harm than good. Recently, tests have been created to spot gene defects related to breast, ovarian, and colon cancers.

Another controversial issue regarding the Human Genome Project has been the cost. Millions of dollars have been spent on the research. Some people think the money could be better spent on research that has an immediate impact on human life.

Words to Know

Cells: The smallest living units of the body which together form tissues.

Deoxyribonucleic acid (DNA): The double-helix shaped molecule that serves as the carrier of genetic information for humans and most organisms.

Gene: A discrete unit of inheritance, represented by a portion of DNA located on a chromosome. The gene is a code for the production of a specific kind of protein or RNA molecule, and therefore for a specific inherited characteristic.

Genetic disease: An inherited disease.

Genome: A complete set of the DNA for a species.

For More Information

"DOE Genomes." *U.S. Department of Energy Office of Science.* <http://www.doegenomes.org/> (accessed April 22, 2006).

"The Genomic Revolution." *American Museum of Natural History.* <http://www.amnh.org/exhibitions/genomics/> (accessed April 22, 2006).

"Human Genome Project Information." *U.S. Department of Energy.* <http://www.ornl.gov/sci/techresources/Human_Genome/home.shtml> (accessed April 21, 2006).

"Overview of the Human Genome Project." *National Human Genome Research Institute.* <http://www.genome.gov/12011238> (accessed April 22, 2006).

[*See Also* **Vol. 1, Designer Genes; Vol. 1, Genetic Discrimination; Vol. 1, Genomics.**]

■■■

Human Growth Hormone

Description

Human growth hormone (HGH) is a chemical released from a pea-sized structure below the brain called the pituitary gland. The pituitary gland is considered the body's control center. It tells other glands in the body to produce chemicals (called hormones) that control body functions.

Scientific Foundations

Growth hormone helps children grow. Another name for this hormone is somatotropin. Some people make too much or too little growth hormone. This can lead to disease.

Too little growth hormone can cause a condition called pituitary dwarfism, meaning little growth. Children who do not make enough growth hormone are usually shorter than other children their age. They may have more fat around their stomachs and face, and lower-than-normal levels of sugar (glucose) in their blood. Adults who have damage to their pituitary gland may fail to make enough growth hormone. This condition, called adult growth hormone deficiency, causes weight gain, along with weak muscles and bones.

If a child's body produces too much growth hormone, a rare disorder called gigantism results. Gigantism causes bones to grow very fast. The person becomes very tall. People who have gigantism have very large hands and feet, and thick fingers and toes. If the body produces too much growth hormone after a person stops growing, the condition is called acromegaly. *Acro* means "end" and *megaly* means "enlarged." This condition usually strikes adults between age thirty and fifty. Cancerous tumors of the pituitary gland can cause too much growth hormone to be released.

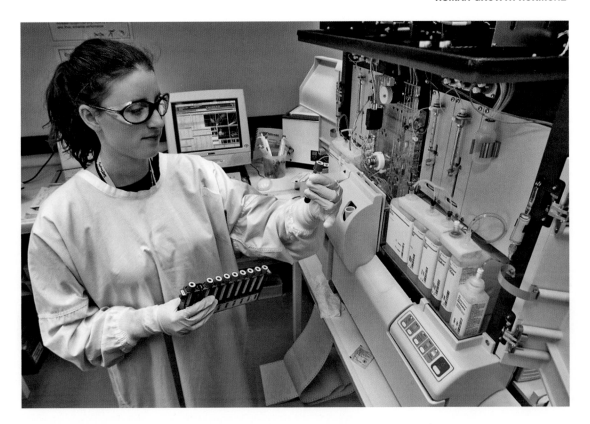

A laboratory technician checks a blood sample during testing for human growth hormone, a banned subtance in athletic competitions. © Reuters/ Corbis.

Development

Cases of slowed and rapid growth have been seen for centuries. The Roman military commander Gaius Plinius Secundus (23–79 CE) wrote about families of short people (dwarfs) in Asia and Africa. Religious writings talked about giant people, particularly a giant man with twenty-four fingers and toes. The first medical description of acromegaly was published in 1886. French neurologist Pierre Marie (1853–1940) wrote about a condition that caused bones in the nose, jaw, fingers, and toes to become very large, and discovered it was caused by a tumor in the pituitary gland. Marie is credited with inventing the term acromegaly.

Because the pituitary gland sits at the bottom of the brain, many scientists did not experiment with it. However, in 1909 neurosurgeon Harvey Cushing (1869–1930) said he treated acromegaly by taking out part of a woman's pituitary gland. A few years later, two scientists each discovered that removing the pituitary gland caused slow growth.

Andre the Giant

Andre Rene Roussimoff, otherwise known as "Andre the Giant" (1946–1993), was born in Grenoble, France to normal-sized parents. He displayed symptoms of gigantism early in life, standing six feet, seven inches tall by the time he was a teenager.

Andre made the best of his condition and began a career in professional wrestling. He called himself the "Eighth Wonder of the World." He was hired by the World Wrestling Federation to perform in America under the name Andre the Giant. He appeared in *Sports Illustrated* magazine, and began acting in television and movies. His most famous role was that of Fezzik, in the 1987 film, *The Princess Bride*.

Andre grew until he reached seven feet, four inches in height and five hundred pounds in weight. This continuing growth put a strain on his heart, which eventually could not keep up with the demands of his body.

Growth hormone was discovered in the 1920s. About thirty years later, scientists figured out how to remove growth hormone from the human pituitary gland. They gave it to children with growth hormone deficiencies and discovered it helped them grow. This discovery led to the development of growth hormone replacement therapy. The first growth hormone replacement therapy medicine was taken from the pituitary glands of dead bodies (cadavers). It was given through a shot (injection). Between 1958 and 1985, the medicine was used to treat more than 8,000 children with growth hormone deficiencies.

In 1985, scientists discovered that some people who had received the growth hormone made from dead bodies developed a deadly brain disorder called Creutzfeld-Jakob disease. The U.S. Food and Drug Administration (FDA) said that the medicine could no longer be sold. Scientists started looking for new ways to create growth hormone medicine.

The first artificial (synthetic) human growth hormone, called Protropin, was developed in 1985 by the Genetech corporation in San Francisco. A year later, the Indianapolis-based drug maker Eli Lily created an artificial human growth hormone that was exactly the same as the one produced by the human pituitary gland. They called their product Humatrope. In 2003, the FDA said the drug could be used to increase height in short children who did not have a growth hormone deficiency. By 2005, available synthetic growth hormones included Genotropin, Norditropin, and Saizen.

Current Issues

Numerous experiments have been carried out using human growth hormone. In recent years, medical researchers have wondered if human growth hormone could keep people from aging. Studies have

Words to Know

Acromegaly: A disease caused by the release of excess growth hormone, resulting in excessive growth of some bones.

Gigantism: A rare disease caused by the release of too much growth hormone while a child is still developing.

Genotropin: A human-made form of human growth hormone.

Growth hormone deficiency: A condition in which the body makes too little growth hormone.

Leukemia: A cancer of the blood-producing cells in bone marrow.

Pituitary gland: In humans, a structure (organ) below the brain that releases human growth hormone.

shown that adults who take human growth hormone lose fat while gaining a lot of muscle mass. How growth hormone effects normal aging remains a popular area of research.

Growth hormone helps the body metabolize (break down) the components of foods. The failure to properly break down such products can lead to conditions that cause excessive weight gain. Researchers have reported that a type of human growth hormone could be used to treat obesity.

Human growth hormone has also been given as an experimental treatment in certain patients whose intestines do not work properly.

There is concern that people may experiment with human growth hormone to improve their athletic abilities. Research shows some young athletes take growth hormone supplements illegally in hopes of putting on more muscle and building strength. Human growth hormone has not been shown to improve athletic performance but has many negative side effects.

Critics have questioned the FDA's approval of Humatrope for children who do not have growth hormone deficiencies. Some believe that the drug is too expensive (ten to twenty thousand U.S. dollars per year) to be used to boost a child's height by only a few inches.

Other research suggests that people who take growth hormone have higher rates of a type of cancer called leukemia. Common side effects of growth hormone include headaches and muscle pain.

■ ■ ■

For More Information

"Acromegaly." *National Institute of Diabetes and Digestive and Kidney Diseases.* <http://www.endocrine.niddk.nih.gov/pubs/acro/acro.htm> (accessed April 22, 2006).

"Adult Growth Hormone Deficiency." *The Pituitary Network Association.* <http://www.pituitary.org/disorders/gh_deficiency.aspx> (accessed April 22, 2006).

"Growth Hormone." *The Hormone Foundation.* <http://www.hormone.org/learn/growth.html> (accessed April 21, 2006).

"Growth Hormone Deficiency." *National Institutes of Health Medline Plus.* <http://www.nlm.nih.gov/medlineplus/ency/article/001176.htm> (accessed April 21, 2006).

"Growth Hormone to Prevent Aging: Is it a Good Idea?" *Mayo Clinic.* <http://www.mayoclinic.com/health/growth-hormone/HA00030> (accessed April 22, 2006).

Howard, Patrick and Barbara Haberman. "Andre the Giant." <http://www.andrethegiant.com/bio.html> (accessed July 18, 2006).

[*See Also* **Vol. 1, Protein Therapies.**]

In-Vitro Fertilization

Description

Fertilization is when an egg cell and a sperm cell come together to make an zygote, a cell that has all the DNA needed to make a new individual. In mammals (warm-blooded animals, including humans), fertilization happens inside the female, but it can also be made to happen in a glass dish. *Vitro* is the Latin word for glass, so fertilization in the laboratory is called in-vitro fertilization.

In-vitro fertilization (IVF) is used in cloning, animal breeding, and to overcome fertility problems in human beings. Fertility is the ability to get pregnant. To begin IVF, a woman is given a drug to encourage the growth of follicles on the ovaries. Follicles are small balls of cells that each contain an egg ready for fertilization. After about ten days, another drug is given that prepares the ovary (which stores eggs) to release the eggs. A needle is then inserted into the vagina and through its wall to suck prepared eggs from the ovaries. These eggs are combined with sperm in glassware to fertilize them.

The resulting fertilized cells (zygotes) are allowed to grow for two or three days until they are embryos containing six or eight cells. Several of the embryos are then put into the woman's uterus (the womb, where the baby will grow until birth) through a tube. If any of the embryos implant in the wall of her uterus and begin to grow, she is pregnant.

On average, a woman must go through three rounds of implantation before getting pregnant. In the United States in 2006, the cost per round was at least $7,500, making the cost of conceiving with IVF at least $22,500—often much more. For many people, therefore, IVF was not an affordable choice.

In-vitro fertilization

How human eggs are fertilized in the laboratory

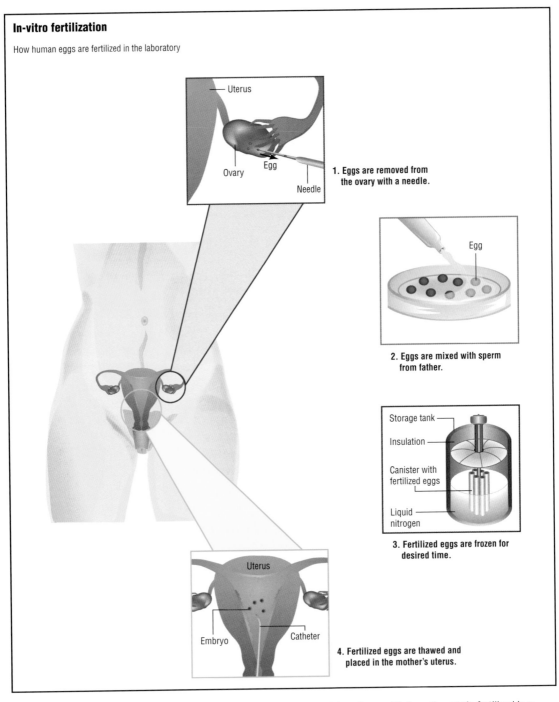

Uterus

Ovary Egg

Needle

1. Eggs are removed from the ovary with a needle.

Egg

2. Eggs are mixed with sperm from father.

Storage tank

Insulation

Canister with fertilized eggs

Liquid nitrogen

3. Fertilized eggs are frozen for desired time.

Uterus

Embryo Catheter

4. Fertilized eggs are thawed and placed in the mother's uterus.

During in-vitro fertilization, eggs and sperm are removed from the potential mother and father; the egg is fertilized in a lab; and the embryo is returned to the mother to grow until birth. *Illustration by GGS Inc.*

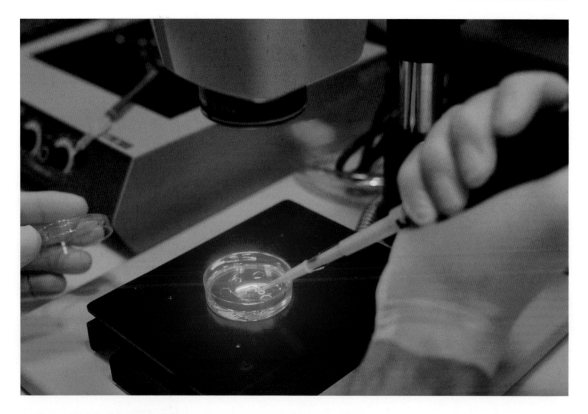

Scientific Foundations

Almost all living things pass on their DNA (deoxyribonucleic acid, their genetic information) to the next generation when they reproduce. DNA is present in almost every cell in humans. Throughout their lives, cells use their DNA copy as a recipe book to make large, complex molecules called proteins. Most cells in the human body contain or two copies of the human genome divided up into forty-eight microscopic packages called chromosomes. The egg cells produced by females and the sperm cells produced by males each contain only twenty-three chromosomes. When they come together, they produce a cell containing a new mixture of chromosomes with the correct number, forty-six. The fertilized cell divides into two, those two cells divide into four, and so on, beginning a growth process that can produce an adult person. In-vitro fertilization simply allows the beginning of this process to happen outside the female body instead of inside.

Technician injecting sperm into a laboratory dish containing a human egg in an in-vitro fertilization procedure. © Owen Franken/Corbis.

Development

Two doctors in Great Britain, Patrick Steptoe and Robert Edwards, began trying to solve conception-related infertility in 1966. They

500,000 Frozen Embryos

Today there are about 430 fertility clinics in the United States alone. These are medical businesses that use in-vitro fertilization (IVF) to help women become pregnant. Many of the embryos that are made during the IVF process never get used. They are not thrown away. Instead, they are kept frozen in liquid nitrogen, which is far colder than the freezing point of water. In 2002, the RAND corporation estimated that there were already 400,000 embryos in frozen storage; by 2006 there were probably more than 500,000. There is no agreement about what to do with these embryos. They could be used for stem-cell research, but religious conservatives view them as human beings and so consider their destruction for any purpose as murder. In 2001, President George W. Bush banned federal money for medical research using stem cells (special cells in that can grow into any other kind of cell) from leftover IVF embryos and has promoted what some call the "adoption" of leftover IVF embryos by women wishing to become pregnant. In 2005, the U.S. Food and Drug Administration declared that IVF embryos are "tissue," not people.

were able to extract eggs from the body and fertilize them in vitro, but were not able to implant them successfully in a woman's uterus. They finally succeeded in 1977, and the world's first "test-tube" baby, named Louise Joy Brown, was born in July 1978.

Since that time, many thousands of babies have been born that were conceived in vitro. In 2005, it was estimated that about 1 percent of babies in the United States—more in some other countries, for example 4 percent in Denmark—were conceived using IVF.

Current Issues

The Catholic Church and some conservative Protestant groups oppose IVF. In the words of the official Catechism (statement of beliefs) of the Catholic Church, methods like IVF "dissociate the sexual act from the procreative act. The act which brings the child into existence is no longer an act by which two persons give themselves to one another," but one that "entrusts the life and identity of the embryo into the power of doctors and biologists and establishes the domination of technology over the origin and destiny of the human person." Furthermore, conservative religious groups view the fertilized egg cells that are produced by IVF as human beings. Since more fertilized eggs are produced in IVF than are used, IVF is, in their view, destructive of human lives.

Words to Know

Fertilization: The union of an egg cell with a sperm cell to make a zygote, or cell that may divide repeatedly to become an embryo and potentially a full-grown creature.

Genome: A complete set of the DNA for a species.

Zygote: The cell resulting from the fusion of male sperm and the female egg. Normally the zygote has double the chromosome number of either gamete, and gives rise to a new embryo.

Whether IVF is right or wrong is not a scientific question but a religious or ethical one. Disagreement about this question will continue in our society for the foreseeable future.

Children conceived using IVF are about 3.7 times more likely to have cerebral palsy (a disease of the nervous system) than children conceived naturally. In 2006, research showed that this is because children conceived using IVF have a higher chance of being born prematurely (too soon).

■ ■ ■

For More Information

BBC (British Broadcasting Company). "Brain Worry Over IVF Children." February 8, 2002. <http://news.bbc.co.uk/1/hi/health/1807351.stm> (accessed September 2, 2006).

Gregory, Linda. *Essential IVF: Basic Research and Clinical Applications*. Boston: Kluwer Academic Publishers, 2004.

Henig, Robin. *Pandora's Baby: How the First Test Tube Babies Sparked the Reproductive Revolution*. Boston: Houghton Mifflin, 2004.

Mundy, Liza. "Souls On Ice: America's Embryo Glut and the Wasted Promise of Stem Cell Research." *Mother Jones* (July/August 2006).

[See Also **Vol. 1, Human Cloning; Vol. 1, Germline Gene Therapy.**]

Insulin, Recombinant Human

Description

Insulin is a hormone that is normally produced by specialized cells located in the pancreas (a gland found in the human abdomen). A hormone is a chemical messenger—a chemical produced in one tissue of the body and then transported to other tissues where it produces a reaction. The presence of insulin is critical in the regulation of the use of carbohydrates and fats consumed as food and used for energy by the body.

In the disease called diabetes, the production of insulin is abnormal or does not occur. As a consequence, the form of sugar called glucose either is not broken down properly or cannot be broken down at all into the smaller units that help power the body.

Scientific Foundations

The insulin from pigs and cows was sometimes given to diabetics (people with diabetes) as medicine, but the insulin from these animals is not identical to human insulin. This means that some people will develop an immune system reaction to the animal versions, which can be painful and potentially unhealthy in the long-term. The immune system is designed to identify foreign substances in the body and attack them, and it is this reaction that causes harm to the body. These concerns led to the use of recombinant DNA technology to produce recombinant human insulin, as described in the next section.

Insulin is a relatively small protein whose sequence is simple. Proteins are the primary components of living cells, and perform most of their vital functions. Insulin is made up of only fifty-one chemical parts called amino acids, whereas some proteins can be comprised of hundreds or thousands of amino acids. Thirty amino

Recombinant human insulin

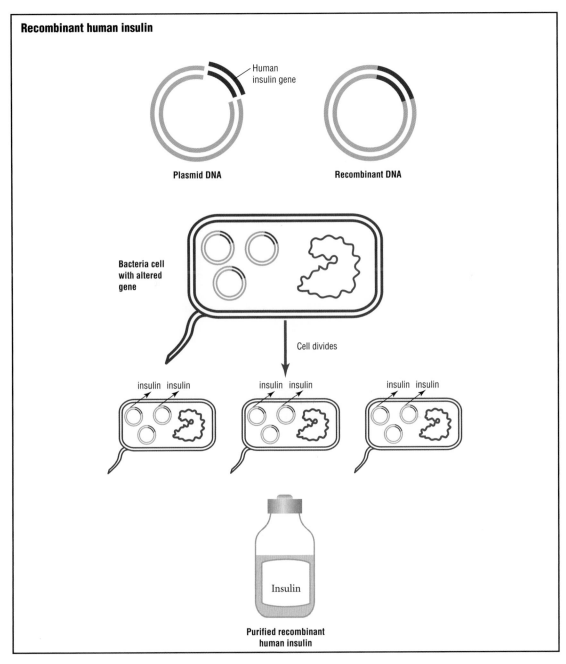

The process of creating recombinant human insulin. Plasmids are structures that carry genetic information in bacteria. Once the bacteria produce more insulin as they divide, it can be extracted and purified into drug form. *Illustration by GGS Inc.*

Insulin Paved the Way for Biotechnology

The ability to deliberately insert the genes from one organism into the genome of another organism only came about in 1973. Almost immediately, researchers and commercial biotechnology companies recognized the potential of DNA technology in the manufacture of insulin. While the insulin obtained from pigs and cows was life-saving for diabetics, allergic reactions were possible. By harnessing the bacterium *Escherichia coli* to express the inserted human gene for insulin, a plentiful and profitable supply of insulin was ensured. By the end of the 1970s, recombinant human insulin was in the marketplace, demonstrating the potential for biotechnology. Over 130 recombinant drugs are now used to treat many types of cancer, arthritis, and for vaccines.

acids are arranged in one chain, and the remaining twenty-one are arranged in a second chain. The two chains are bonded together.

The genetic information that carries the instructions for assembling these amino acids is located on one of the arms of chromosome 11. (Humans have forty-six chromosomes.) To produce recombinant human insulin, this human is inserted into a bacterium (plural, bacteria). Bacteria are one-celled germs that exist in most places on Earth, and sometimes cause disease. The bacterium that is inserted with the human insulin gene is *Escherichia coli* (*E. coli*).

E. coli is normally found in the intestinal tract of humans and other mammals and does not cause disease. Other versions of the bacterium are not as harmless, and can contaminate food and water. For the production of insulin, the version of *E. coli* used has been deliberately crippled so that it cannot grow outside the test tube. After the human insulin gene has been inserted the bacterium, it then "knows" how to produce that insulin protein. When the bacterium divides, subsequent generations of bacteria also produce the protein. After the insulin is harvested from the bacteria cells, it is refined and made into medicine for diabetics. Large amounts of recombinant human insulin can be produced in this way.

Development

Since the discovery of insulin in 1921 by Canadian researchers Frederick Banting (1891–1941) and Charles Best (1899–1978), and their demonstration that the compound could cure diabetes in an animal model, diabetics who require insulin have relied on regular injections of the compound to function normally. In the past, the insulin that was routinely used by diabetics was obtained from pigs or cows.

Words to Know

Chromosome: A thread-shaped structure that carries genetic information in cells.

DNA: A double-helix shaped molecule inside cells that carries the genetic information.

Escherichia coli: *E. coli*, a species of bacteria that lives in the intestinal tract and that are often associated with fecal contamination.

Gene: A discrete unit of inheritance, represented by a portion of DNA located on a chromosome. The gene is a code for the production of a specific kind of protein or RNA molecule, and therefore for a specific inherited characteristic.

Hormone: A chemical substance produced by the body. Hormones are created by one organ of they body but they usually carry out functions in other organs or parts of the body.

Insulin: A substance made by the body (or by genetically engineered bacteria) that the body needs to regulate the amount of sugar in the blood.

Recombinant DNA: DNA that is cut using specific enzymes so that a gene or DNA sequence can be inserted.

With the development of techniques that permitted the genetic material (deoxyribonucleic acid or DNA) from one organism to be inserted and expressed in the genetic material of a different organism, the ability to harness bacteria for the production of human insulin was realized. In 2006, recombinant human insulin (marketed as Humulin®) was the overwhelming source of insulin for diabetics around the world.

Current Issues

The production of recombinant human insulin remains notable because it is still one of the few animal proteins produced by bacteria that is absolutely identical to the human counterpart. This accuracy of production, and the resulting overwhelming acceptance and approval of recombinant human insulin as a life-saver for diabetics continues to be a powerful example of the potential for biotechnology, in the face of vocal opposition.

Research continues into improving the yield of recombinant insulin, and in ensuring that its manufacture is free from contamination.

■ ■ ■

For More Information

Balbas, Paulina, and Timothy Malone, eds. *Recombinant Gene Expression: Reviews and Protocols*. Totowa, NJ: Humana Press, 2004.

Fredrickson, Donald S. *The Recombinant DNA Controversy: A Memoir, Science, Politics, and the Public Interest 1974–1981*. Herndon, VA: ASM Press, 2001.

Scheiner, Gary. *Think Like a Pancreas: A Practical Guide to Managing Diabetes with Insulin*. New York: Marlowe & Company, 2004.

[*See Also* **Vol. 1, Designer Genes; Vol. 1, Gene Therapy; Vol. 1, Pharmacogenetics.**]

Metabolic Engineering

Description

Numerous chemical reactions take place in the human body on a daily basis. Most of these reactions occur repeatedly in the same body systems. For instance, the digestive system controls to break down of food, whereas the circulatory system ensures proper blood circulation in the body. These biological systems are a series of chemical reactions. The combined effect of all the chemical reactions in the human body is referred to as metabolism. Metabolism is important to general health and growth.

Metabolic engineering consists of techniques that allow us to better understand metabolic processes that can be altered to benefit mankind. Metabolic engineering has the potential to contribute immensely towards the growth of health care, medical sciences, and various industries.

Metabolic engineering can be used to improve food production for such products as cheese, wine, and beer. It is helpful in finding cures for diseases, for the mass production of antibiotics, to improve agricultural practices, and to enable effective means of energy production. Metabolic engineering can also assist in the development of eco-friendly ways for cleaning up the environment.

Scientific Foundations

All living bodies, including plants and animals, are made of cells. Each cell in a body is programmed to carry out a number of chemical reactions. Metabolism comprises all of these reactions. There are two different types of metabolic processes. Anabolic reactions take place to form a compound (chemical molecule), while catabolic reactions are responsible for the break down of compounds. Enzymes are substances that catalyze (or speed up) metabolic reactions.

These genetically modified *E. coli* bacteria in solution make a drug called hydromorphone, an artificial version of morphine, a powerful painkiller. *James King-Holmes/Photo Researchers, Inc.*

Metabolic reactions typically follow set sequences, called metabolic pathways. Scientists study these pathways to understand the functioning of cells, tissues, organs, and eventually the complete body system. Enzymes catalyze each step in a cellular pathway, so determining the specific enzymes participating in a reaction is important. Metabolic engineering involves discovering and analyzing such metabolic pathways.

Development

Since the time English naturalist Charles Darwin (1809–1882) introduced his theory of evolution, people have known that minor changes occur from one generation to another. Although they share several

Metabolic Engineering as a Comprehensive Subject

Metabolic engineering is a multidisciplinary area requiring knowledge and implementation of other principles including recombinant deoxyribonucleic acid (DNA) technology (in which DNA from different organisms is combined), microbiology, cell biology, biochemistry, mathematical sciences, and chemical engineering.

similarities, children are different from their parents. Some of their differences are better suited for survival. Some do not have any effect, while others may be harmful. Nature always prefers those changes (also known as mutations) that increase survival rates of an organism. During the natural course of evolution, mutations accumulate over millions of years to such an extent that the organism showing modifications stops resembling the parent species and becomes a new species.

Metabolic engineering is a relatively new science that is developed on the underlying principles of evolution. It allows scientists to create mutations and study their effects in a much shorter span of time and in a laboratory setup. By modifying the genetic composition of cells, scientists can enhance desired mutations that either improve quality or increase production of various bioproducts (cheese, medicines, and so on) for industrial use.

Cells and their components are so small that it is difficult to study them in detail. Studying the genetic information in cells did not become possible until the advent of some sophisticated techniques such as the polymerase chain reaction (PCR), in which the smallest quantities of genetic material can be amplified to an extent where they can be easily examined.

Invented in 1985, PCR enables scientists to clone (copy) and investigate the genes responsible for the creation of various com-

How was Erythromycin Discovered?

Erythromycin, a common antibiotic for treating infections caused by bacteria, was discovered from a bacterium in 1952. Its structure was identified in 1965, and the process of its creation was published in 1981. However, it was only in the 1990s that its manufacture was completely understood. With the new information gained, researchers have now found a laboratory method for mass-producing erythromycin.

Words to Know

Anabolic: To build the body. Often used to describe a group of hormones sometimes abused by athletes in training to temporarily increase the size of their muscles.

Catabolic: To break down. The break down of complex molecules into simpler molecules.

Catalyst: Any agent that accelerates a chemical reaction without entering the reaction or being changed by it.

Metabolism: Chemical changes in body tissue that convert nutrients into energy for use by all vital bodily functions.

pounds the body uses. PCR also aids analysis of the complete genetic material of several organisms, allowing scientists to look at genetic differences across a population.

Current Issues

Metabolic engineering helped create several beneficial bioproducts—products derived through living systems. Microorganisms and single-cell creatures are much simpler than their multi-cellular counterparts and have less genetic material and fewer biochemical reactions to be investigated. Consequently, researchers are more successful in engineering metabolic pathways in microorganisms.

The primary objective of metabolic engineering is to improve human life. It is being used to create varieties of plants that are resistant to pest infestation, yield a higher quantity of produce, or generate more nutritious goods. Metabolic engineering has also been used to study heart and liver diseases.

Apart from the complexity of organisms, other issues have slowed the progress in metabolic engineering. Sometimes, scientists who discover certain beneficial microbes also get legal protections that restrict others from performing investigative studies on the newly discovered microorganism. In other instances, it is not possible to study the metabolic pathways of some microorganisms because they cannot be cultured in the laboratory for various reasons.

■■■

For More Information

Lee, Sang Yup, and E. Terry Papoutsakis, eds. *Metabolic Engineering (Biotechnology and Bioprocessing Series)*. New York: Marcel Dekker, 1999.

"Metabolic Engineering Project Inventory." *Metabolic Engineering Working Group.* <http://www.metabolicengineering.gov/project.htm#Background> (accessed August 7, 2006).

"Metabolic Profiling Glossary." April 24, 2006. *CHI, Cambridge Healthtech Institute.* <http://www.genomicglossaries.com/content/metabolic_engin eering.asp> (accessed August 7, 2006).

Shimon, Gepstein, and Lewinsohn Efraim. "Implementation of Metabolic Engineering to Improve The Aroma of Fruits." *Plant Physiology Online.* September 2002. <http://3e.plantphys.net/article.php?ch=13&id=274> (accessed August 7, 2006).

Stephanopoulos, Gregory N., Aristos A. Aristidou, and Jens Nielson. *Metabolic Engineering: Principles and Methodologies.* San Diego, CA: Academic Press, 1998.

Yang, Yea–Tyng, George N. Bennett, and Ka–Yiu San. "Genetic and Metabolic Engineering." *Electronic Journal of Biotechnology.* December 5, 1998. <http://www.ejbiotechnology.info/content/vol1/issue3/full/3/> (accessed August 7, 2006).

[See *Also* **Vol. 3, Biodegradable Packaging and Products; Vol. 3, Bioremediation; Vol. 2, Genetic Engineering.**]

■■■

Multiple Sclerosis Drugs

Description

Multiple sclerosis (MS) is a disease that affects the central nervous system (CNS). MS causes the gradual breakdown of the nerve cell's myelin sheath. Myelin is a fatty coating found on neurons (nerve cells) that protects and aids the brain in instructing the body and mind to respond to stimuli. The name multiple sclerosis refers to the many scars formed on the sheath. MS is a chronic, inflammatory disease, and is classified as an autoimmune disease because it is thought to arise from the body's attack on its own immune system and nervous system.

MS is the most common acquired disease of the nervous system. It affects an estimated one million people worldwide; 350,000 of them are in the United States. MS primarily affects adults between the ages of twenty and forty, and is more common among women than men. MS can affect sensation, vision, muscle strength, and mood, and it results in difficulty with coordination and speech. Although MS in itself is often not a terminal disease (one that causes death), patients suffer from pain and impaired mobility in severe cases.

Although much is known about MS and the damage it does, it is yet unknown what exactly triggers the disease, and there is no complete cure. There are, however, many drug treatments available that may slow the progression of MS, lessen the frequency and severity of symptoms, and overall reduce the disability associated with the disease.

MS drugs have shown to be effective in clinical trials (testing on people) for improving the physical condition of MS patients. In addition, the drugs are able to reduce the number of MS lesions (areas of damage) in the brain and spinal cord. Each drug is used on a regular basis, usually anywhere from once a day to once a week. The drugs are injected, usually by the patient or someone close to the patient.

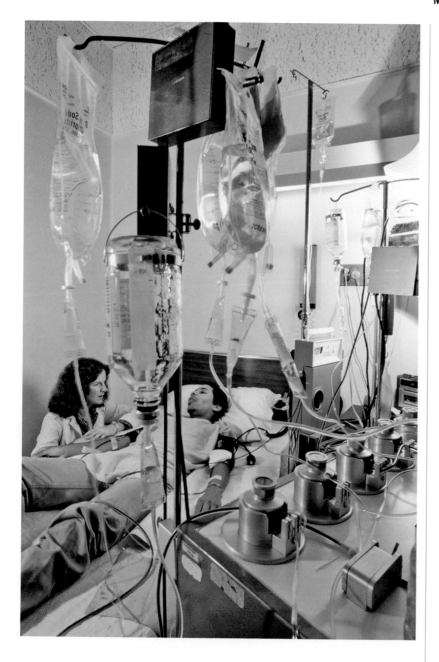

Man undergoing plasmapheresis treatment for multiple sclerosis. In this treatment, blood is removed from the patient and the harmful agents that attack the nerve cells are filtered out before returning the blood to the body. © *Annie Griffiths Belt/Corbis.*

Scientific Foundations

In 1868, French neurologist Jean-Martin Charcot was the first to classify MS as a distinct disease. In the course of his studies, Charcot identified three signs of MS: dysarthia (problems with speech), ataxia (problems with coordination), and body tremors.

Since that time, the National Multiple Sclerosis Society has divided MS into four types for the purposes of identification and treatment: relapsing-remitting, secondary-progressive, primary-progressive, and progressive relapsing. Relapsing-remitting involves unpredictable relapses and attacks followed by remission (periods of no attacks). When symptoms go away between remission periods, it is called benign MS. It is the second most common type of MS. Secondary-progressive patients first go through a relapsing-remitting phase, which is followed by less severe attacks (but total remission does not occur). It is the most common type of MS.

Primary-progressive involves MS symptoms that never go away; however, they increase and decrease in intensity over time. Progressive-relapsing patients have initial MS symptoms that steadily decrease in intensity, but with sudden and often severe attacks occurring from time to time. Primary-progressive and progressive-relapsing types of MS occur the least often of the four types.

Development

Interferons were the first class of drugs available to treat MS. These drugs block immune proteins, called MHCII (major histocompatibility complex II), which are associated with destroyed myelin in nerve cells. Interferon drugs used for MS include IFN1b (Betaseron®) and IFN1a (Avonex®). Copaxone® (glatiramer acetate, formerly called copolymer-1), is another type of drug. Copaxone is a artificially created molecule that resembles a protein found in myelin.

These three drugs (Avonex, Betaseron, and Copaxone) are commonly referred to as the ABC drugs. All three have been shown to reduce the rate of relapses (recurrence of symptoms of the disease) in persons with MS. These drugs are administered by injection only and have many side effects, including pain and skin injury at the injection site, nausea, vomiting, headaches, and depression. Long-term use of interferons like Avonex and Betaseron may result in the development of antibodies (a protein produced by the body to eliminate foreign substances or fight disease), lessening their effects.

Corticosteroid drugs may also be used as a treatment for MS. Corticosteroids reduce pain by suppressing the immune system's attack on myelin. However, steroids do not improve the long-term course of the disease and will lose effectiveness over time. There is no agreement on the best form of corticosteroid use or dosage for MS.

Tysabri® is the first monoclonal antibody to be produced to treat MS. An antibody is produced by the immune system to help fight disease and viral infection. A monoclonal antibody is spe-

Eureka! There's Gold in MS Drugs

In the last part of nineteenth century, French neurologist Jean-Martin Charcot used gold injections to treat MS because it was shown to be an effective treatment for syphilis, another disease that can affect the nervous system. While this idea may at first seem ridiculous, recent research at Harvard Medical School has shown that gold and other metals, such as platinum, work by stripping bacteria and virus particles from the grasp of a key immune system protein, thus making the protein inactive. The protein MHCII normally holds pieces of invading bacteria and virus to the cell surface. When the cell recognizes that these invaders are present, it starts a normal immune response. In an autoimmune disease, this response goes awry and the body turns on itself causing diseases like type I diabetes, lupus, or rheumatoid arthritis.

cially designed in a laboratory to recognize one specific type of foreign substance. Tysabri is only available by injection and, like other MS drugs, has some side effects, including nausea, headache, abdominal pain, and infection.

MS drugs that are still in development include those that are being currently used for cancer and for lowering cholesterol. The link between these drugs and their method of blocking the progression of MS is being determined. There is still much research being devoted to learning more about MS, finding better treatment options, and, some day, discovering a cure.

Current Issues

Tysabri was initially approved by the Food and Drug Administration (FDA) in November 2004 as a treatment to reduce the frequency of relapsing MS. When the drug is administered, the cells that cause the damage and inflammation to the myelin sheath are bound and prevented from moving from the bloodstream into the brain. Clinical trials showed a 66 percent reduction in the rate of relapses. MRI (magnetic resonance imaging) scans showed that Tysabri prevented scarring of the myelin sheath.

Almost a year later, Tysabri was voluntarily removed from the market by its manufacturers because two people who took the drug developed a progressive disease known as PML. Since then, no new cases of PML have been reported.

After a safety evaluation, and hearing emotional testimonials from people who suffer from MS, the FDA approved Tysabri's return to the market in March 2006, listing certain conditions for

Words to Know

Monoclonal antibody: Antibodies produced from a single cell line that are used in medical testing and, increasingly, in the treatment of some cancers.

Neuron: A nerve cell. Neurons may be either sensory (involving the senses) or

motor (related to the motion of the body).

Stimuli: An agent, action, or condition that elicits a response.

Terminal: Causing, ending in, or approaching death; fatal.

the drug's use. Most importantly, Tysabri must be used alone, and not in conjunction with any other medicinal therapy. In addition, the patient must show that they cannot tolerate any of the other MS drugs currently on the market.

■ ■ ■

For More Information

Clinical And Medical Research. "MS: Basic Facts." <http://www.pubmedcentral.nih.gov/articlerender.fcgi?artid=1069024> (accessed July 29, 2006).

Coyle, Patricia and June Halper. *Meeting the Challenge of Progressive Multiple Sclerosis*. New York: Demos Medical Publishing Inc., 2001.

National MS Society. "A History of MS: The Basic Facts." <http://www.nationalmssociety.org/Brochures-HistoryofMS1.asp> (accessed August 4, 2006).

Weiner, Howard L. *Curing MS*. New York: Three Rivers Press, 2005.

[See Also **Vol. 1, Corticosteroids; Vol. 1, Painkillers; Vol. 1, Protein therapies.**]

Nuclear Transfer

Description

Nuclear transfer is a laboratory procedure that removes the nucleus (the central part of the cell that contains its genetic information) of a mature cell and places it into an immature female egg cell. The female cell, whose own nucleus has been removed, is then able to reproduce. The nucleus from the mature cell is called the donor nucleus, and it then directs the cell development and ultimately the expression of basic physical characteristics. Such an artificially made egg cell normally forms an embryo and develops into a living plant or animal.

Scientific Foundations

Cloning is defined as creating a genetic copy of a living thing, anywhere from a simple cell to an organism, such as a sheep. The copies (or clones) made with cloning have the same genetic blueprint (gene structure) and, if raised in a similar environment, similar physical characteristics as the original. Cloning uses nuclear transfer techniques and other genetic technologies.

The procedure for nuclear transfer uses a small vacuum to keep the donor cell in place. A thin needle is stuck through the membrane of the cell and inserted into the interior of the cell. The nucleus is then removed through the hollow needle. Later, the needle is inserted into the recipient cell (after its original nucleus has been removed in a similar way) and the donor nucleus is placed inside.

Although cloning might be considered a new technique, and nuclear transfer a new technology, the attempt to alter future generations of plants and animals is not new. Farmers have crossbred (or cloned) plants for thousands of years. They hoped, in many cases, to make new plants that would grow faster and stronger, produce larger

How cells are cloned with the technique of nuclear transfer.
When the cloned cells multiply, they become a copy of the donor of the body cell.
Illustration by GGS Inc.

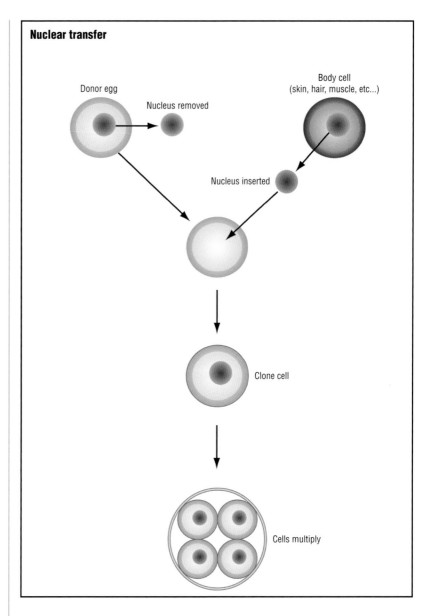

Nuclear transfer

Donor egg

Nucleus removed

Body cell
(skin, hair, muscle, etc...)

Nucleus inserted

Clone cell

Cells multiply

seeds, or make better tasting fruits. Genetic engineering began in the late twentieth century when scientists modified the genetic material, deoxyribonucleic acid (DNA), of a plant to change its characteristics. Whereas crossbreeding by farmers was only modestly successful, scientists are now able to clone thousands of plants very inexpensively over a short period. The cloning of animals, however, still takes much time, is costly, and results in small groups of plants or animals.

A "Fantastical" Experiment

In 1952, scientists Robert Briggs and Thomas J. King used nuclear transfer to clone frogs. Although they later claimed to be unaware of Hans Spemann's work their experiment was similar to what Spemann proposed in 1938 as "a 'fantastical' experiment." Briggs and King tried to clone tadpoles using donor nuclei obtained from older cells (differentiated cells) but found that the embryos did not develop or that they developed abnormally and that genetic potential diminished as cells from older and become more specialized (differentiate). In many cases they could not clone organisms from adult cells.

Development

German embryologist Hans Spemann (1869–1941) was the first to propose nuclear transfer. In 1938, Spemann published his experimental conclusions in which he described the use of a slip of hair to divide a fertilized salamander egg into a nucleus and a cytoplasm (the material surrounding the nucleus inside a cell). After the nucleus divided four times—changing into a sixteen-cell embryo—Spemann removed the hair so the nucleus and cytoplasm could join back together. The cell then began to divide again. Spemann tightened the hair again, which caused the cell to divide into two embryos and grow into identical salamanders.

In 1948, American embryologist Robert Briggs (1911–83) began studying the possibility of nuclear transfer (without knowing about Spemann's earlier research) while performing experiments related to chromosomes (structures within the nucleus that contain DNA) developing within the nucleus. American embryologist Thomas King (1921–2000) helped him with the surgical techniques. They used a North American leopard frog because its eggs are larger than most other animals' eggs. Using a tiny needle, King applied suction to a single cell from an embryo containing thousands of cells. When the cell was opened, the nucleus was removed and inserted into an egg whose nucleus had been earlier removed. After improving their technique, Briggs and King published their findings in 1952. Other scientists tried similar experiments after reading their article.

Current Issues

Nuclear transfer has the potential to reproduce genetically altered animals that can produce drugs to fight diseases like Alzeheimer's and Parkinson's. Animals cloned as a result of nuclear transfer might provide organs to transplant into humans needing new organs.

Words to Know

Deoxyribonucleic acid (DNA): The double-helix shaped molecule that serves as the carrier of genetic information for humans and most organisms.

Embryo: A stage in development after fertilization.

Embryologist: A scientist who studies embryos and their development.

Cloning animals may help endangered species avoid extinction, or even bring back extinct animals, similar to what happened in the movie *Jurassic Park* (1993). Many people are in favor of cloning for its medical and other benefits. Other people are against cloning because of ethical and religious reasons.

Critics of animal cloning say that cloned animals, including humans, could be born with serious defects. They argue that some of the world's past dictators tried to breed out characteristics in people that they felt were undesirable. Some religious groups argue that cloning goes against their beliefs.

■ ■ ■

For More Information

Klotzko, Arlene Judith. *A Clone of Your Own?: The Science and Ethics of Cloning.* New York: Cambridge University Press, 2006.

MedlinePlus, U.S. National Library of Medicine and National Institutes of Health. "Cloning." <http://www.nlm.nih.gov/medlineplus/cloning.html> (accessed July 20, 2006).

Morgan, Rose M. *The Genetics Revolution: History, Fears, and Future of a Life-altering Science.* Westport, CT: Greenwood Press, 2006.

Panno, Joseph. *Animal Cloning: The Science of Nuclear Transfer.* New York: Facts on File, 2005.

Pence, Gregory E. *Cloning After Dolly: Who's Still Afraid?* Lanham, MD: Rowman and Littlefield Publishers, 2004.

President's Council on Bioethics. "Human Cloning and Human Dignity: An Ethical Inquiry." July 2002. <http://www.bioethics.gov/reports/cloning-report/index.html> (accessed July 20, 2006).

Woodward, John, ed. *The Ethics of Human Cloning.* Detroit, MI: Thomson, Greenhaven Press, 2005.

[*See Also* **Vol. 2, Animal Cloning; Vol. 1, Bioethics; Vol. 2, Biotech in the Dairy Industry; Vol. 1, Human Cloning; Vol. 2, Genetically Engineered Animals.**]

Organ Transplants

Description

An organ transplant is a surgical procedure to put a healthy body part (organ) into a person whose organ no longer works. Organs that can be transplanted include the heart, kidneys, lungs, pancreas, and liver.

According to the United States Division of Transplantation, about seventy-four people get an organ transplant every day. However, many people die waiting for transplants because there are not enough donated organs. In April 2006, more than 91,000 people in the United States were waiting for an organ transplant.

Hearts and lungs can only be taken from a person who has just died. This has to be done right away because organs died very quickly after death. A person who is legally dead is often kept on special machines to keep the body functioning until the organ can be removed.

Kidneys and livers may be donated by a person who is alive, since the liver grows back and most people are born with two kidneys.

Scientific Foundations

One of the biggest problems facing transplant patients is rejection. Rejection means the body looks at the new organ as an invader and attacks it. In 1983, the drug cyclosporine was approved to help prevent rejection. The drug's approval lead to a big increase in the number of organ transplant procedures.

In 1999, the National Institutes of Health (NIH) Clinical Organ Transplant Program was formed to develop and test new ways of preventing rejection. The development of new transplantation techniques and better anti-rejection drugs in recent years has helped people with organ transplants live longer. The number of heart- and lung-transplant patients living three years or more after

This twelve-year-old boy is playing with his old diseased heart, after his successful heart transplant surgery. *AP/ Wide World Photos.*

their surgery continues to rise. The percentage of patients who lived for at least three years jumped from 55 percent between 1988 and 1994 to 64 percent between 2000 and 2003.

Scientists have been looking into the causes of death following transplants. A study found that patients who get a severe lung injury called primary graft dysfunction after a lung transplant are much more likely to die within the first month than those who did not have the problem. Researchers are working on new ways to better predict and treat transplant-related lung problems.

Tracking Donors and Patients

People who need a transplant must join the Organ Procurement and Transplantation Network (OPTN), a national program run by the United Network for Organ Sharing (UNOS). UNOS keeps a database of all patients waiting for transplants. The organization also determines who gets which organs. A national computerized system helps match donated organs to a person who needs one. The transplanted organ must work with the person's blood type. Other considerations are organ size, how badly the person needs a transplant, how long they have waited for it, and the patient's location.

Development

Transplants date back thousands of years. The Chinese were believed to have tried transplanting a heart as early as the second century BCE. Roman myths suggest that people tried transplanting a leg from one man to another. In 1902, Hungarian surgeon Emerich Ullmann (1861–1937) performed the first successful kidney transplant in a dog.

The first human-to-human kidney transplant took place in the late 1950s, when surgeons at a hospital in Boston, Massachusetts successfully took a kidney from one man and put it inside his twin brother, who was dying from kidney failure. The lead surgeon, American-born Joseph Murray (1919–), won the Nobel Prize in Physiology or Medicine in 1990 for his work.

Soon, physicians tried to transplant other organs. After four unsuccessful years, the first successful human liver transplant took place in 1963 at the University of Colorado. Meanwhile, South African physician Christiaan Bernard (1922–2001) completed the world's first heart transplant. The patient lived for eighteen days. The first successful heart transplant in the United States took place a year later. Houston, Texas physician Denton Cooley transplanted a heart into a forty-seven-year-old man during a procedure at St. Luke's Episcopal Hospital. The patient lived for 204 days.

The same year, the United States passed a law (Uniform Anatomical Gift Act) that established a donor card. People who wished to donate their organs after death carried the card with them. The law also allowed families to say yes or no to organ donation.

In 1984, the National Organ Transplant Act took effect. This law made the sale of human organs illegal. It also set up a nationwide program called the Organ Procurement and Transplantation Network (OPTN) to take in and distribute donated organs.

Words to Know

Immune system: A system in the human body that fights off foreign substances, cells, and tissues in an effort to protect a person from disease.

Immunosuppressive drugs: Medicines that turn off the body's defense (immune) system. They are used to fight organ transplant rejection.

Organ Procurement and Transplantation Network (OPTN): A program that promotes organ donation and oversees the national distribution of organ transplants.

Primary graft dysfunction: A severe lung injury that occurs in some lung transplant patients.

Rejection: An event that occurs when the body's defense (immune) system attacks a transplanted organ.

United Network for Organ Sharing (UNOS): A Richmond, Virginia company that runs the Organ Procurement and Transplantation Network.

Current Issues

Every day, someone who is waiting for an organ transplant dies. The shortage of donated organs is a big concern. The demand for organs is simply larger than the supply. People on the waiting list for organs do not know how long they will wait to receive one. Long wait times not only cause a person's health to get worse, they also create more expensive medical costs because the person must often stay in a hospital until a transplant donor is found.

Donated organs must be matched as closely as possible to the patient so that the risk of rejection is low. However, even with a good match, the body still thinks of the new organ as a foreign substance. Organ transplant patients must take medicines that turn off the body's defense (immune) system. Such medicines are called immunosuppressive drugs. Most transplant patients must take some type of medicine for the rest of their life.

Immunosuppressive drugs can have dangerous consequences. Because they suppress the immune system, the body has a hard time fighting off even the simplest of infections. Patients who take these medicines also have a higher risk of certain cancers. Side effects of immunosuppressive drugs include high blood pressure, high cholesterol, and an increased risk of diabetes.

■ ■ ■

For More Information

Children's Organ Transplant Association. <http://www.cota.org/site/c.dqLQI3OEKpF/b.496377/k.CC4B/Home.htm> (accessed April 21, 2006).

Donate Life. <http://www.organdonor.gov/> (accessed April 22, 2006).

Donor Action. "Alleviating the Organ and Tissue Shortage." <http://www.donoraction.org/> (accessed April 21, 2006).

Global Organization for Organ Donation. <http://www.global–good.org/> (accessed April 21, 2006).

"In the Spotlight." *Transplant Living.* <http://transplantliving.org/> (accessed April 22, 2006).

International Association for Organ Transplantation. <http://www.iaod.org/> (accessed April 22, 2006).

"It's All About Life." *United Network for Organ Sharing (UNOS).* <http://www.unos.org/> (accessed April 22, 2006).

"You Have the Power to Donate Life." *Coalition on Donation.* <http://www.shareyourlife.org/> (accessed April 21, 2006).

[See Also **Vol. 1, Anti-Rejection Drugs.**]

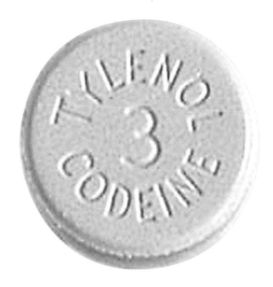

Tablet of Tylenol #3 with codeine. © *Thomson Micromedex.*

■■■

Painkillers

Description

Painkillers, also called analgesics, are medicines that help relieve pain. There are many different types of painkillers. The most common types of painkillers include anti-inflammatory drugs, non-narcotics, and opioids (narcotics).

Anti-inflammatory drugs reduce swelling and soreness. They are often used to treat muscle, bone, and joint pain. People with osteo-arthritis or arthritis (diseases that cause joint pain and bone changes) sometimes take anti-inflammatory drugs. Anti-inflammatory pain-killers are classified according to whether or not they contain a steroid, a powerful chemical that reduces swelling. Those without steroids, such as aspirin and ibuprofen, are called non-steroidal anti-inflammatory drugs (NSAIDs).

Some NSAIDs (like aspirin) are available over-the-counter (without a doctor's prescription). Stronger NSAIDs require a prescription. They include naproxen, ketoprofen, and diclofenac.

The most common non-narcotic painkiller is acetaminophen (Tylenol®). It works on mild-to-moderate pain and costs less than other pain medicines. Acetaminophen is the main ingredient in hundreds of different painkillers. It can be bought in grocery stores and pharmacies without a prescription. Acteaminophen is the most popular type of painkiller used in hospitals.

Opioids are the strongest painkillers. They are listed as narcotics because act quickly and can be addicting. These drugs are usually given to people with post-surgical pain, cancer, long-term (chronic) back pain, and severe headaches. Morphine is the strongest opioid painkiller. Codeine is a weaker type, but still powerful. Acetamino-phen is commonly combined with codeine (Tylenol #3). Opioid pain killers can only be purchased with a prescription.

Scientific Foundations

Painkillers relieve pain through differing biochemical actions. Aspirin and other NSAIDs work to stop the body from producing a chemical called prostaglandin. Along with other functions, prosta-glandin causes muscles to tighten and blood vessels to constrict, often leading to pain and swelling. By blocking prostaglandin, muscles relax and blood vessels dilate (widen), reducing pain and swelling. Although the exact action of opioid pain relievers is not known, scientists assume they act directly on pain receptors (nerve cells) in the central nervous system.

Development

Opioid medicines have been used for thousands of years. They date back to 300 BCE, when people learned that the seeds of the poppy flower, made into a powder and named opium, gave a feeling of well-being to those who smoked it. In 1803, German scientist Friedrich Wilhelm Sertürner (1783–1841) identified the powerful pain-killing chemical in the opium powder as morphine. Many nineteenth century medicines were based on a mixture containing alcohol and opium. This product was called "tincture of opium," or laudanum.

The drug manufacturer E. Merck & Company of Darmstadt, Germany, began making morphine in 1827. Today, researchers use the sap of the poppy flower to create synthetic (not from a natural source, such as a plant) drugs such as oxycodone that copy opium's pain-relieving effect.

Aspirin was the first type of painkiller sold in the United States. The ancient Romans used a raw form of aspirin from the willow tree to cure aches and pain. In the late 1800s, a scientist at Friedrich Bayer

New Uses for Painkillers

Scientists are also investigating different ways to use existing painkillers. For example, aspirin and other NSAIDs may be able to prevent cancer of the colon, stomach, breast, and lung. An early study involving people with severe memory and reasoning impairment (dementia) found that acetaminophen helped make them more alert and active. Other research suggests that certain NSAIDS may slow down the progress of Alzheimer's disease, a severe brain disease that causes dementia and behavior problems, usually in older people.

& Company in Germany developed a synthetic version of aspirin called acetylsalicylic acid, and found that it helped relieve arthritis pain.

In 1955, the Johnson & Johnson company McNeil Consumer Products introduced liquid acetaminophen for children. The drug was the first aspirin-free pain medicine.

Low doses of ibuprofen, the most popular type of NSAID, became available without a prescription in the 1980s. There are many brands of ibuprofen, including Advil®, Motrin®, and Nuprin®.

COX-2 inhibitors are the newest type of NSAIDs. These drugs block a different pain-causing chemical than older anti-inflammatory drugs. Researchers developed these drugs because existing NSAIDs sometimes caused stomach problems such as ulcers. COX-2s reduced the risk of stomach troubles and were proclaimed to be valuable pain relievers, especially for people with a history of stomach problems. Three COX-2 drugs were developed: celecoxib (Celebrex®), rofecoxib (Vioxx®), and valdecoxib (Bextra®). However, researchers soon learned that some patients taking COX-2s had a higher risk of heart attacks and strokes. The U.S. Food and Drug Administration (FDA) recommended drug manufacturers stop selling rofecoxib and valdecoxib, and in 2005, they stopped being sold.

Current Issues

Researchers continue to look for safer, more effective painkillers. Significant progress has been made in understanding how a person actually feels pain. This knowledge is being used to develop new ways to safely block pain signals. One new non-narcotic drug, ziconotide, derived from a natural chemical produced by snails, works by blocking particular minerals in the nerve cell that transmit

Words to Know

Analgesic: A compound that relieves pain without loss of consciousness.

Arthritis: Inflammation of the joints.

Narcotic: A drug that depresses the central nervous system and is usually addictive.

Opium: A natural product of the opium poppy, *Papaver somniferum*. Cutting the immature pods of the plant allows a milky liquid to seep out and be collected. Air-dried, this is crude opium.

Steroid: A group of organic compounds that belong to the lipid family and that include many important biochemical compounds including the sex hormones, certain vitamins, and cholesterol.

pain signals to the brain. Ziconitide is delivered directly to the spinal fluid and is reserved for severe or chronic pain. Another new drug, pregabalin, targets the specific nerve pain caused by complications from certain diseases, such as diabetes or shingles.

Painkillers are powerful drugs and may cause side effects. Considerable concern has been raised over the safety of all NSAIDs, especially COX-2 inhibitors. Medical evidence found that people who regularly take large doses of such painkillers have an increased risk of heart attack, stroke, and bleeding in the stomach.

On April 7, 2005, the FDA ordered drug manufacturers to add a warning label to all NSAIDs. The label, called a black-box warning, states that the drugs could increase a person's risk of serious, possibly life-threatening events, particularly heart attacks, strokes, and stomach bleeding. The agency also warned that people who recently had heart surgery should not take some types of NSAIDs.

The bad news regarding COX-2s and NSAIDs resulted in increased sales for the makers of acetaminophen products. Acetaminophen is considered one of the safest painkillers. It does not cause the stomach problems often seen with NSAIDs. However, large amounts of the drug can cause liver disease. A study published in 2005 stated that daily use of the drug could increase blood pressure in women.

Among the most effective but problematic painkillers are the opioid narcotic drugs. While persons with persistent or severe pain can benefit from them, these drugs are physically addictive (causing users to become dependent on them) and commonly abused. Large amounts of opioid drugs can prevent a person from coughing, and in severe cases, cause breathing to stop. Other side effects include constipation, nausea, and vomiting. Those who take opioid drugs for long periods of time for medical reasons must stop taking them gradually to avoid withdrawal symptoms (negative reactions to not having the drug). While the law requires stringent quality and supply controls for opioids used in medical settings, they are frequently sold illegally. Narcotics sold on the street, including morphine and heroin, can be contaminated with dangerous ingredients.

■ ■ ■

For More Information

American Academy of Pain Medicine. "The Use of Opioids for the Treatment of Chronic Pain." <http://www.painmed.org/productpub/statements/pdfs/opioids.pdf> (accessed on March 18, 2006).

American Chronic Pain Foundation. <http://www.theacpa.org/> (accessed on March 21, 2006).

National Foundation for the Treatment of Pain. <http://www.paincare.org> (accessed on March 21, 2006).

National Institute of Neurological Disorders and Stroke. "NINDS Chronic Pain Information Page." <http://www.ninds.nih.gov/disorders/chronic_pain/chronic_pain.htm> (accessed on March 21, 2006).

[*See Also* **Vol. 1, Aspirin.**]

■■■

Paternity Testing

Description

The word paternity means to be someone's father. Paternity testing is a way to know with great certainty whether or not a man is a child's father by comparing their genetic material.

Paternity testing is used, for example, if the mother has had intercourse with more than one man at around the same time. The mother may need to prove the father's identity before asking for money to support the child or for the child's inheritance money. It can also be done for matters of immigration, child custody (the legal right of a parent to care for and make decisions regarding their child), or adoption.

Scientific Foundations

Deoxyribonucleic acid (DNA) is the genetic material that is present in each cell of the human body. It is unique to each person and determines traits such as hair color, eye color, and height. DNA is made up of a sequence of bases—adenine (A), cytosine (C), guanine (G), and thymine (T). The order of these bases determines the individual's traits. DNA is tightly packed into structures called chromosomes.

With the exception of identical twins, every person's DNA is slightly different. A few differences in the sequence of bases are what make one person look and act different from another person. The closest DNA matches are between family members, since each child inherits DNA from his or her mother and father.

Sperm and egg cells each carry twenty-three chromosomes. During reproduction, when the sperm fertilizes the egg, the chromosomes from the father and mother combine. This gives the child a full set of forty-six chromosomes—half from the father, and half from the mother.

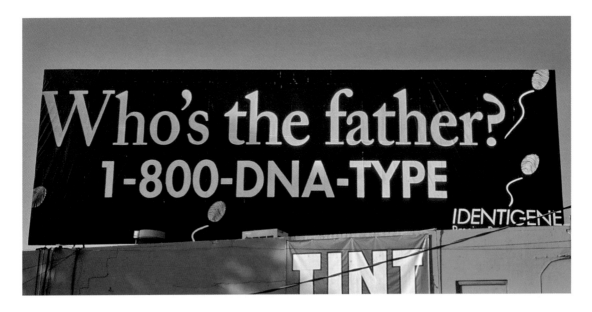

Because a child receives half of his or her DNA from the father, it is possible to test to find out whether a man is the child's biological father. Scientists can take blood or other tissue from the child and the supposed father and compare the DNA to see if they match.

Development

A German scientist named Friedrich Miescher discovered the building blocks of DNA in 1869, but it took more than one hundred years for scientists to understand how to use DNA to identify a person. In 1985, a British geneticist (a scientist who studies genes) named Alec Jeffreys discovered that certain DNA sequences repeated over and over again. He also found that the repeated sections could differ slightly from one person to the next. Jeffreys discovered a way to identify DNA variations between people. His discovery paved the way for DNA fingerprinting in crime investigations, as well as for paternity testing.

A paternity test can be done while the baby is still in the mother's womb, or after the child has been born. A small sample of fluid or tissue is taken from the child, and a sample is taken from the man who is believed to be the father. Although paternity tests are usually done in a laboratory, there are tests that take a swab of tissue from the father and child's cheek that can be done at home.

To confirm paternity, scientists look for certain sections of the child's DNA that show variations. At each chromosome are two fragments of DNA, one that the child inherited from the father, and one that the child inherited from the mother. These are called alleles.

Paternity Tests Before Birth

A child's paternity can be tested while he or she is still in the womb. The procedures used to take a DNA sample during a woman's pregnancy are called chorionic villus sampling and amniocentesis. In chorionic villus sampling, small pieces of tissue that are attached to the mother's uterus (the hollow organ in a woman's body that houses the growing fetus) are removed. These pieces of tissue contain the baby's genetic material. Amniocentesis is done by passing a needle through the mother's stomach. A small sample of amniotic fluid (the fluid around the developing fetus) is removed. The fluid has cells in it that contain the baby's DNA. Samples from both of these tests are taken to a lab for DNA testing. A comparison to the father's DNA can then be done.

First, scientists remove DNA from tissue samples taken from the mother, the child, and the potential father. They use a special type of molecular scissors called restriction enzymes to cut the DNA into fragments. The cut fragments are separated by length using a special gel. Then the fragments are placed on a type of nylon film. Special radioactive (giving off high-energy rays) strands of DNA called probes are also placed on the film. These probes seek out and stick to specific base sequences. When the sheet containing the probes is exposed to an x ray, the probes form a visible pattern.

Scientists take DNA from the mother and compare the pattern with that of the child's DNA. Once they have identified the fragment from the mother, they know that the other fragment must be from the father. Then they use DNA taken from the man who is thought to be the father, to see if it matches that fragment. If it does match, the man is almost certainly the father.

Current Issues

DNA testing is very accurate. It can tell whether a man is a child's father with about 99.9 percent certainty. It can tell with 100 percent certainty whether a man is not the father.

There are certain ethical (having to do with morality, or what is perceived as being the right thing to do) issues surrounding paternity testing, though. A father might try to use it to avoid having to pay child support, for example. A man might want a child tested if he thinks his wife has been unfaithful to him. Or a man who left his family years ago might come back home and request a paternity test to prove that he is the father of the child he left behind. There

Words to Know

Allele: Any of two or more alternative forms of a gene that occupy the same location on a chromosome.

Amniocentesis: A method of detecting genetic abnormalities in a fetus; in this procedure, amniotic fluid is sampled through a needle placed in the uterus; fetal cells in the amniotic fluid are then analyzed for genetic defects.

Amniotic fluid: The fluid that surrounds the developing fetus in the womb.

Chorionic villus sampling: Testing a sample of cells from the tissue surrounding the embryo. It can be used to determine a child's paternity before he or she is born.

Chromosome: A thread-shaped structure that carries genetic information in cells.

Custody: The legal right of a parent to care for and make decisions regarding their child.

Deoxyribonucleic acid (DNA): The double-helix shaped molecule that serves as the carrier of genetic information for humans and most organisms.

Ethical: Having to do with morality, or what is perceived as being the right thing to do.

Geneticist: A scientist who studies genes.

Paternity: The genetic father of an offspring.

Radioactive: The production of high-energy rays as a result of changes in the atomic structure of matter.

Restriction enzyme: A special type of protein that can recognize and cut DNA at certain sequences of bases to help scientists separate out a specific gene.

is concern that having a paternity test in these cases could emotionally hurt the children involved, or that it could be done without the mother's consent.

■ ■ ■

For More Information

Blunkett, David. *Who Is Really Who?: The Comprehensive Guide to DNA Paternity Testing*. London, England: John Blake Publishing, 2006.

U.S. Government. "History of Forensic DNA Analysis." <http://www.dna.gov/basics/analysishistory/> (accessed April 30, 2006).

Victorian Institute of Forensic Medicine. "DNA Paternity Testing." <http://www.vifm.org/paternity_gov.html> (accessed April 30, 2006).

[See Also **Vol. 1, Bioethics; Vol. 1, DNA Fingerprinting; Vol. 1, DNA Sequencing; Vol. 1, Forensic DNA Testing; Vol. 3, Polymerase Chain Reaction.**]

Penicillins

Description

Penicillins are prescription medicines used to treat infections that are caused by bacteria (a one-celled germ that can cause disease). Penicillin is a type of antibiotic, a drug that kills bacteria. Penicillin does not kill viruses, so it does not work for a cold or the flu.

Scientific Foundations

There are many different types of penicillin. They are grouped into two categories: natural or human-made. Natural penicillin is called biosynthetic penicillin. It is produced directly from mold. Penicillin type G (benzylpenicillin) is the only natural penicillin used today. This type of penicillin must be given with a needle (injection).

Penicillin created in the laboratory is called semi-synthetic penicillin. Scientists create this type of medicine by slightly changing the structure of natural penicillin. Popular types of human-made penicillin include penicillin V, ampicillin, and amoxicillin.

Penicillin fights many diseases, but not all. Some germs cannot be killed with penicillin, so researchers have been trying to come up with newer types of antibiotics. Some physicians say penicillin should not be used to treat children who have strep throat, because newer, less expensive drugs called cephalosporins work better.

Many people are allergic to penicillin. Scientists are working on a skin test that can be used to figure out who might have a bad reaction to the drug.

Development

Scottish scientist Alexander Fleming (1881–1955) accidentally discovered penicillin in 1928 while working at St. Mary's Hospital

A laboratory culture dish growing penicillin mold.
P. Barber/Custom Medical Photo Stock, Inc.

in London. He covered a plate with bacteria, but then left it at room temperature for a long time. When he looked at the plate later, he noticed a green mold growing on the plate. The bacteria near the mold were dying. The mold was later identified as *Penicillium notatum*, or penicillin for short. Under a microscope, the penicillin had the shape of a pencil.

Fleming experimented with the penicillin for a while. He discovered the penicillin mold was not dangerous. He believed it could fight some illnesses, but he could not get it into a form that still worked when given to humans. In 1929, he published a paper in the *British Journal of Experimental Pathology* on his discovery of penicillin and its potential uses, but the scientific community did not seem interested. As a result, penicillin's disease-fighting ability remained unexplored for more than ten more years. During World War II (1939–1945), German biochemist Ernst Boris Chain (1906–1970) and Australian pathologist Howard Walter Florey (1898–1968) found a way to turn the raw penicillin into a brown powder that still killed bacteria even

Penicillin Saves Nurse First

In March 1942, young nurse Anne Sheafe Miller lay near death in a Connecticut hospital with a temperature near 107 degrees Fahrenheit (42 degrees Celcius) caused by a streptococcal infection. After trying everything available to save her life, including sulfa drugs, blood transfusions, and surgery, doctors gave Nurse Miller an injection of a small amount of an experimental drug, penicillin. Overnight, Miller's fever decreased, and by the next day, she was alert and eating meals. Miller became the first person whose life was saved by penicillin, and afterward, American pharmaceutical companies quickly geared up to mass-produce the drug, first for soldiers overseas, then for the public at large. Anne Miller lived until she was ninety years old.

after a few days. They gave it to mice, and found it made bacteria infections go away. Soon, the drug was being produced in a large quantity, and used to treat people who were injured during the war. In 1945, Fleming, Florey, and Chain received the Nobel Prize in Physiology or Medicine for their discoveries related to penicillin.

Chain and Florey's work also revealed that there were several different forms of penicillin. All of them worked in a similar fashion but, under a microscope, each looked slightly different. Medical persons gave a form of the drug called penicillin V to World War II soldiers who had infected cuts (wounds). This was a considerable achievement. Before the discovery of penicillin, minor wounds turned into serious bacteria infections that eventually caused death. The use of penicillin during the war helped save many lives. By the time the war was over, companies in the United States were producing 650 billion units of penicillin each month.

Shortly after the war, Oxford chemist Dorothy Crowfoot Hodgkin (1910–1994) revealed the complex structure of penicillin. Her discovery allowed scientists to come up with ways to make artificial (synthetic) forms of the drug.

Current Issues

Penicillin was once considered a wonder drug. However, it is not used as often as it was in the past because of widespread antibiotic resistance. Antibiotic resistance is major public health threat in which bacteria cannot be killed with antibiotic medicines. Just a few years after natural penicillin was being made and used in large supply, scientists realized that it could no longer kill certain germs. Such resistance makes bad bacteria become stronger, leading to "super germs." This can make an infection become much worse. For example, ear infections caused by

Words to Know

Anaphylactic shock: A violent, sometimes fatal, response to an allergen after initial contact.

Antibiotic: A compound produced by a microorganism that kills other microorganisms or retards their growth. Genes for antibiotic resistance are used as markers to indicate that successful gene transfer has occurred.

bacteria are difficult to successfully treat with antibiotic drugs. In such cases, treatment is a guessing game. A physician will need to give the patient different antibiotics, until one works.

The first type of bacteria to show resistance to penicillin was *Staphylococcus aureus*. This type of bacteria can lead to pneumonia, a serious disease that causes swelling of the lungs.

Antibiotic resistance can occur in people who take penicillins and other antibiotics on a regular or repeated basis. People who use antibiotics when it is not necessary or who do not take all of their antibiotic medicine have a higher risk for resistance.

Penicillin can cause stomach aches and diarrhea. Women who take penicillin sometimes develop a yeast infection in their vaginas. This common condition causes extreme itchiness.

Many people are allergic to drugs made with penicillin. If a person who is allergic to penicillin is given such a drug, they can have a life-threatening condition called anaphylactic shock, which causes breathing problems, swelling, itchy bumps (hives), and a sudden, severe drop in blood pressure.

Penicillin can interact with a number of medications, including blood thinners, thyroid drugs, blood pressure drugs, birth control pills, and other antibiotics.

■ ■ ■

For More Information

Nobelprize.org. "The Discovery of Penicillin." <http://nobelprize.org/educatio nal_games/medicine/penicillin/readmore.html> (accessed August 10, 2006).

University of Edinburgh. "The Microbial World; Penicillin: The Story of an Anti-biotic." <http://helios.bto.ed.ac.uk/bto/microbes/penicill.htm> (accessed April 20, 2006).

[See Also **Vol. 1, Antibiotics, Biosynthesized; Vol. 3, Antimicrobial Soaps.**]

■■■

Pharmacogenetics

Description

A person's response to medication often depends on their genes. Pharmacogenetics is the study of how people with certain inherited genes will react to specific medications. By learning how people with certain genes respond to a particular drug, doctors can know in advance what kind of reaction a patient with a similar genetic makeup might have.

Medications are usually one-size-fits-all. Although today's medicines can treat disease very effectively, sometimes doctors have to try many drugs until they find one that works for their patient. Many drugs cause side effects; some can even be life threatening. One study found that reactions to medications kill about 100,000 people and send more than two million people to the hospital each year.

Scientific Foundations

Deoxyribonucleic acid (DNA) is the genetic material in each cell of the human body. It is made up of a sequence of chemical bases—adenine (A), cytosine (C), guanine (G), and thymine (T). The order of these bases tells the body's cell how to make proteins, the main components of living things. Which proteins are produced determines an individual's traits. Proteins direct all of the functions of the body, from hair and eye color, to the likelihood of getting certain diseases.

When drugs enter the body, they come in contact with proteins. How the proteins and drugs interact determines whether a person will get better, stay the same, or have a harmful reaction to the drug. That interaction also determines how the person's body will break down and remove the drugs. People produce slightly different

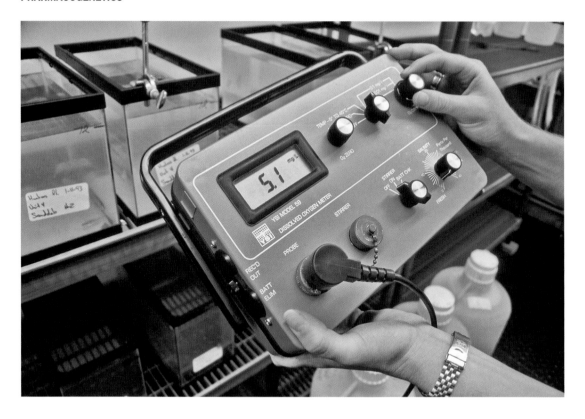

Chemist using an oxygen meter to perform a bioassay test. Bioassays are sometimes used to measure how well a drug is working in a biological system. © Bob Rowan; Progressive Image/Corbis.

proteins, so one person may react to the same medication differently than another person.

Development

Since the 1950s scientists have been able to recognize that inherited differences in certain proteins could affect the way people respond to medications. For decades, doctors have been able to test a person's blood to find out if they are a match for an organ transplant or blood transfusion (a procedure to replace blood lost during an accident, illness, or surgery). The next step was to find out how to genetically test people to learn in advance how they will react to medications. To do that, scientists needed to look closely at people's DNA.

Scientists were first able to find the order of chemical bases in a section of DNA (called sequencing) in the 1970s. Identifying a sequence for a specific protein is difficult considering there are three billion base pairs in the human genome (all of the genes in a human being).

By the end of the 1990s, improvements in technology allowed scientists to automate much of the gene-sequencing process. In 2003, scientists of the Human Genome Project announced that they had

Pharmacogenetics Versus Pharmacogenomics

The words pharmacogenetics and pharmaco-genomics sound almost exactly the same, but their meanings are slightly different. Pharmacogenetics is the study of genetic variations that affect the way a person responds to a certain medication. Pharmacogenomics, on the other hand, looks at genetic variations in groups of people that make them more likely to develop a disease, or respond to medications in a certain way.

sequenced all of the 20,000–25,000 genes in the human body. This made it possible to identify sections of DNA that code for certain proteins. Their discovery paved the way for the science of pharmacogenetics.

The Human Genome Project helped identify the tiny DNA changes that make one person different from another. Humans are almost identical genetically, but have tiny variations in their DNA called single nucleotide polymorphisms, or SNPs (pronounced "snips"). SNPs are changes to a single nucleotide in the DNA sequence. An example of a SNP would be a change in a sequence of DNA from ATGAGA to ATGACA. This very slight change can affect whether a person develops a disease or reacts to a certain drug.

SNPs occur every 100 to 300 bases along the three billion bases of the human genome. Most SNPs are outside of the coding area, which means they do not code for proteins. The SNPs that lie in a coding sequence are important to scientists because they can change the function of a protein.

SNPs are identified by taking a sample of DNA from the blood or tissue of several different people. The DNA is then sequenced to determine the order of base pairs in each segment. A single gene can contain several million bases, so scientists have to use special chemicals to cut them into fragments. A gel is used to separate the DNA fragments by their sequence (for example, all fragments ending in A, all fragments ending in C, etc.). Scientists then compare the sections to find SNPs. This method used to be done by hand, which took a long time. By the 1990s, computers were able to do the sequencing work much faster.

Current Issues

Pharmacogenetics, or personalized medicine, has the potential to save both money and lives. It could, for example, be used to screen potential study participants for clinical trials of a new drug. This

Words to Know

Deoxyribonucleic acid (DNA): The double-helix shaped molecule that serves as the carrier of genetic information for humans and most organisms.

Genome: A complete set of the DNA for a species.

Pharmacogenetics: The study of how a person's genetic makeup affects his or her response to medications.

Pharmacogenomics: The study of how human genetic variations affect responses to medications.

Sequencing: Finding the order of chemical bases in a section of DNA.

Single nucleotide polymorphisms: A change to a single nucleotide (A, C, T, or G) in a DNA sequence.

Transfusion: A technique used to replace blood lost during an accident, illness, or surgery.

would help ensure that anyone who might have a reaction to a drug is not included in the trial. This screening process would make trials smaller and less expensive, and could save consumers money on medications. Pharmacogenetics could also help prevent dangerous drug reactions by knowing in advance which people may have a reaction to a certain drug.

Despite the promise of pharmacogenetics, there are several hurdles scientists have to overcome. First, they will need to look at millions of SNPs to know which ones are involved in certain drug responses. Second, even if they know that some people will have a reaction to a kind of medicine, there may not be an alternate drug available to give those people. Lastly, drug companies may not want to spend the research money to develop drugs that will only work on a small number of people.

■ ■ ■

For More Information

Human Genome Project Information. "Pharmacogenomics." <http://web.ornl.gov/sci/techresources/Human_Genome/medicine/pharma.shtml> (accessed May 2, 2006).

National Center for Biotechnology Information. "One Size Does Not Fit All: The Promise of Pharmacogenomics." March 31, 2004. <http://www.ncbi.nlm.nih.gov/About/primer/pharm.html> (accessed May 2, 2006).

National Human Genome Research Institute. "DNA Sequencing." Last reviewed November 2005. <http://www.genome.gov/10001177> (accessed May 2, 2006).

National Institutes of Health. ''Tomorrow's Medicines—Personalized Medicines.'' December 8, 2004. <http://nihseniorhealth.gov/takingmedicines/personalizedmedicines/01.html> (accessed May 2, 2006).

[*See Also* **Vol. 1, Antibiotics, Biosynthesized; Vol. 1, Anti-Rejection Drugs; Vol. 1, Blood Transfusions; Vol. 1, DNA Sequencing; Vol. 1, DNA Vaccines; Vol. 1, Organ Transplants.**]

■■■

Protein Therapies

Description

Protein therapy refers to a medical treatment that involves the insertion of specific proteins into cells or areas surrounding cells, in order to stimulate or block biological reactions. Proteins are large molecules that are the main components of living cells. Protein therapy is temporary, since a protein does not persist indefinitely, but is degraded over time.

The potential of protein therapy has been demonstrated for the relief of damage caused by autoimmune reactions—where the immune system reacts against the body's own organs and tissues—and the uncontrolled growth of cancer cells, as two examples.

Scientific Foundations

The basis of protein therapy is the use of specific proteins as either triggers of chemical reactions in cells, or to block other proteins that themselves can act as the trigger. The addition of a protein can also stimulate cell signals that, in turn, drive other reactions.

Protein therapy is still in its infancy, but has already demonstrated great potential in adjusting the reaction of the immune system. Normally, the immune system attacks anything that is foreign in the body. This can be quite valuable when the body is invaded by a bacteria or virus that causes an illness. However, an immune response can be unhealthy if it is directed at a person's own tissues and organs. Autoimmunity, as this abnormal reaction is called, is the basis of a number of diseases, including rheumatoid (ROO-muh-toid) arthritis and systemic lupus erythematosus (pronounced LOO-puhs er-uh-THEM-uh-toe-suhs). Protein therapy can be used to block the chemical reactions that cause autoimmune reactions.

Protein Therapy May Spur Drug Development

Any drug that is intended for human use must meet rigorous criteria to establish its effectiveness and safety. This involves testing the drug on humans, which always carries some risk. Some clinical trials of gene therapies have been disastrous, since the dose of the drug could not be rapidly adjusted. Protein therapy may help alleviate this problem.

Proteins are naturally degraded in the body. Because the therapeutic protein must be given to a patient regularly, the amount of the protein can be quickly changed. If signs of trouble are detected, the protein concentration can be lowered. Conversely, if no positive effects are apparent, the protein dose can be increased. Regulation of the protein level can be accomplished with a few hours. This ability to fine-tune the dose is making protein therapy an attractive strategy in the clinical evaluation of treatments for immune-related diseases, neurological disorders, and infectious diseases.

Protein therapy has also shown promise in directing the development of stem cells—special cells that have the potential to develop into virtually any type of mature body cell. The ability to precisely tailor the development of stem cells could allow these cells to be used to regenerate body tissues.

Protein therapy differs from gene therapy. In gene therapy, the gene that codes for the creation of the therapeutic protein is supplied, and the action of this gene within the body subsequently produces the desired protein. Supplying the protein directly is time saving, since the protein does not have to be produced by cells in the body. On the other hand, the proteins supplied by protein therapies need to be administered regularly, because proteins normally break down over time.

Development

One application of protein therapy is in slowing the process of programmed cell self-destruction, known as apoptosis. While useful in maintaining a turnover of cells in the body, excessive or premature apoptosis can be harmful, as in the destruction of insulin-producing cells in the pancreas that underlies diabetes. The introduction of proteins that protect cells has successfully blocked pancreatic cell apoptosis in laboratory studies. Reduced apoptosis also would prolong the life of cells intended for transplantation, which would allow patients more time to travel to a transplant center.

Words to Know

Apoptosis: Programmed cell death in which a controlled sequence of events (or program) leads to the elimination of cells without releasing harmful substances into the surrounding area. Many types of cell damage can trigger apoptosis, and it also occurs normally during development.

Autoimmune disorder: Disorders that are caused by misdirected immune response in

which lymphocytes mount an attack against normal body cells.

Immune system: A system in the human body that fights off foreign substances, cells, and tissues in an effort to protect a person from disease.

Liposome: A sphere composed of lipid.

Protein: Complex molecules that cells use to form most of the structures and control chemical reactions within a cell.

Paradoxically, another protein therapy strategy seeks to trigger even greater apoptosis. Researchers have demonstrated that by supplying an artificial version of part of a protein called p53—which functions to suppress cancer tumors by increasing the amount of cell apoptosis that occurs—the destruction of cancer cells can be boosted.

Another potential application for protein therapy is in the relief of rheumatoid arthritis. Researchers have successfully eased the painful symptoms of the disease in volunteers by supplying a therapeutic protein in pill form. The supplied protein blocks the action of another protein, and thus slows the overactive immune response that occurs with that disease.

Current Issues

Protein therapy is an area at the cutting edge of research. The potential of the strategy is already apparent in the regulation of autoimmune responses and the regulation of apoptosis in various types of cells. The challenges now are to tailor protein therapy so that it can be used in people safely and with confidence that it will produce a beneficial result with minimal (or no) side effects.

An immediate challenge is to deliver the therapeutic protein so that it reaches its intended cell target and is not destroyed along the way. It may be possible to supply the protein in a pill that will resist degradation in the stomach. Another route that has been successfully used for the targeted delivery of some injected drugs is to package the protein inside molecules made in the laboratory called liposomes (LIP-a-sohmes). Liposomes are hollow spheres made of lipids (fats) that can be filled the therapeutic protein.

Finally, prolonging the activity of a therapeutic protein in the body is desirable, since it would then have to be given to the patient less often. Designing proteins to resist degradation is another research goal.

■ ■ ■

For More Information

Jo, Daewoong, et al. "Intracellular Protein Therapy with $SOCS_3$ Inhibits Inflammation and Apoptosis." *Nature Medicine* 11 (August 2005): 892–898.

Medical News Today. "Snapin: A Protein with Therapy Potential for Autism." August 25, 2005. <http://www.medicalnewstoday.com/medi calnews.php?newsid=29628> (accessed July 5, 2006).

[See Also **Vol. 1, Chemotherapy Drugs; Vol. 1, Enzyme Replacement Therapy.**]

■■■

Skin Substitutes

Description

Sometimes when people are badly burned, or have a disease such as diabetes that prevents their wounds from healing, their natural skin does not grow back. Doctors need to cover the area, both to make it look more natural and to protect against infection. To cover an area of lost skin, doctors have used skin grafts (healthy skin that is used to replace damaged skin) from dead bodies or from the patient's own body. If the burns are too deep for this to be done, doctors can use artificial skin substitutes.

Skin grafts can often be rejected by the body's natural defenses, and artificial skin is only temporary. So scientists have been developing new, tissue-engineered (also called bioengineered—artificial products that are made from natural biological materials) skin substitutes that heal more like real skin.

Scientific Foundations

Skin is the largest organ in the body. It is made up of two layers: the dermis and the epidermis. The dermis is the bottom layer. It contains blood vessels, nerve cells, and sweat glands. On top of the dermis is the epidermis, the part of the skin that can be seen. The epidermis contains cells that produce keratin, a substance that makes skin strong. The epidermis also constantly makes new skin cells. The old cells rise to the surface, where they turn into dead skin and flake off.

Although skin is able to regrow when it is damaged, it cannot regrow when both the dermis and epidermis have been destroyed. This sometimes happens when someone is badly burned, or has a disease that prevents their wounds from healing.

Skin substitutes

How artificial skin helps burns heal

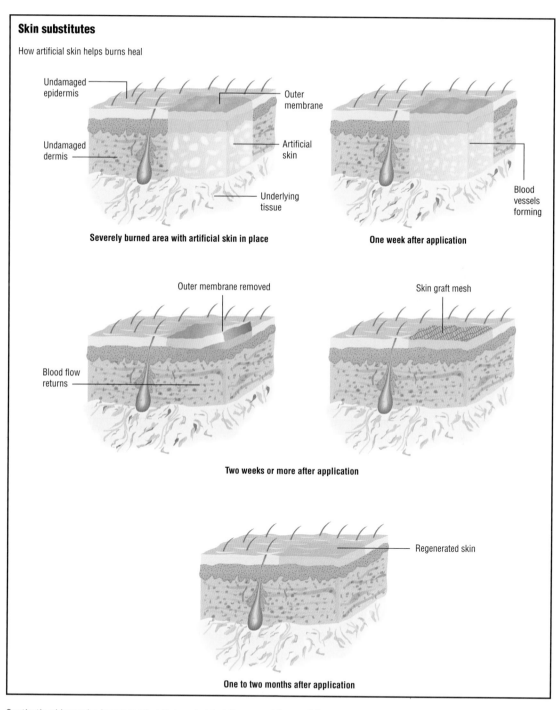

Severely burned area with artificial skin in place

One week after application

Two weeks or more after application

One to two months after application

Synthetic skin works by protecting the underlying tissues while providing a structure that allows regrowth of the skin. *Illustration by GGS Inc.*

Building a New Body

In the 1980s, scientists Robert Langer and Joseph Vacanti discovered that they could grow human skin in a lab. Their discovery not only enabled scientists to create skin substitutes, but it also paved the way for the creation of entire organs. The scaffold they discovered could be shaped like an organ, for example a liver. Then organ cells from the patient or a donor could be put on the scaffold. The cells would grow and divide, forming a new organ. The idea was to implant the organ in the patient's body and have the scaffold dissolve away. The challenge is to get blood vessels to regrow so that the organ can integrate naturally into the patient's body.

Doctors often use skin substitutes to cover open wounds. Skin substitutes protect against fluid loss and infection, and help the wound heal. There are four different types of skin substitutes that can be used to replace lost skin: autografts, allografts, synthetic skin, and tissue-engineered skin.

An autograft uses epidermal skin from another part of the patient's body. An allograft uses skin from a cadaver (a dead body) or from a pig. An allograft is only temporary because the person's body will eventually recognize the skin as foreign and reject it. Synthetic skin is usually made of silicone (an artificial material made of the element silicon and oxygen), collagen (a type of protein that makes up connective tissue), and a support layer of fiber. It is also temporary, because it cannot grow into the person's skin. Tissue engineered skin is a newer technology. It is made from real human cells and is designed to permanently replace lost skin.

Development

In the past, burn victims were left vulnerable to infection without skin to protect them. People with diabetes and other conditions that prevented wounds from healing would sometimes need to have their affected limbs amputated (cut off) in order to save their lives. Up until the late twentieth century, skin could only be surgically replaced using grafts from the patient's own body or from a donor. But patients sometimes did not have enough extra skin for a graft, and donor skin can be rejected.

As early as the 1970s, scientists learned how to grow human tissue in a lab. In 1986, Robert Langer (1948–) of the Massachusetts Institute of Technology and Joseph Vacanti of Massachusetts General Hospital pioneered a new method for growing human tissues. They

Words to Know

Allograft: Transplanted tissues or organs from donors of the same species.

Amputate: To cut off a limb or part of the body.

Autograft: A type of skin graft that uses tissue from another part of the patient's own body, and therefore has cells with the same genes.

Biodegradable: Able to be broken down by natural processes.

Cadaver: A dead body.

Circumcision: Removal of the foreskin of the penis.

Collagen: A type of protein that makes up connective tissue.

Dermis: The inner layer of skin. It is made up of connective tissue that gives skin its strength.

Diabetes: A disease in which the body cannot make or properly use the hormone, insulin.

Epidermis: The outer layer of the skin consisting of dead cells. It is the primary protective barrier against sunlight, chemicals, and other possible harmful agents. The epidermal cells are constantly being shed and replenished.

Fibroblast cells: Cells in the dermis layer of the skin that give rise to connective tissue.

Graft: A transplanted tissue.

Keratinocytes: Skin cells that make a protein called keratin, which protects the skin.

Silicone: A controversial substance that has been used in breast and other types of implants. It is classified as a high-risk category material by the FDA.

Tissue engineered (also called bioengineered): Artificial products that are made from natural biological materials.

figured out how to grow skin using a type of biodegradable (able to break down naturally) scaffolding as a framework. The first type of artificial skin made with real human cells was approved by the U.S. Food & Drug Administration in 1997.

Tissue-engineered skin is made using healthy skin cells from a donor (sometimes tissue that is removed from the foreskin of male babies during circumcision). The cells are seeded onto a scaffold. This is like a framework that molds the cells into a particular shape. The scaffolds are biodegradable, which means that they are absorbed into the skin without having to be removed surgically.

Scientists use natural skin-making cells to seed the scaffold. Then they make the cells multiply until they fill in the scaffold and create what looks like real skin. When the patient is ready, the skin is stretched over the wound. No stitches are needed—the tissue-engineered skin becomes integrated with the patient's natural skin. Some types of tissue-engineered skin are made from an artificial epidermis with a dermis made of real cells. Other types contain both dermal and epidermal cells. The cells in tissue engineered skin function much natural human skin.

Current Issues

Tissue-engineered skin can be made to look and feel like real skin, but it does not act entirely like skin. For example, it cannot grow blood vessels, so it has no real blood supply to feed it. This can cause the body to reject the skin, or cause the skin to lose function. Tissue-engineered skin also cannot grow hair, sweat, or heal (scab over) like natural skin because it lacks the cells to do these things.

■ ■ ■

For More Information

Brill, Leon R., and Jeffrey A. Stone. "New therapeutic options for lower-extremity ulcers." *Patient Care for the Nurse Practitioner* (October 1, 2004).

Cornell University. "Skin Substitutes." <http://www.mse.cornell.edu/courses/mse461/Notes/skin_substitutes/skin_substitutes.html> (accessed May 3, 2006).

Forbes. "Plastic Man." December 23, 2002. <http://www.forbes.com/forbes/2002/1223/296_print.html> (accessed May 3, 2006).

Kirn, Timothy F. "Biologic Wound Therapies have Limited Utility." *Skin & Allergy News* 43, no. 3 (2003): 41.

The Whitaker Foundation. "Bioengineered Skin." <http://www.whitaker.org/glance/skin.html> (accessed May 3, 2006).

[See Also **Vol. 1, Anti-Rejection Drugs; Vol. 1, Bone Substitutes; Vol. 1, Collagen Replacement; Vol. 1, Organ Transplants; Vol. 1, Tissue Engineering; Vol. 1, Xenotransplantation.**]

Somatic Cell Therapy

Description

Somatic cell therapy, or cell therapy, is a set of techniques and scientific processes that are used to repair diseased cells of a human body by replacing them with healthier and scientifically processed new cells. This modern therapy can be used to treat a variety of diseases and conditions, such as cancer, spinal cord injuries, Parkinson's disease, and diabetes. A somatic cell is any cell in the human body except for egg cells and sperm cells.

In the case of diseases that cause the body's organs not to work properly, drug treatments may not work well over long periods of time. After that time, the only option that often remains is organ transplant, which is difficult and expensive to do and often fails. Scientists are hoping to develop somatic cell therapy so that plenty of healthy cells can be created to replace the disease-causing cells, resulting in a new treatment option.

Scientific Foundations

Cells are called the building blocks of life. They are the structural and functional units of a living organism. All organisms are either unicellular (composed of one cell) or multicellular (composed of many cells). In multicellular organisms, like animals and humans, different cells perform all the functions that are responsible for the overall performance of the organ or tissue that they compose.

Different type of cells make up the human body (such as blood cells, skin cells, or muscle cells), but all of them arise from a single cell—the fertilized egg, or zygote. These cells then replicate, or make copies of themselves. The cells that are produced during the early stages of human development are not specialized for any

A laboratory worker with a cell culture to be used as cell therapy in heart transplants. © *Dung Vo Trung/CORBIS SYGMA.*

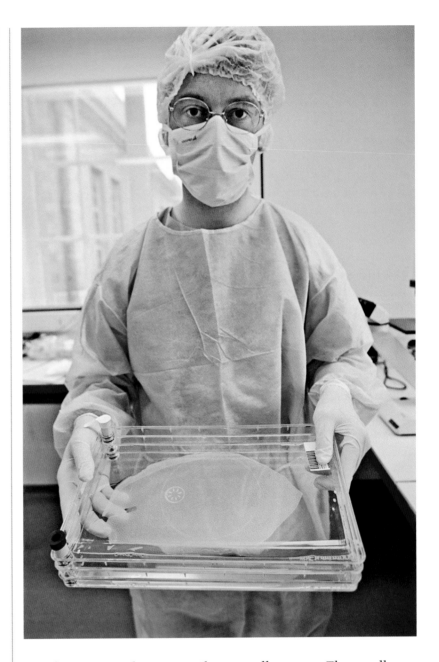

specific organ and can contribute to all organs. These cells are known as embryonic stem cells. These cells progressively develop into specialized cells such as liver cells or kidney cells. Another type of stem cell, the adult stem cell, is found in specialized tissues, such as bone marrow (the soft material inside bones). They can generate all of the cells found in the blood.

Development

In 1968, a successful bone marrow transplant gave momentum to adult stem cell research. The concept of stem cells received more attention in the early 1980s, when improved technology for microscopic research and cultivation of stem cells in laboratories was developed. As mentioned earlier, there are two main types of stem cells, embryonic stem cells and adult stem cells.

In 1998, embryonic stem cells were developed by isolating cells from the inner cell mass of early embryos. Embryonic stem cells have become popular with medical researchers because they are easily available and can potentially be used to make any body cell. Adult stem cells, on the other hand, are obtained from adult tissues. Both embryonic and adult stem cells are capable of self-renewal as well as progressive development into specialized cells. Scientists can manipulate stem cells so that they can be used to replace damaged cells in the diseased organs in the body. This is called stem cell therapy.

A specific type of stem cell therapy is known as somatic cell nuclear transfer. This is a genetic procedure for cloning that involves removing the nucleus (the structure in each cell that contains genetic information) from a patient's somatic cell, usually a skin cell. This nucleus is then inserted into an egg cell from which the nucleus has already been removed. The egg cell now contains the patient's genetic material. It is allowed to divide in the laboratory until it forms a hollow sphere of cells called a blastocyst. The cells from the inner wall of the blastocyst are removed and used to develop a new stem cell line that has the patient's genetic material. Somatic cell therapy can be done in the body as well as outside the body.

According to scientists, the results of stem cell research and experiments have been very promising so far. Bone marrow transplants are an example of cell therapy in which the stem cells in a donor's marrow are used to replace the bone marrow cells of a patient who has leukemia or other cancers. Cell therapy has also been used to graft new skin cells to treat burn victims. In addition, it has been used in experiments to grow a new cornea for a sight impaired person. Experts suggest that with stem cell therapy, we may soon have effective cures for cancer, Parkinson's disease, diabetes, kidney disease, and paralysis caused by spinal injuries.

In a recent development, pancreatic cells grown from stem cells were implanted into the body of a diabetic patient and they began to produce insulin. Pancreatic cells are found in the pancreas, the

The First Somatic Cell Therapy

The first approved somatic cell therapy was performed on a four-year-old girl, Ashanti DeSilva, in September 1990. DeSilva had a very weak immune system caused by a deficiency of an enzyme known as adenosine deaminase (ADA). The therapy conducted on DeSilva helped her body produce the amount of ADA it needed for her immune system to work properly, and it saved her life. Today DeSilva is quite healthy and leads a normal life. However, she continues to receive gene therapy regularly, since the cells she receives only work for a few months.

gland in the human body that produces digestive enzymes and insulin. Nonetheless, there are several scientific challenges that have to be overcome before the true power of stem cell therapy can be fully harnessed.

Current Issues

Somatic cell therapy is a relatively new science, but dramatic results in this area have caused great optimism in the scientific community. However, there are several technical challenges and ethical issues that have caused intense debate in society. It is still difficult for scientists to work with stem cells. After the cells are identified, scientists need to develop the right biochemical solution that will enable the stem cell to develop and differentiate into the cell type they want. In addition, the cells that are implanted into the human body must learn to function in harmony and coordination with the body's natural cells. The possibility of tissue rejection by the body's immune system is another challenge. Finally, uncontrolled growth of the new transplanted cells could lead to diseases, such as cancer.

In the last few years, owing to their potential role in cloning humans, ethical concerns have arisen over embryonic stem cell research and somatic cell nuclear transfer. Extraction of embryonic stem cells may destroy the embryo and, in the words of the several critics, destroy a human life. However, advocates of stem cell research argue that the embryonic cells do not yet have any human characteristics.

In 1973, the U.S. government prohibited the use of federal funds for human embryo research. Ever since, there has been a continuing debate about whether the government should cancel or continue

Words to Know

Adult stem cell: A renewable and unspecialized cell found among specialized cells in a tissue or organ.

Cells: The smallest living units of the body which together form tissues.

Clone: A cell or organism that contains the identical genetic information of the parent cell or organism.

Embryonic stem cell: A stem cell found in embryos about a week old. Descendants of one of these cells can be any kind of tissue. These cells can reproduce indefinitely in the laboratory.

Enzyme: A protein that helps control the rate or speed of chemical reactions in the cell.

Nucleus: A compartment in the cell which is enclosed by a membrane and which contains its genetic information.

Somatic cell: Cells that are part of the body but are not in the germline (able to pass their DNA on to future generations). Any type of cell in the body that is not a sperm or egg cell.

---

the ban. In 2000, President Bill Clinton allowed funding of research on cells derived from aborted human fetuses, but not from embryonic cells. In 2001, President George W. Bush restricted federal funding to research using existing human embryonic stem cell lines created before to his announcement.

The future of cell therapy continues to be debated by doctors, scientists, and society as a whole. However, scientists around the world agree that before somatic cell therapy becomes a reality, significant research is still required.

■ ■ ■

For More Information

Focus on Social Issues. "Gene Therapy: A Brief History." June 23, 2004. <http://www.family.org/cforum/fosi/bioethics/genetics/a0032608.cfm> (accessed June 25, 2006).

Genetic Science Learning Center at the University of Utah. "Stem Cell Therapies Today." <http://learn.genetics.utah.edu/units/stemcells/sctoday/> (accessed June 25, 2006).

Genetic Science Learning Center at the University of Utah. "What Are Some Issues in Stem Cell Research?." <http://learn.genetics.utah.edu/units/stemcells/scissues/> (accessed June 25, 2006).

Keating, A., et al. *Regenerative and Cell Therapy: Clinical Advances.* New York: Springer, 2004.

National Institute for Medical Research. "Stem Cell Therapy and Research." 2001. <http://www.nimr.mrc.ac.uk/millhillessays/2001/stemcells.htm> (accessed June 25, 2006).

North Carolina Center for Genomics and Public Health. ''Gene Therapy.'' <http://www2.sph.unc.edu/nccgph//phgenetics/therapy.htm> (accessed June 25, 2006).

Stem Cell Research Foundation. ''Frequently Asked Questions.'' <http://www.stemcellresearchfoundation.org/About/FAQ.htm> (accessed June 25, 2006).

Templeton, Nancy S. *Gene and Cell Therapy: Therapeutic Mechanisms and Strategies*. Boca Raton, FL: CRC Press, 2003.

[*See Also* **Vol. 1, Stem Cell Lines; Vol. 1, Stem Cells, Adult; Vol. 1, Stem Cells, Embryonic.**]

Stem Cell Lines

Description

There are about 200 types of cells in the human body: blood cells, brain cells, muscle cells, liver cells, skin cells, and more. All these types of cells (except egg, sperm, and red blood cells) contain a complete set of human DNA molecules. DNA is short for deoxyribo-nucleic acid, the molecule used by all living things to pass on traits to offspring. Because they contain a complete set of DNA, all cells could in theory make any other kind of cell. In practice, however, this does not happen. A DNA molecule in a cell is always telling the cell how to build molecules, like a book of recipes being used to cook many dishes. There are also molecules that attach to DNA and make differ-ent parts of it active or inactive—turn some of its recipes on or off. Different cell types grow differently because different parts of their DNA are turned on or off.

Single cells make new cells by growing to a certain size, copying their DNA, and then splitting in two. Each half gets a copy of the DNA and becomes a new cell. However, once a cell's DNA has been set for a certain kind of function, such as being a nerve cell, that cell can no longer divide.

There is only one kind of cell that can keep on dividing in the body, and that is a stem cell. There are several kinds of stem cells. All of them can give rise to other kinds of cells. Some stem cells—those found in embryos a few days old—can give rise to all 200 kinds of body cells. This is exactly what happens when a fertilized egg cell grows into a baby: the fertilized egg divides into two cells, then four, then eight, and so on as the embryo grows. A series of cells descended from each other is called a cell line. In an embryo, one cell line becomes heart muscle cells, another brain cells, another skin cells, and so on, until a baby is formed who has all 200 or so types of cells.

How embryonic stem cells are used

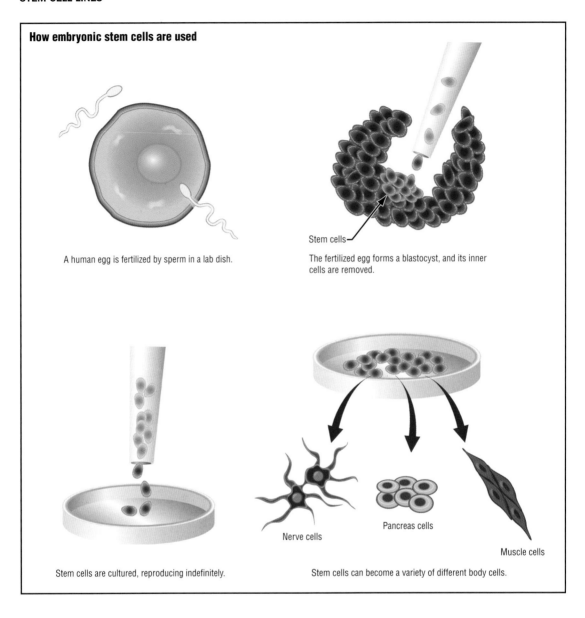

A human egg is fertilized by sperm in a lab dish.

Stem cells

The fertilized egg forms a blastocyst, and its inner cells are removed.

Nerve cells

Pancreas cells

Muscle cells

Stem cells are cultured, reproducing indefinitely.

Stem cells can become a variety of different body cells.

How embryonic stem cells are used to produce different types of body cells. The cells that are cultured from a single blastocyst become a stem cell line. *Illustration by GGS Inc.*

Once the body is formed, it still contains stem cells. But these stem cells are not as flexible as the ones in the young embryo. They can divide to produce some kinds of cells, but not others. For this reason, the stem cells in the young embryo are called "pluripotent" (pronounced ploor-IP-oh-tent). *Pluri* means "many" and *potent* means "having power." A pluripotent stem cell has the power to produce many kinds of cells.

The stem cells in the body are called adult stem cells (even though babies and children have them too). Adult stem cells make only one type of cell or sometimes several types, but never as many types as embryonic stem cells make. Adult stem cells make it possible for skin, muscle, and other tissues to heal after being damaged. Each kind of tissue has its own kind of stem cell.

Stem cells are special because they have the power to give rise to other kinds of cells. There are some medical treatments that use this power, and many more are being investigated.

Scientific Foundations

When taken out of the body, ordinary cells can be made to make new cells in a dish of nutrients. (The nutrient or food used is a thick liquid called a culture medium that is specially made for cells to live in.) But they can only reproduce or divide about fifty times. After that, they die out. This limit on the number of generations is called the Hayflick limit, after American professor of anatomy Leonard Hayflick (1928–), the person who discovered it in 1965. But embryonic stem cells have no Hayflick limit. No one knows how long an embryonic stem cell line can continue. Once a line of stem cells has been found, it can be kept going for years and be studied in laboratories around the world. Some human embryonic stem cell lines have been living since 1998. Adult stem cell lines do not last in this way because after a while they differentiate, that is, the new cells begin to look like cells from a particular tissue rather than like stem cells. Then they die out.

Development

Scientists have known for over a century that just a few cells in the embryo give rise to all the different kinds of cells in the body. However, it was not until about forty years ago that they began to understand the differences between stem cells and ordinary cells. Embryonic cells from mice were first isolated in the 1960s and used to start cell lines. Adult stem cells were first used to treat disease in the 1960s. The stem cells in bone marrow, which give rise to blood cells and some other types of cell, can be used to treat the kind of cancer known as leukemia.

It was not until 1998 that human embryonic stem cells were found. They were taken from embryos at a very early stage of growth—only three to five days after fertilization (the coming together of an egg and a sperm to make a single cell). At that time, the embryo is a ball of a few dozen cells. It has no brain, heart, limbs, or other organs.

Treating Parkinson's Disease

As of 2006, some scientists believed that they were close to finding a way to use stem cells to treat Parkinson's disease. In Parkinson's disease, the nerve cells that control the muscles break down. The limbs of people with Parkinson's disease shake or stiffen, and these people can no longer move normally. One out of every fifty people over sixty-five years old has Parkinson's disease. Researchers have found that they can treat Parkinson's disease in mice using embryonic stem cells. They add a gene to the stem cells to make them grow into nerve cells, then add the new cells to the brains of the sick mice. Once there, the new cells grow and the mice can move around better. Even if the same method will work for people, it will probably be years before an effective treatment is developed.

Current Issues

There are two kinds of issues or arguments about stem cells. First, there are factual questions about stem cells that scientists have not answered yet. Scientists do not know how to tell stem cells to make new cells of the right kind exactly where they are needed, so they cannot yet treat most diseases and injuries using stem cells. Also, they do not know where adult stem cells come from. A new kind of stem cell, the spore-like cell, was only discovered in 2001. The spore-like cell is very small and tough. Scientists still know very little about spore-like stem cells.

Second, there are ethical issues. Ethical issues are arguments about right and wrong. Some people think that it is wrong to use embryonic stem cells in research or to cure diseases because, they say, even when the embryo is only a few days old, shaped like a ball of ten or fifty cells that all look alike, it is already a human being with full human rights. Because of the objections from people who have these beliefs, the government of the United States has refused to fund the creation of new human embryonic stem cell lines since the late 1990s and has barred federal government funding for research using human embryonic stem cells since 2001. However, it is still legal for people to create and use human embryonic stem cell lines with private (non-government) money. Other people argue that the government should fund embryonic stem cell research because the benefits to sick people could be so great. They do not agree that the embryo is a human being at such an early stage of development.

Words to Know

Adult stem cell: A renewable and unspecialized cell found among specialized cells in a tissue or organ.

Cell line: Series of cells descended from each other like the generations of a family.

Culture medium: A substance that supports the growth of bacteria so they may be identified.

Deoxyribonucleic acid (DNA): The double-helix shaped molecule that serves as the carrier of genetic information for humans and most organisms.

Embryonic stem cell: A stem cell found in embryos about a week old. Descendants of one of these cells can be any kind of tissue. These cells can reproduce indefinitely in the laboratory.

Parkinson's disease: Disease of the nerves that causes the patient to gradually lose control of their muscles. Loss of a chemical in the brain called dopamine causes shaking and muscle stiffness.

Spore-like stem cell: An unspecified cell that remains in a dormant state in the body until they are stimulated to divide and form specialized cells.

Stem cell: An unspecialized cell that can divide to form other types of specialized cells in the body. Stem cells give rise to cells that have specialized form and function such as nerve or muscle cells.

There are no ethical arguments about research on adult stem cells, since adult stem cells can be taken from a living person without hurting them, or from a person who died from age, disease, or accident.

■ ■ ■

For More Information

National Institutes of Health. "Stem Cell Basics." August 12, 2005. <http://stemcells.nih.gov/info/basics/> (accessed June 5, 2006).

Parson, Ann B. *The Proteus Effect: Stem Cells and Their Promise for Medicine.* Washington, DC: Joseph Henry Press, 2004.

Shaw, Jonathan. "Stem-cell Science." *Harvard Magazine* (May-June 2004). This article can also be found online at <http://www.harvardmagazine.com/on-line/050466.html>

[*See Also* **Vol. 1, Bioethics; Vol. 1, Bone Marrow Transplant; Vol. 1, Somatic Cell Therapy; Vol. 1, Stem Cells, Adult; Vol. 1, Stem Cells, Embryonic.**]

■■■

Stem Cells, Adult

Description

An adult human body contains about 100 trillion cells. Most cells do not last a lifetime. Some cells, like those that line the throat, last only about a week. Others, like muscle cells, can last for fifteen years or more. Whenever a cell dies, it must be replaced by a new one. New cells come from a special type of cell that is found in every kind of body tissue. These cells are called adult stem cells (because new cells "stem from" or arise from them). Adult stem cells do not do the specialized jobs of the cells around them; they do not contract like muscle cells, or send messages like nerve cells, or sense light like the cells at the back of the eye. Their main job is to make new specialized cells to replace those that die.

Stem cells must make new stem cells, too, to replace themselves as they die off. This is called long-term self-renewal. Because of self-renewal, there are always fresh stem cells in all the tissues of the body, ready to replace lost cells.

There are about 200 types of cells in the human body: blood cells, brain cells, muscle cells, liver cells, skin cells, and more. Most of these tissues have their own stem cells, which usually produce new specialized cells for just that one kind of tissue. Stem cells are rare. For example, in the bone marrow, where blood cells are made, only about one cell in 10,000 or 15,000 is a stem cell.

Besides the adult stem cell—which, despite its name, is also found in babies and children—there is at least one other kind of stem cell, the embryonic stem cell. Embryonic stem cells are found in embryos about three to five days after fertilization (the joining of the egg and sperm cell). At that time, the embryo consists of a ball of a dozen or so cells that all look alike. Embryonic stem cells are different from adult stem

Luc Douay, whose team at the St. Antoine Faculty of Medicine in Paris developed a technique to produce functional, mature, human red blood cells from adult stem cells. *VOISIN/Photo Researchers, Inc.*

cells because an embryonic stem cell can give rise to any kind of cell in the body. Adult stem cells do not have this ability.

Embryonic stem cells can also be kept alive for many generations outside the body, in a laboratory dish. They split, grow, and split again, producing new copies of themselves, year after year. Adult stem cells cannot do this. After a certain number of generations, adult stem cells start to look like the specialized cells of the tissue they were taken from, and then they lose their ability to keep on dividing. A laboratory culture of adult stem cells will die off after about a year. But a culture of embryonic stem cells can live for many years—nobody knows how long.

Scientific Foundations

There are two ways to tell whether a cell found in the body is a stem cell or not. The first is to label the cells and then track them in the body to see if they give rise to specialized cells (for example, muscle cells). Labeling is usually done by adding radioactive material to the cells; they can then be tracked by measuring their radioactivity. (Radioactivity is the ability that some elements have to give off energy and smaller particles when they disintegrate.) The other way to see if a kind of cell is a stem cell is to take the cells out of the body and raise them in dishes in the laboratory. If they can be made to give rise to specialized cells, they are stem cells.

Development

For over a hundred years, biologists have known that the body must have something like adult stem cells. They knew that skin cells and blood cells died quickly and must be replaced somehow. Every second, the body loses two million red blood cells and makes two million more. But red blood cells cannot make other red blood cells because they do not have any deoxyribonucleic acid (DNA, the molecule that all living things use to pass on traits to their offspring). Therefore, another kind of cell must make red blood cells.

In the 1950s, researchers began to hunt for the stem cells that make blood cells. In 1961, a Canadian team discovered stem cells in the bone marrow. These cells are called hematopoietic cells (pronounced hee-mat-o-poy-ET-ik), which is Greek for "blood-making." Hematopoietic stem cells make all the blood cells in the body, including white blood cells, red blood cells, and platelets.

In the kind of cancer called leukemia, cells in the bone marrow start to reproduce out of control. Since 1968, some kinds of leukemia have been treated using hematopoietic stem cells. Doctors take healthy hematopoietic stem cells from the patient's bone marrow and grow them outside the body. Then they kill all the other cells in the bone marrow, including the cancer, with radiation. The hematopoietic stem cells can then be put back into the bone marrow,

Not Just Junk

In 2001, a whole new type of cell, the spore-like stem cell, was discovered by Dr. M. P. Vacanti and his co-workers. The Vacanti group showed that extremely small cells—only a thirtieth or less the volume of a normal cell—exist in almost all tissues of the body. They called these cells "spore-like" because spores can survive extreme cold, extreme heat, and lack of oxygen, and so can these cells. Nobody had ever noticed the spore-like cells before because they are so small. One scientist, when Vacanti first pointed them out under a microscope, told him they were "just junk." But the Vacanti group showed that the tiny spore-like cells are living stem cells by culturing them in laboratory dishes and watching them give rise to cells resembling the tissues they are taken from. Very little is known yet about what spore-like stem cells do.

where they grow and spread and replace all the kinds of bone-marrow cells and blood cells that the body needs. Experiments with mice have shown that a single hematopoietic cell can repopulate the entire blood-cell and immune system of the body, which contains trillions of cells.

Current Issues

In recent years, scientists have found that there are stem cells in all (or almost all) of the tissues in the body. But they still do not know where exactly the stem cells come from. They also do not know whether most adult stem cells can give rise to types of cells other than the tissues they are found in. This property is important because doctors may be able to use it to treat some diseases. For example, if adult stem cells could be forced to make new nerve cells, people paralyzed by severed spinal cords might be able to grow new nerves and use their bodies again. (The spinal cord is the large bundle of nerves that connects the brain to most of the body.)

It is still easier to treat diseases with embryonic stem cells than with adult stem cells. However, scientists would rather use adult stem cells. There are two reasons for this. First, some people think it is wrong to use embryonic stem cells because they come from embryos. These people believe that even when an embryo is only a few days old and has no brain, heart, or other organs, it is already a human person and must not be used for anybody else's benefit. Although most doctors and scientists do not share this belief, the government of the United States, which pays for most of the medical research in the country, will not pay for research that uses embryonic stem cells.

Words to Know

Adult stem cell: A renewable and unspecialized cell found among specialized cells in a tissue or organ.

Embryonic stem cell: A stem cell found in embryos about a week old. Descendants of one of these cells can be any kind of tissue. These cells can reproduce indefinitely in the laboratory.

Hematopoietic cell: A cells in the bone marrow that gives rise, by splitting, to all the various kinds of blood cells. *Hemato-* means blood and *-poietic* means making.

Spore-like stem cell: An unspecified cell that remains in a dormant state in the body until they are stimulated to divide and form specialized cells.

Stem cell: An unspecialized cell that can divide to form other types of specialized cells in the body. Stem cells give rise to cells that have specialized form and function such as nerve or muscle cells.

A second reason that scientists would rather use adult stem cells is that a patient's own stem cells could be used to treat their disease. This is already done with leukemia treatments. The body would welcome cells that come from its own cells, rather than trying to fight them off as invaders. However, it is still not practical to treat any human disease using adult stem cells, except for using hematopoietic cells to treat leukemia.

Knowledge about stem cells is growing quickly, and in the next few years diseases other than leukemia will begin to be treated using stem cells.

■ ■ ■

For More Information

National Institutes of Health. "Report on Stem Cells: Chapter 4: The Adult Stem Cell." August 12, 2005. <http://stemcells.nih.gov/info/scireport/chapter4.asp> (accessed June 6, 2006).

Parson, Ann B. *The Proteus Effect: Stem Cells and Their Promise for Medicine.* Washington, DC: Joseph Henry Press, 2004.

Shaw, Jonathan. "Stem-cell Science." *Harvard Magazine* (May-June 2004). This article can also be found online at <http://www.harvardmagazine.com/on-line/050466.html>

[*See Also* **Vol. 1, Bioethics; Vol. 1, Bone Marrow Transplant; Vol. 1, Somatic Cell Therapy; Vol. 1, Stem Cells, Embryonic; Vol. 1, Stem Cell Lines.**]

■■■

Stem Cells, Embryonic

Description

Embryonic stem cells are the cells in an embryo (a human being in its earliest stages of development) that will ultimately develop into every cell, organ, and tissue in the body. Because of their ability to become many different cell and tissue types, scientists believe that embryonic stem cells have the potential to treat many different diseases. They also have the potential to generate entire human organs, which could help the thousands of people who are waiting for organ transplants. However, research is just beginning into the nature of these cells, and any treatments that may come from embryonic stem cells are many years in the future.

Scientific Foundations

In human reproduction, a sperm from the man fertilizes an egg from the woman. The nuclei (plural of nucleus, the center part of a cell that controls all its functions) from the egg and the sperm merge, forming a zygote (a fertilized egg). The cells begin to divide. After about a week, they form a ball of about 100 cells, called a blastocyst. The inner part of the blastocyst contains the stem cells. These cells are pluripotent, which means that they can develop into any cell or tissue in the body.

Scientists would like to be able to grow embryonic stem cells in a lab, then coax those cells to become the type of cell that is missing or malfunctioning in a certain disease. Embryonic stem cells have several possible uses:

- To grow cells that produce dopamine for patients with Parkinson's disease (a nervous system disorder caused by a lack of the neurotransmitter dopamine, which causes shaking and muscle stiffness).

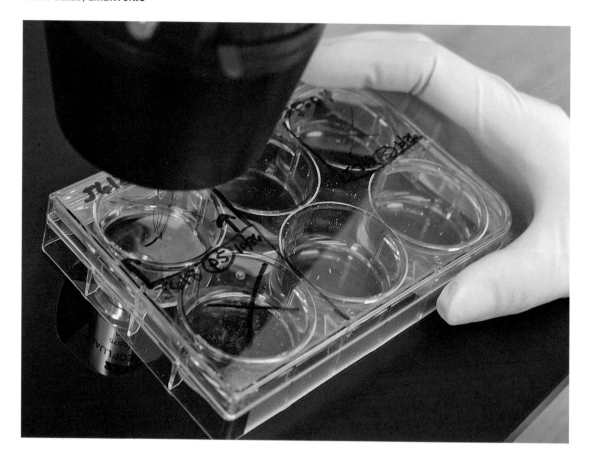

Embryonic stem cells in a plate of liquid nutrients being examined in a laboratory. © *Kat Wade/San Fransisco Chronicle/Corbis.*

- To grow pancreatic cells that produce the hormone insulin for people with diabetes (a disease in which the body cannot make or properly use insulin).

- To grow nerve cells to replace those damaged in people with spinal cord injuries.

- To grow new heart muscle tissue to replace tissue that is damaged during a heart attack.

Development

In 1981, two different research groups were able to isolate embryonic stem cells from mice. In 1997, researchers were finally able to pull stem cells from human embryos. American researcher Dr. James Thomson and his team of researchers at the University of Wisconsin were the first to discover a method for isolating and growing human embryonic stem cells.

Researchers who work with embryonic stem cells usually obtain frozen embryos at the blastocyst stage leftover from fertility clinic

The Ethics of Embryonic Stem Cell Research

In 2001, United States President George W. Bush prohibited the use of federal money for embryonic stem cell research, with the exception of the twenty lines that already existed. In other countries, stem cell research is not only accepted, it is encouraged. In the United Kingdom and Singapore, the governments have invested a great deal of money in stem cell research. One study by researchers at the University of Michigan and Stanford University found that scientists in other countries were beginning to outpace the United States in embryonic stem cell research.

procedures. These are embryos that would normally be destroyed. Scientists then remove stem cells from the inner part of the blastocyst. Removing these cells destroys the blastocyst. The cells are placed in a culture dish that contains nutrients. In the culture dish, the cells grow and multiply many times. After a few months, thirty original cells may have divided into millions of embryonic stem cells. Cells that do not differentiate (change into a more specialized cell type) after growing for several months are called a stem-cell line. These are the cells that have the greatest potential to treat disease. A stem-cell line can be frozen and used over and over again in the lab.

To get stem cells to differentiate into blood cells, muscle tissue, or any other type of tissue, scientists can change the chemical composition of the dish in which they are cultured. Or, they can add certain genes (pieces of DNA that specify the production of proteins, which determine how the body functions) to the cells.

Current Issues

There is much public debate about the ethics (what is right and wrong) of destroying embryos to harvest their stem cells. When stem cells are taken out of an embryo, that embryo no longer can be implanted into a woman's uterus and grow into a baby. Critics of embryonic stem cell research say that destroying embryos is murder, regardless of its scientific potential. In 2006, researchers grew stem cells from a single cell taken from an embryo without destroying it, and are working to perfect the technique.

There is also the issue of federal funding of embryonic stem cell research. U.S. President George W. Bush said in 2001 that federal money could not be used for embryonic stem cell research, with the exception of the stem cell lines that were already in existence at

Words to Know

Blastocyst: A cluster of cells resulting from successful fertilization of an ovum (egg) by a sperm. This is the developmental form that must implant itself in the uterus to achieve pregnancy.

Diabetes: A disease in which the body cannot make or properly use the hormone, insulin.

Differentiate: To become a specialized type of cell.

Embryo: A stage in development after fertilization.

Ethics: The study of what is right or wrong.

Genes: Pieces of DNA that carry instructions for traits and diseases.

Leukemia: A cancer of the blood-producing cells in bone marrow.

Parkinson's disease: Disease of the nerves that causes the patient to gradually lose control of their muscles. Loss of a chemical in the brain called dopamine causes shaking and muscle stiffness.

Zygote: The cell resulting from the fusion of male sperm and the female egg. Normally the zygote has double the chromosome number of either the sperm or egg, and gives rise to a new embryo.

the time. Although government has not forbidden embryonic stem cell research, many universities and research centers rely on federal money to operate.

Because of the public debate about embryonic stem cells, many researchers are investigating the use of adult stem cells as another option for treating disease. Adult stem cells are already being used to treat blood disorders such as leukemia. Although adult stem cells can replace damaged or malfunctioning cells, their ability to differentiate is much more limited than that of embryonic stem cells. Therefore, the stem cells present in human bone marrow could probably never be used to create nerve cells for people with spinal cord injuries, for instance.

■ ■ ■

For More Information

Dolan DNA Learning Center. ''How Embryonic Stem Cell Lines are Made.'' <http://www.dnalc.org/stemcells.html> (accessed May 4, 2006).

Holland, Suzanne, Karen Lebacqz, and Laurie Zoloth, editors. *The Human Embryonic Stem Cell Debate: Science, Ethics, and Public Policy*. Cambridge, MA: The MIT Press, 2001.

National Institutes of Health. ''Stem Cell Information: Frequently Asked Questions.'' Last updated October 5, 2005. <http://stemcells.nih.gov/info/faqs.asp> (accessed May 4, 2006).

NPR. "Q&A: Embryonic Stem Cells: Exploding the Myths." May 3, 2006. <http://www.npr.org/templates/story/story.php?storyId=5376892> (accessed May 3, 2006).

University of Michigan. "U.S. Falling Behind in Embryonic Stem Cell Research, Study Says." April 6, 2006. <http://www.umich.edu/news/index.html?Releases/2006/Apr06/r040606b> (accessed May 4, 2006).

[*See Also* **Vol. 1, Bioethics; Vol. 1, Gene Therapy; Vol. 3, Government Regulations; Vol. 1, Stem Cell Lines; Vol. 1, Stem Cells, Adult; Vol. 1, Therapeutic Cloning.**]

Synthetic Biology

Description

Synthetic biology is the activity of designing and making new biological parts, products, and systems that do not occur in nature. It also involves redoing existing biological systems for new purposes. Based in biology, chemistry, and engineering, synthetic biology involves making artificial biological systems rather than natural ones. Thus, synthetic biologists, or synthetic biology engineers, are researching the possibility of developing living machines (what are called bioengineered microorganisms) from chemical ingredients. Bioengineered microorganisms are tiny living things that have been changed artificially so they can be used in a particular way. They could help solve many of the world's problems in agriculture, human health and medicine, manufacturing, renewable energy and energy production, and the environment.

For example, with respect to human health, according to the National Center for Infectious Diseases, between 700,000 and 2.7 million people die from malaria each year around the world. The drug artemisinin, which comes from a plant, treats malaria but is too expensive for use in poor countries where most of the cases occur. However, synthetic biologists artificially made a medicine that works like artemisinin but is much less costly.

With respect to renewable energy, synthetic biologists are working to develop artificial systems to turn waste into energy and to turn sunlight into hydrogen. For example, cellulose, a major part of plants, could be a source of renewal energy if synthetic biologists find a way to use bioengineered microorganisms to take out energy stored in cellulose.

The environment may benefit from synthetic biology if synthetic biologists can develop bioengineered microorganisms to break down and decontaminate pollutants that are threats to humans. For example, synthetically made cells could be made to swim to a hazardous waste spill and decontaminate it.

Scientific Foundations

Synthetic biologists are involved with biological molecules in the twenty-first century like electronic engineers were involved with electrons (particles smaller than an atom that have a negative electric charge) in the twentieth century, and like mechanical engineers were involved with machine components in the nineteenth century. Electronic engineers made standardized electronic devices such as capacitors, resistors, and transistors that were used to make products in the electronics industry. Now, synthetic biology engineers are developing standardized biological devices for products in the biotechnology industry. These biological devices are compared to LEGO® toys because they can be put together in different ways.

By making standardized biological parts with different characteristics, bioengineers can build inexpensive devices and materials to process information, produce energy, change chemicals, make materials, provide food, and deal with human health and the environment. A type of engineered enzyme is now being used in laundry detergents. Recently, an Israeli computer scientist built a computer from biological molecules that was able to perform simple mathematical calculations.

Development

During the last half of the twentieth century, the advancement of synthetic biology has been helped by the discovery of the structure of deoxyribonucleic acid (DNA, an organism's genetic material), the mapping of the human genome (an organism's complete genetic content), and other developments in genetics. In 1978, Swiss biologist Werner Arber (1929–), American molecular biologist Daniel Nathans (1928–1999), and American biologist Hamilton O. Smith (1931–) received the Nobel Prize in Physiology or Medicine for their work with restriction enzymes in genetics research. Restriction enzymes are proteins that break apart DNA. The term synthetic biology was used for the first time to describe Arber, Nathans, and Smith's work.

Based on their work, other researchers in the last two decades of the twentieth century were able to modify the DNA molecule, along with analyzing individual genes. For example, biotechnology companies now use restriction enzymes to make synthetic medicines such as human insulin for diabetes patients.

The World's First Synthetic Biology Department Established

On July 2003, the world's first synthetic biology department was established within the Physical Biosciences Division at Lawrence Berkeley National Laboratory, which is part of the U.S. Department of Energy and is managed by The University of California. A research facility, named the Berkeley West Biocenter, has been established that involves the areas of synthetic biology, cell and molecular bio-logy, cancer research, and quantitative biology.

The Biocenter scientists involved with synthetic biology work inside the Berkeley Center for Synthetic Biology. They try to understand and design biological systems and their components. In turn, the scientists develop techniques to help solve many problems that so far cannot be solved using naturally occurring means.

The first international conference on synthetic biology was held at the Massachusetts Institute of Technology in June 2004. The second conference was held in May 2006 at the University of California at Berkeley. Most of the work on synthetic biology occurs in the United States. However, several research groups work in Japan, Europe, and Israel. Leading U.S. companies involved with synthetic biology include Amyris Biotechnologies (Emeryville, California), Codon Devices (Cambridge, Massachusetts), and Synthetic Genomics (Rockville, Maryland).

Current Issues

Synthetic biology is a promising field that should create new products in such fields as agriculture, industry, medicine, and energy. As with many new technologies, risks sometimes occur in society. For instance, unintentional dangers can occur to human health. Other times, intentional weapons are made to hurt people. Some people worry about the safety and security of products made with synthetic biology. They fear that unnatural organisms could cause environmental problems or that synthetic biology products could be misused by terrorist groups.

Special safeguards are being put into place to make sure that dangerous bioengineered products are used for the right purpose. Hypothetically, terrorists could use standardized biological materials to recreate the smallpox virus or other deadly diseases. Even though medicines can be made through synthetic biology to cure

Words to Know

Bioengineered: The process of using engineering to solve medical problems.

Chromosome: A thread-shaped structure that carries genetic information in cells.

Deoxyribonucleic acid (DNA): DNA—The double-helix shaped molecule that serves as the carrier of genetic information for humans and most organisms.

Enzyme: A protein that helps control the rate or speed of chemical reactions in the cell.

Gene: A discrete unit of inheritance, represented by a portion of DNA located on a chromosome. The gene is a code for the production of a specific kind of protein or RNA molecule, and therefore for a specific inherited characteristic.

Microorganism: An organism too small to be seen without a microscope, such as a virus or bacterium.

malaria, they can also be made into biological weapons that could kill large numbers of people.

Because the field of synthetic biology is in its early stage of development, issues concerning social, ethical, and legal problems are mostly being discussed by scientists and researchers. Environmental and ethics groups are beginning to raise their concerns with synthetic biological products as well.

■ ■ ■

For More Information

Andrianantoandro, Ernesto, Subhayu Basu, David K. Karig, and Ron Weiss. "Synthetic Biology: New Engineering Rules for an Emerging Discipline." *Nature.com.* <http://www.nature.com/msb/journal/v2/n1/full/msb4100073.html>

Brent, Robert. *Nature Biotechnology.* "A Partnership between Biology and Engineering." Volume 22 (October 2004): 1211. This article can also be found online at <http://www.molsci.org/files/Nature_v22_p1211–1214.pdf> (accessed July 21, 2006).

Luisi, Pier. *The Emergence of Life: From Chemical Origins to Synthetic Biology.* London, UK: Cambridge University Press, 2006.

The Nobel Foundation. "The Nobel Prize in Physiology or Medicine, 1978: 'for the discovery of restriction enzymes and their application to problems of molecular genetics.'" *NobelPrize.org.* <http://nobelprize.org/nobel_prizes/medicine/laureates/1978/> (accessed July 21, 2006).

"Synthetic Biology." *Berkeley West Biocenter, Berkeley Lab and University of California, Berkeley.* <http://www.lbl.gov/pbd/synthbio/potter.htm> (accessed July 24, 2006).

Tucker, Jonathan B., and Raymond A. Zilinskas. ''The Promise and Perils of Synthetic Biology.'' *The New Atlantis*. <http://www.thenewatlantis. com/archive/12/tuckerzilinskasreferenced.htm> (accessed July 21, 2006).

[*See Also* **Vol. 3, Biological Weapons; Vol. 3, Biorubber; Vol. 1, DNA Sequencing; Vol. 2, Genetic Engineering; Vol. 2, Genetically Modified Organisms.**]

■ ■ ■

Therapeutic Cloning

Description

Therapeutic cloning is the creation of an embryo (a human being in the earliest stages of development) by scientists in a lab in order to pull stem cells from it. Embryonic stem cells can grow into every type of cell and tissue in the body, such as heart cells, blood cells, or muscle cells. They may be used to treat diseases such as Parkinson's (a disease of the central nervous system that causes a person to shake and their muscles to become rigid) and Alzheimer's (a condition that affects the brain and interferes with thinking and memory), or to repair a spinal cord damaged by injury, among other uses. Eventually, embryonic stem cells may be able to grow into entire organs.

Therapeutic cloning is not the same as human cloning. With therapeutic cloning, an embryo is created only for the purpose of using its stem cells. With human cloning, an entire human being is created. Therapeutic cloning destroys the embryo before it can be implanted in a woman's uterus and have the chance to grow.

Scientific Foundations

During human reproduction, a sperm from the man fertilizes an egg from the woman. The fertilized egg begins to divide to form an embryo. Half of the genetic material in the embryo is from the mother; the other half is from the father. The cells in the inner part of the embryo are called pluripotent—they have the ability to become any type of cell or tissue in the body.

Scientists can also make an embryo in a lab using an egg that has had its nucleus (the part of the egg that contains deoxyribonucleic acid [DNA]) removed and an adult cell from anywhere in the

The Race to Clone

In November 2001, scientists at the company Advanced Cell Technology (ACT) in Massachusetts announced that they had created the first cloned human embryo. Although they technically created an early embryo, they were only able to get one of the eight eggs involved in their research to divide to six cells. In 2004, a team of scientists in South Korea led by professor Hwang Woo-Suk announced that they had cloned more than thirty human embryos, but the team was later accused of faking part of their research.

In 2005, researchers in Britain were able to clone an embryo from a human cell. Despite ethical concerns by some groups, research centers around the world continue to press forward with therapeutic cloning studies.

body. They insert the DNA from the adult cell into the egg, then stimulate the egg and cell to divide and form an embryo. The genetic material in a cloned embryo primarily comes from the adult cell used to create it.

Development

In 1953, American scientist James Watson (1928–) and British scientist Francis Crick (1916–2004) announced that they had discovered the structure of DNA in cells. Their discovery paved the way for all future research in human genetics. A series of advances in the technology of genetics eventually let scientists to clone the first human embryos for therapeutic research in 2001.

Therapeutic cloning is done by removing the nucleus, the "brain" of the cell which contains the genetic information (DNA), from an unfertilized egg. The nucleus is added to the DNA from a somatic cell taken from an adult (usually the patient who needs the treatment). A somatic cell is any cell in the body (for example, a blood cell or a liver cell) with the exception of a reproductive cell (sperm and egg). The egg is stimulated with a small electric shock or special chemicals to make it start to divide.

After a few days, the egg forms a ball of about one hundred cells. This ball of cells is a very young embryo called a blastocyst. The inner part of the blastocyst contains the stem cells. Scientists remove the stem cells from the embryo and grow them in a dish. The idea is to coax the embryonic stem cells to become a specific type of cell (for example, heart cells). Those cells would then be implanted in the patient to repair damage caused by disease or injury.

Words to Know

Blastocyst: A cluster of cells resulting from successful fertilization of an ovum (egg) by a sperm. This is the developmental form that must implant itself in the uterus to achieve pregnancy.

Embryo: A stage in development after fertilization.

Ethics: The study of what is right or wrong.

Nucleus: A compartment in the cell which is enclosed by a membrane and which contains its genetic information.

Pluripotent: Pertaining to a cell that has the capacity to develop into any of the various tissues and organs of the body.

Current Issues

Although embryonic stem cells hold great promise for treating diseases, scientists are still learning how to coax them to become the types of cells they want. For example, in the case of spinal cord injury, scientists first need to get embryonic stem cells to become nerve cells. Then, they have to implant those cells in the spinal cord and get them to act like real nerve cells.

Another issue deals with the ethics (the study of what is right or wrong) of creating human embryos for the purposes of scientific research. Some people are against therapeutic cloning. They say that an embryo is a life, and that destroying it is killing a human being. In 2001, United States President George W. Bush limited federal funding of therapeutic cloning research to the embryonic stem cell lines that were already in existence at the time. The United States subsequently proposed a ban on all therapeutic cloning, but it failed to pass through Congress.

There is also concern among some groups that the practice of therapeutic cloning could lead to the cloning of people. However, embryos cloned for therapeutic purposes are destroyed when their stem cells are removed.

Another less controversial therapy uses adult stem cells to repair diseased cells and tissue. Although adult stem cells do not have the potential to become as many different types of cells as embryonic stem cells can become, researchers are trying to manipulate adult stem cells in a way that will increase their potential for medical treatments.

For More Information

Cibelli, Jose B., Robert P. Lanza, and Michael D. West. "Therapeutic Cloning: How It's Done." *Scientific American*. November 24, 2001. <http://www.sciam.com/article.cfm?articleID=00016CF7-CE54-1CF4-93F6809EC5880000> (accessed May 5, 2006).

"Cloning for Treatments." *CNN.com*. <http://www.cnn.com/interactive/health/0202/cloning2/frameset.exclude.html> (accessed May 6, 2006).

"Federal Policies on Cloning." *Center for Genetics and Society*. October 4, 2004. <http://www.genetics-and-society.org/policies/us/cloning.html> (accessed May 7, 2006).

"Human Embryo Created Through Cloning." *CNN.com*. November 26, 2001. <http://archives.cnn.com/2001/TECH/science/11/25/human.embryo.clone/> (accessed May 6, 2006).

Kolata, Gina. "The Promise of Therapeutic Cloning." *The New York Times*. January 5, 2003. <http://query.nytimes.com/gst/fullpage.html?sec=health&res=9805E7D61F3FF936A35752C0A9659C8B63> (accessed May 6, 2006).

[*See Also* **Vol. 1, Bioethics; Vol. 1, Somatic Cell Therapy; Vol. 1, Human Cloning; Vol. 1, Nuclear Transfer; Vol. 1, Stem Cells, Embryonic.**]

■ ■ ■

Tissue Banks

Description

Tissue banks are facilities that collect, process, identify, store, and distribute tissues used for tissue transplantations into human beings. Tissues are groups of cells within the human body, such as arteries, blood, bones, bone marrow, cartilage, corneas, heart valves and muscles, skin, sperm, tendons, and veins. There are four main groups of tissues: connective tissue (cells holding together parts of the body), epithelium tissue (layers of cells protecting internal organs and external surfaces), muscle tissue (cells containing pieces that stretch and bend), and nerve tissue (cells surrounding the brain, spinal cord, and nervous system).

Some tissue banks specialize in certain tissues. When this specialization occurs, they are called by such names as blood banks, sperm banks, and skin banks, to name a few.

The most common tissue collected at tissue banks is blood. This blood is used in blood transfusions, often for patients undergoing surgeries. Other tissues commonly transplanted include blood vessels, bones, bone marrow, cartilage, corneas (skin covering the eyeball), skin, and tendons (tissue that connects a muscle and a bone).

There are many different types of problems that require surgeries involving tissue replacement. Consequently, many tissue banks exist throughout the world. A variety of procedures may require the transplantation of tissues include orthopedic surgeries to repair torn tendons of the knee, ophthalmologic surgeries to treat diseased corneas in the eye, and cardiovascular surgeries to correct malfunctioning heart valves.

Scientific Foundations

The popularity of tissue transplantation created the need for tissue banks. Tissue transplantation is the process of taking tissue from the

Worker in a brain bank at Harvard Brain Tissue Research Center in Belmont, Massachusetts. This tissue bank holds 5,000 brains. © *Reuters/Corbis.*

body of a donor and placing it into the body of a recipient. Two types of transplantation are possible: allograft and autograft. Allograft tissue is donated by one person so that it can be stored and preserved for transplantation into another person.

Autograft tissue is tissue taken from a person who needs a tissue transplantation and, then, stored and preserved so that it can be later placed into another part of that same person's body. Skin is commonly transplanted in this way. An autograft transplant is usually a safer and faster way to transplant tissue. Allograft tissue takes longer to transplant into the body, but, only one site (the transplant site) needs to heal since the tissue comes from another human. Since tissue transplants of both types are not subject to rejection by the immune system like organ transplants, immunosuppression (anti-rejection) drugs are not needed during and after the surgery.

Development

In the first quarter of the twentieth century, medical researchers developed surgical techniques to perform tissue transplants of bones,

American Association of Tissue Banks

The American Association of Tissue Banks (AATB, http://www.aatb.org/) is a non-profit scientific organization founded in 1976 to provide high quality tissues to hospitals and surgeons for transplant into patients. Beginning in 1986, the AATB began offering an Inspection and Accreditation Program for qualifying tissue banks. The AATB also offers individuals within the tissue bank field an examination called the Certification of Tissue Bank Personnel. The examination tests a person's knowledge of such important topics as donor and tissue suitability, retrieval of tissues, tissue processing, techniques of decontamination, quality control, labeling, recordkeeping, product testing, and various clinical applications and procedures.

corneas, and tendons. The U.S. Navy Tissue Bank, established in 1949, provided the first bone and tissue processing and storage facility in the United States. It was essentially the first U.S. tissue bank. French immunologist Jean-Baptiste-Gabriel-Joachim Dausset (1916–) introduced matching of blood types between tissue donors and recipients (what is now generally called tissue matching for all types of tissues) in 1958.

Between the late 1970s and the early 1980s, tissue banks were first organized to meet the need to gather, store, and distribute tissues to hospitals. By 1986, many nonprofit bone banks were in operation in the United States. In 1993, the U.S. Food and Drug Administration (FDA) began to regulate some aspects of U.S. tissue banks. Additional regulations were implemented in 1997, including the registration of all tissue processors. Further regulations came in during the first decade of the twenty-first century.

Current Issues

Tissue banks process tissues that are needed for hundreds of thousands of people in the United States each year. According to the FDA, about one million tissue transplants were performed in the United States in 2004, nearly three times as many as in 1990. However, many questions are raised concerning the use of human tissues in transplantations as more are used in biotechnology applications, medical treatments, and scientific research. Laws regarding the use of human tissues have not kept pace with scientific developments, and this has added to the debates. Some of the major issues regarding the use of human tissues include: the ethical versus the unethical uses of tissues; legal aspects of using tissues; safeguards for tissue donors and recipients; commercial uses of tissues; and safety of tissues for medical purposes.

Words to Know

Allograft: Transplanted tissues or organs from donors of the same species.

Autograft: A type of skin graft that uses tissue from another part of the patient's own body, and therefore has cells with the same genes.

Epithelium: The layer of cells that covers external and internal surfaces of the body. The many types of epithelium range from flat cells to long cells to cubed cells.

Hepatitis: General inflammation of the liver; may be caused by viral infection or by excessive alcohol consumption.

Human immunodeficiency virus (HIV): The virus that causes AIDS (acquired human immunodeficiency syndrome); HIV stands for human immunodeficiency virus.

Immunosuppression: The act of reducing the efficiency of the immune system.

Parkinson's disease: Disease of the nerves that causes the patient to gradually lose control of their muscles. Loss of a chemical in the brain called dopamine causes shaking and muscle stiffness.

Tissue: Groups of cells with a similar function.

Transplantation: Moving cells or tissues from their point of origin in one organism to a secondary site in the same or a different organism.

Many problems have occurred as tissues are processed from donors to recipients through tissue banks. Diseases and infections have occurred when tissues are not handled properly. In addition, the tissue bank industry was mostly unregulated from its beginnings in the 1970s to the late 1990s. Consequently, in 2004, the FDA issued additional and stricter safety standards for tissue banks to prevent disease and infection from being passed in tissue transplants. In addition, the FDA requires all tissue banks to be registered and regularly inspected. Currently, all tissue banks are screened for tissues that may contain dangerous diseases such as hepatitis B and hepatitis C (liver diseases) and human immunodeficiency virus (HIV, the virus that causes AIDS).

In recent years, issues regarding fetal tissue banks and the use of fetal tissues have been raised in the United States and around the world. Fetal tissue is tissue that is taken from a human fetus (an unborn child from three months of pregnancy to birth). Critics of the use of fetal tissues question the ethics of using tissues from aborted human fetuses for any type of research. Proponents state that suffering from diseases, such as Parkinson's disease, could be ended, or at least reduced, by further research involving fetal tissues.

For More Information

American Association of Tissue Banks (AATB). <http://www.aatb.org/> (accessed July 5, 2006).

New York Organ Donor Network. "Tissue Transplantation Facts." <http://www.nyodn.org/transplant/tissue.html> (accessed July 5, 2006).

Phillips, Glyn O., et al. *Advances in Tissue Banking.* Hackensack, NJ: World Scientific Publishing, 1997.

United Network of Organ Sharing (UNOS). <http://www.unos.org/> (accessed July 5, 2006).

U.S. Senate. Committee on Governmental Affairs. Permanent Subcommittee on Investigations. *Tissue Banks.* Washington, D.C., U.S. Government Printing Office, 2001.

[*See Also* **Vol. 1, Anti-Rejection Drugs; Vol. 1, Bone Marrow Transplant; Vol. 1, Organ Transplants.**]

■■■

Tissue Engineering

Description

Tissue engineering is the collection of procedures used to make biological replacement tissues and organs such as blood vessels, blood, bones, cartilage, muscles, skin, stem cells, and bladders from synthetic or natural materials. It involves the fields of clinical medicine, bioengineering, and materials science and engineering. Tissue engineering uses natural cells and engineered materials to replace damaged or defective tissues and organs.

The need for transplant tissues and organs is growing in the United States and in industrial countries around the world. However, the supply of human and animal tissues has not met the demand for transplants. Lately, artificially grown tissues are helping to supply needed tissues for transplants. For example, the U.S. Food and Drug Administration (FDA) approved tissue engineered skin for burn victims and patients with serious skin sores or ulcers. It is likely that cartilage and bone will soon be grown to reduce arthritis pain; and that blood vessels, cardiac valves, and muscle tissues will be made to minimize cardiovascular disease.

In the future, custom-made bone marrow, corneas, hearts, kidneys, and livers will help minimize illnesses. The major U.S. research institutions pursuing tissue engineering include Columbia University, Massachusetts Institute of Technology, University of Pennsylvania, the University of Michigan, the University of Minnesota, Rice University, Stanford University, and the University of California at Berkeley. It was reported in 2001 that biotechnology companies that develop tissue-engineered products have a market worth of nearly $4 billion, and that they are spending, on average, 22.5 percent more every year.

Scientific Foundations

Cells are the main substance used for tissue engineering. Living cells used for research consist of several groups that are categorized by their source. Autologous cells are those taken from a donor who is also the recipient of the implanted tissues (in other words, using one's own tissue cells), while allogenic cells come from a donor who is different from the recipient, such as a brother and a sister. Xenogenic cells are provided from a donor who is of another species than the recipient. For example, tissue cells from a pig may be grown and implanted into a human. Isogenic cells come from identical organisms such as twins. Stem cells are identical cells with the ability to divide in a laboratory culture and grow into different types of specialized cells.

Generally, cells used for tissue engineering are grown on three-dimensional structures that are specially designed so the cells develop into functioning tissues. Once grown, the tissues are transplanted into the patient. Given enough time, the tissues are absorbed into the neighboring tissues and eventually look just like the original tissues.

Alloderm®, an artificial tissue made from human skin, being used in surgery to repair the stomach of a man severely injured in motorcycle crash. © Sapone, Patti/Star Ledger/Corbis.

First Human Receives Tissue-Engineered Organ

American physician Anthony Atala, director of the Institute for Regenerative Medicine at Wake Forest University School of Medicine, reported in March 2006 that for the first time a human received an organ artificially grown in the laboratory. Several bladders had been grown from the cells of young patients between the ages of four and nineteen years who had poor bladder function from birth. These bladders replaced the damaged bladders in these patients. Atala reported that he had been working since 1990 to build bladders from the patient's own cells. In the future, Atala will be working on developing twenty different types of tissues and organs grown artificially in the laboratory.

Development

American bioengineer Yuan-Cheng Fung, of the University of California at San Diego (UCSD), originated the term and idea of tissue engineering in 1985. At that time, Fung led the UCSD team in their National Science Foundation (NSF) research proposal titled, "Center for the Engineering of Living Tissues." Fung proposed the term again in 1987 at a NSF panel meeting, which led to a special NSF panel meeting on tissue engineering later that year. The first formal meeting involving tissue engineering met in 1988.

Between 1988 and 1993, the concept spread throughout the scientific community. In 1993, American physicians Robert Langer (1948–) and Joseph Vacanti published a tissue engineering paper in the journal *Science* that described their new process for growing human tissues. They defined tissue engineering as "an interdisciplinary field that applies the principles of engineering and life sciences toward the development of biological substitutes that restore, maintain, or improve tissue function." This definition formed the foundation for later work within tissue engineering.

Current Issues

Several problems have slowed the development of tissue engineering. First, the implanted cells are not always provided enough oxygen and nutrients to make them function properly. Secondly, once tissues have been successfully made, there is concern about how they are stored. Personal data is collected in order to identify the stored tissues. Thus, the privacy of donors can be at risk if such information is used for purposes other than medical.

Since human embryos are sometimes used in tissue engineering, critics say that tissue engineering is unethical. Those in favor of

Words to Know

Cartilage: A connective tissue found in the knees, tip of the nose, and outside of the ears; it provides flexibility and resilience to these structures.

Embryo: A stage in development after fertilization.

Nutrient: A substance that provides nourishment.

using human embryos state the numerous medical benefits produced from their use. Animal experiments are also performed in research involving tissue engineering. Similar ethical problems have been raised about using test animals.

There are many current and future uses for tissue engineering. Some of these uses include replacement or repair of defective or damaged bones, connective tissue, muscles, corneas, and blood vessels; replacement of skin due to serious burns; and restoration of cells involved in chemical activities within the body such as hormones. So far, cartilage, bone, and skin have been made in the laboratory. The making of blood vessels, blood, and organs such as the heart, lung, pancreas, and liver are expected to occur in the near future.

Before many of these uses can be accomplished, several technologies must first be completely developed. Two of these technologies involve the improved growth of cells without impurities and long-term storage of tissues that can be accessed around the world.

Tissue engineering can help reduce medical costs because fewer and less expensive treatments for major medical problems are needed. Since the use of transplant operations can be reduced, fewer complications, drugs, and recovery times are possible. In addition, improvements in the quality of life for patients should result. According to the Advanced Technology Program (ATP) of the National Institute of Standards and Technology, tissue-engineered medical solutions could drastically decrease the country's total healthcare costs.

■ ■ ■

For More Information

Arnst, Catherine. "The Dynamic Duo of Tissue Engineering." *Business-Week*. July 27, 1998. http://www.businessweek.com/1998/30/b3588008.htm (accessed July 24, 2006).

"The Body Shop." *Public Broadcasting Service*. http://www.pbs.org/saf/1107/features/body.htm (accessed July 24, 2006).

Lanza, Robert, Robert Langer, and Joseph P. Vacanti, eds. *Principles of Tissue Engineering*. San Diego, CA: Academic Press, 2000.

Sipe, Jean D., Christine A. Kelley, and Lore Anne McNichol, eds. *Reparative Medicine: Growing Tissues and Organs*. New York: New York Academy of Sciences, 2002.

Viola, Jessica, Bhavya Lal, and Oren Grad. "The Emergence of Tissue Engineering as a Research Field." *National Science Foundation*. http://www.nsf.gov/pubs/2004/nsf0450/exec_summ.htm (accessed July 24, 2006).

"Wake Forest Physician Reports First Human Recipients of Laboratory-Grown Organs." *Wake Forest University Baptist Medical Center*. April 3, 2006. http://www1.wfubmc.edu/news/NewsArticle.htm?Articleid=1821 (accessed July 24, 2006).

[*See Also* **Vol. 1, Bone Substitutes; Vol. 1, Organ Transplants; Vol. 1, Skin Substitutes.**]

Vaccines

Description

Vaccines are substances that trigger the body's defenses against a germ so that it can defend itself against the germ. Once a person has received the vaccine for a particular kind of germ, that person is immune to (will not become sick from) that kind of germ. For some diseases the immunity lasts for a few years, and for others it lasts a lifetime. Giving a vaccine (usually by injecting it directly into the blood or muscle with a needle) is called vaccination. Since vaccination makes a person immune to a disease, it is also called immunization.

Vaccines teach the body's active immune system how to defend the body against a specific germ. The active immune system is a network of cells throughout the body, mostly in the blood, that attacks cells and other bits of material that do not belong in the body.

Vaccines have been developed for over twenty diseases caused by viruses and bacteria, including smallpox, flu, hepatitis B, meningitis, rabies, rubella, polio, and whooping cough. For example, scientists say that as many as 500 million people were killed by smallpox during the twentieth century. But starting in 1967, a worldwide campaign to vaccinate smallpox succeeded in completely wiping out the disease in only about ten years. Today, the only smallpox virus known to remain on Earth is in storage in heavily-guarded laboratories in the United States and Russia.

Scientific Foundations

The blood contains cells called lymphocytes. These blood cells can go through stages, and there are always lymphocytes in the blood that are in all three stages: some are called naive cells, some are active cells, and some are memory cells. Naive (pronounced neye-EEV)

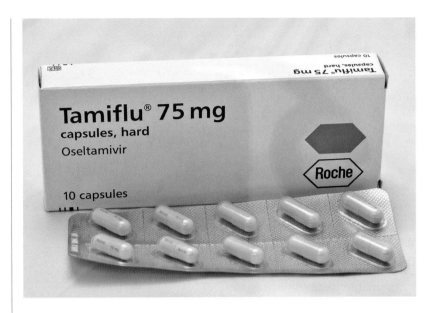

When influenza vaccines are not available, anti-viral drugs such as Tamiflu® usually shorten the course of the disease. *SPL/Photo Researchers, Inc.*

means inexperienced. Naive cells are inexperienced because they have not yet met a pathogen. When they do, they know it is a pathogen because it has certain chemicals on its surface that label or tag it as not belonging in the body. These chemicals are called antigens. When a naive lymphocyte finds an antigen, it becomes active. Active lymphocytes swallow up and remove pathogens.

When the infection is gone, most of these active lymphocytes die. However, some remain in the blood permanently. These are called memory cells. If they ever again meet the antigen that they first met when they were naive cells, they become active cells again, attacking the pathogen. They also divide quickly, making more active cells to attack that pathogen. This way, the body can attack an infection as soon as it appears.

Most vaccines work by putting antigens in the body, sometimes as part of dead or weakened pathogens. The antigens do not make us sick, but they do turn some naive lymphocytes into active cells and then memory cells. When living pathogens tagged with those antigens enter the body—smallpox or polio viruses, for example— the body attacks them at once with active lymphocytes.

This is a simplified account. The actual working of the immune system is more complicated.

Development

For centuries, people have noticed persons who had suffered the disease cowpox are immune to the disease smallpox. Although the

A Vaccine for Alzheimer's?

Alzheimer's disease is a condition where the nerve cells of the brains of elderly people slowly stop working, leading to memory loss, madness, and death. Some scientists think that Alzheimer's is caused by the buildup in the brain of chemicals called amyloid-beta peptides. They are trying to make a vaccine using a kind of vaccine called a DNA vaccine. In this kind of vaccination, DNA is put into body cells. This DNA acts like a recipe for an antibody, which is a substance that helps the body's immune system recognize germs. The antibody made by cells that have received the DNA vaccine are for amyloid-beta peptides. That is, these antibodies cause the body's lymphocytes to attack amyloid-beta peptides and destroy them. Researchers have had good success in mice with DNA vaccine, but are quick to point out that human beings are not simply large mice. What works in mice often does not work in people. It will be years before we can know whether an Alzheimer's vaccine for humans is possible. If it is, it will save millions of people from the suffering of Alzheimer's.

fact that infectious disease is caused by germs was not known, people experimented with vaccinating each other using fluids from people or cows infected with cowpox. (The viruses are close enough so that one can be used as a vaccine for the other, but cowpox is not deadly, unlike smallpox.) In 1796, an English doctor named Edward Jenner (1749–1823) tried the experiment for himself, using a farm boy as an experimental subject, and found that it worked. Vaccination for smallpox became commonplace. Vaccination for rabies was introduced in 1885, and for many other diseases in the years since. Today, research to find vaccines for HIV (human immunodeficiency virus, the virus that causes AIDS) and for other diseases is under way.

Current Issues

For centuries, some persons have opposed vaccination because they thought it would damage their health or their children's health or for religious reasons. Many people continue to oppose various kinds of vaccination. Scientists agree that some people have been killed or injured by vaccination, but most also agree that many more lives more have been saved through vaccination than have been harmed by it.

Words to Know

Alzheimer's disease: A degenerative disease of the central nervous system that generally afflicts elderly people and that can lead to memory loss and death.

Antibody: A molecule created by the immune system in response to the presence of an antigen (a foreign substance or particle). It marks foreign microorganisms in the body for destruction by other immune cells.

Immune system: A system in the human body that fights off foreign substances, cells, and tissues in an effort to protect a person from disease.

Lymphocyte: A cell that functions as part of the lymphatic and immune systems by attacking specific invading substances.

For More Information

Bloom, Barry R. and Paul-Henri Lambert. *The Vaccine Book*. Boston: Academic Press, 2003.

National Institute of Allergy and Infectious Diseases. "Understanding Vaccines: What They Are and How They Work." July, 2003. <http://www.niaid.nih.gov/publications/vaccine/pdf/undvacc.pdf> (accessed September 2, 2006).

U.S. National Institutes of Health. "MedLine Plus: Immunization." August 31, 2006. <http://www.nlm.nih.gov/medlineplus/immunization.html> (accessed September 2, 2006).

World Health Organization (United Nations). "History of Immunization." <http://www.childrensvaccine.org/files/WHO-Vaccine-History.pdf> (accessed September 2, 2006).

[See Also **Vol. 1, DNA Vaccines; Vol. 1, HIV/AIDS Drugs.**]

Xenotransplantation

Description

Xenotransplantation refers to the transplanting of material including cells, tissues, or entire organs from a non-human species, such as a pig, chimpanzee, or baboon, to humans. The intent of xenotransplantation is to provide medical treatment to patients with urgent health problems, such as the deterioration of heart valves (which regulate the flow of blood through the heart) or kidney failure (in which the kidneys can no longer filter blood well enough to keep the person alive).

While transplantation of tissues or organs from another human is preferred, a suitable donor may not be available when a particular organ or tissue is urgently needed. Shortage of human organs is a problem for people in need of a transplant. More than half of those who require a life-saving organ transplant die before a suitable human organ can be found. Xenotransplantation can overcome this limitation. However, a number of practical and ethical considerations cloud the development of the technique.

Scientific Foundations

The use of non-human transplanted material began in the 1960s. In 1963–64, thirteen chimpanzee kidneys were transplanted into thirteen humans. Twelve people died within two months of their operation. However, one person lived nine months before dying, indicating that the use of animal organs had some potential for medical use. In 1964, a chimpanzee's heart was used to replace the failing heart of a person. Within two hours, the transplant was rejected by the body's immune system. Subsequent heart xenotransplants have also failed.

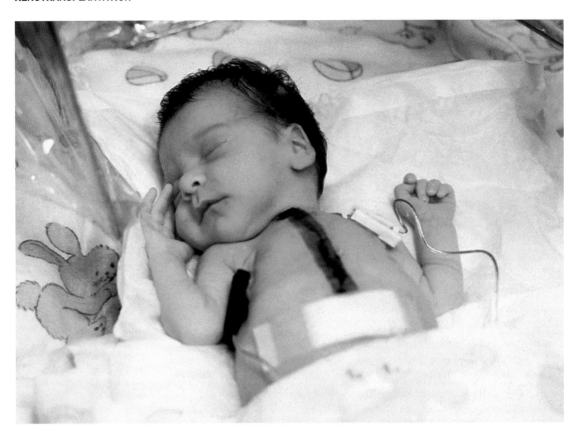

Baby Fae, the first infant to receive a baboon heart, in 1984. The newborn died less than a month after the transplant. © Bettmann/ Corbis.

The efficiency of the human immune system is the underlying reason for the poor track record of xenotransplantation, and immune rejection remains the biggest practical hurdle to successful xenotransplantation. The surface of tissues varies among different species and even between members of the same species. Normally, this is good, because it helps the body to fight diseases brought in by foreign matter, such as bacteria. However, the immune system can also recognize differences in transplanted material and mount an attack on it. Without the use of drugs that suppress the immune system, the transplanted cells will be destroyed and the transplant rejected.

Patients who have had a tissue transplant have a life-long dependence on immunosuppressive drugs to keep the body from rejected the transplant. The use of these drugs carries a risk, since a weakened immune system makes an individual more susceptible to infections that would otherwise be efficiently eliminated. This

A Xenotransplantation Ethical Dilemma

Over 60 million pigs are slaughtered each year to provide pork for the American diet. This creates a huge reservoir of potential donor tissues and organs. But, the considerable differences between pig and human tissue increase the possibility of immune rejection. To deal with this, scientists are genetically engineering pigs to make target tissues more closely related to their human counterparts. Pigs may someday contain organs that do not stimulate an immune response when transplanted into humans.

However, this artificially created similarity carries a risk. Disease-causing organisms that can infect the pig tissue may be more easily capable of causing human illness if present in the transplanted tissue. Is the risk of infection to an individual outweighed by the overall improved health that could result for society as a whole?

risk can be even more serious in the case of xenotransplantation, since an animal disease could, potentially, be transmitted to the human recipient. However, when the only other option is death, this risk can be worth taking.

Development

The concept of xenotransplantation is over a century old. Beginning in 1904, French surgeon Alexis Carrel (1873–1944) and his colleagues experimented with the transplanting of veins. Animal-to-human kidney transplants were first attempted by other scientists in 1906. The uniform failure of these early attempts led to the abandonment of xenotransplantation until the 1950s, when immunosuppressive drugs began to be developed.

Then as now, immune rejection is the paramount practical problem facing xenotransplantation. Because of this barrier, xenotransplantation of organs has mainly been used as an emergency measure as an attempt to buy some time while a more suitable tissue or organ can be located and transported to the patient.

Better success has been obtained when tissues or a component of an organ is transplanted. For example, xenotransplantation of animal heart valves has been performed hundreds of thousands of times since the procedure was first tried using pig heart valves in 1975 and cow valves in 1981.

The use of animal models has aided the development of xenotransplantation. For example, the transplantation of mouse or hamster hearts into rats is a good model of a type of immune rejection

Words to Know

Immune rejection: Immune system rejection of a foreign substance.

Xenograft: Tissues and organs used for transplantation that come from different animal species, like pigs or baboons.

Xenotransplantation: Transplantation of tissue or an organ from one species to another, for example from pig to human.

called acute vascular rejection. Furthermore, transplant studies using pigs as the donors and non-human primates as the recipients have demonstrated that suppression of the immune system is not sufficient to sustain the transplant. Production of protective proteins by the transplanted material is also required.

Current Issues

The spread of an animal infection to a human recipient via the donated tissue or organ (xenozoonosis) remains a concern. In the twenty-first century, more sophisticated detection of disease-causing organisms (pathogens) and even viral genetic material that have become part of the hosts' genetic material has reduced the possibility of xenozoonosis. Yet, xenotransplantation remains risky. The possibility remains that cross-species transfer of material could generate a hybrid pathogen capable of causing widespread illness.

The sacrifice of animals to sustain human health is controversial as well, especially to those who champion animal rights. Raising animals solely to be donors is repugnant to some people. In addition, Muslims and Jews do not consume pork for religious reasons, and this prohibition may cause them to refuse tissues or organs taken from pigs. On the whole, however, the use of animals in organ donations has met with relatively little resistance.

Maintenance of the xenotransplanted material is a more significant challenge. Research is underway to develop techniques for preventing immune rejection while at the same time maintaining an efficiently functioning immune system. In addition, pigs have been genetically changed in the laboratory so that their bodies create human tissues. These transgenic pigs may prove to be ideal sources of transplantable tissues and organs.

For More Information

eMedicine. ''Xenotransplantation.'' May 17, 2004. <http://www.emedicine.com/med/topic3715.htm> (accessed July 6, 2006).

McLean, Sheila, and Laura Williamson. *Xenotransplantation: Law and Ethics.* Aldershot, U.K.: Ashgate Publishing, 2005.

Platt, Jeffrey L. *Xenotransplantation: Basic Research and Clinical Applications.* Totowa, NJ: Humana Press, 2002.

Pontifical Academy for Life. ''Prospects for Xenotransplantation: Scientific Aspects and Ethical Considerations.'' <http://www.vatican.va/roman_curia/pontifical_academies/acdlife/documents/rc_pa_acdlife_doc_20010926_xenotrapianti_en.html> (accessed July 6, 2006).

[*See Also* **Vol. 1, Anti-Rejection Drugs; Vol. 1, Organ Transplants.**]

■ ■ ■

Where To Learn More

Books

Blunkett, David. *Who Is Really Who?: The Comprehensive Guide to DNA Paternity Testing*. London, England: John Blake Publishing, 2006.

Braga, Newton C. *Bionics for the Evil Genius*. Hightstown, NJ: McGraw-Hill, 2006.

Brown, Terry. *Gene Cloning and DNA Analysis: An Introduction*. Malden, MA: Blackwell Publishing, 2006.

Chrispeels, Maarten. *Plants, Genes, and Crop Biotechnology*. Boston: Jones and Bartlett, 2003.

Clay, Jason, and the World Wildlife Fund. *World Agriculture and the Environment: A Commodity-By-Commodity Guide to Impacts And Practices*. Washington, DC: Island Press, 2004.

Cooper, Jon, and Tony Cass. *Biosensors*. New York: Oxford University Press, 2004.

Davenport, John. *Aquaculture: The Ecological Issues*. Malden, MA: Blackwell Science, 2003.

Foster, Lynn E. *Nanotechnology: Science, Innovation and Opportunity*. Upper Saddle River, NJ: Prentice Hall PTR, 2006.

Fumento, Michael. *BioEvolution: How Biotechnology Is Changing Our World*. New York: Encounter Books, 2004.

Gonick, Larry and Mark Wheelis. *The Cartoon Guide to Genetics*. New York: Collins, 1991.

Heasman, Michael. *The Functional Foods Revolution: Healthy People, Healthy Profits?* Sterling, VA: Earthscan, 2001.

Horn, Tammy. *Bees in America: How the Honey Bee Shaped a Nation*. Lexington, KY: University Press of Kentucky, 2005.

Lancaster, M. *Green Chemistry: An Introductory Text*. Cambridge, U.K.: Royal Society of Chemistry, 2002.

Morgan, Rose M. *The Genetics Revolution: History, Fears, and Future of a Life-Altering Science*. Westport, CT: Greenwood Press, 2006.

Parekh, Sarad R. *The GMO Handbook: Genetically Modified Animals, Microbes, and Plants in Biotechnology*. Totowa, NJ: Humana Press, 2004.

Ruse, Michael, and David Castle, eds. *Genetically Modified Foods: Debating Biotechnology*. Amherst, NY: Prometheus Books, 2002.

Saha, Badal C. *Fermentation Biotechnology*. Washington, DC: American Chemical Society, 2003.

Sargent, Ted. *The Dance of Molecules: How Nanotechnology Is Changing Our Lives*. New York: Thunder's Mouth Press, 2006.

Stevens, E. S. *Green Plastics: An Introduction to the New Science of Biodegradable Plastics*. Princeton, NJ: Princeton University Press, 2001.

Thompson, Kimberly M., and Debra Fulghum Bruce. *Overkill: How Our Nation's Abuse of Antibiotics and Other Germ Killers Is Hurting Your Health* and What You Can Do About It. Emmaus, PA: Rodale, 2002.

Wade, Nicholas. *Life Script: How the Human Genome Discoveries Will Transform Medicine and Enhance Your Health*. New York: Simon & Schuster, 2001.

Watson, James D., and Andrew Berry. *DNA: The Secret of Life*. New York: Knopf, 2003.

Web sites

Boston University Biodefense. "Frequently Asked Questions About Biodefense." November 2003. <http://www.gene-watch.org/bubiodefense/pages/faq.html> (accessed June 7, 2006).

CDC (Centers for Disease Control and Prevention). "CDCSite Index A-Z." <http://www.cdc.gov/az.do> (accessed October 8, 2006).

"Creating a Cloned Sheep Named Dolly." *National Institutes of Health*. <http://science-education.nih.gov/nihHTML/ose/snapshots/multimedia/ritn/dolly/index.html> (accessed April 23, 2006).

Food and Agriculture Organization of the United Nations. "Cheese Making." <http://www.fao.org/ag/aga/publication/mpguide/mpguide5.htm> (accessed August 4, 2006).

Food and Drug Administration. <http://www.fda.gov> (accessed October 8, 2006).

"Human Genome Project Information." *U.S. Department of Energy*. <http://www.ornl.gov/sci/techresources/Human_Genome/home.shtml> (accessed April 21, 2006).

Human Genome Project Information. "Pharmacogenomics." <http://web.ornl.gov/sci/techresources/Human_Genome/medicine/pharma.shtml> (accessed May 2, 2006).

Lawrence Berkeley National Laboratory. "Risk-Related Research at Lawrence Berkeley National Laboratory." <http://www.lbl.gov/LBL-Programs/Risk-Research.html> (accessed October 8, 2006).

Library of Congress. "Library of Congress Online Catalog." <http://catalog.loc.gov/cgi-bin/Pwebrecon.cgi?DB=local&PAGE=First> (accessed October 8, 2006).

National Academies. "Health & Medicine at the National Academies." <http://www.nationalacademies.org/health/> (accessed October 8, 2006).

National Center for Biotechnology Information. "One Size Does Not Fit All: The Promise of Pharmacogenomics." March 31, 2004. <http://www.ncbi.nlm.nih.gov/About/primer/pharm.html> (accessed May 2, 2006).

National Center for Biotechnology Information. "PubMed." <http://www.ncbi.nlm.nih.gov/entrez/query.fcgi?DB=pubmed> (accessed October 8, 2006).

National Human Genome Research Institute (NHGRI). "National Human Genome Research Institute (NHGRI)." <http://www.nhgri.nih.gov> (accessed October 8, 2006).

National Institute of Diabetes and Digestive and Kidney Diseases (NIDDKD). <http://www.niddk.nih.gov> (accessed October 8, 2006).

National Library of Medicine. "Environmental Health and Toxicology." <http://sis.nlm.nih.gov/enviro.html> (accessed October 8, 2006).

National Library of Medicine. "History of Medicine." <http://www.nlm.nih.gov/hmd/index.html> (accessed October 8, 2006).

NIBIB - National Institute of Biomedical Imaging and Bioengineering. <http://www.nibib1.nih.gov> (accessed October 8, 2006).

"Nobelprize.org." *Nobel Foundation*. <http://nobelprize.org/index.html> (accessed October 8, 2006).

"Overview of the Human Genome Project." *National Human Genome Research Institute*. <http://www.genome.gov/12011238> (accessed April 22, 2006).

Pharma-Lexicon International. "MediLexicon." <http://www.medilexicon.com/> (accessed October 8, 2006).

Stem Cell Research Foundation. "Frequently Asked Questions." <http://www.stemcellresearchfoundation.org/About/FAQ.htm> (accessed June 25, 2006).

"Synthetic Biology." *Berkeley West Biocenter, Berkeley Lab and University of California, Berkeley*. <http://www.lbl.gov/pbd/synthbio/potter.htm> (accessed July 24, 2006).

U.S. Department of Agriculture. "Inside the Pyramid." <http://www.mypyramid.gov/pyramid/oils.html> (accessed August 9, 2006).

U.S. Department of Energy. "Facts About Genome Sequencing." October 27, 2004. <http://www.ornl.gov/sci/techresources/Human_Genome/faq/seqfacts.shtml> (accessed April 28, 2006).

U.S. Environmental Protection Agency. "What Are Biopesticides?" May 2, 2006. <http://www.epa.gov/pesticides/biopesticides/whatarebiopesticides.htm> (accessed May 29, 2006).

World Health Organization. "20 Questions on Genetically Modified Foods." <http://www.who.int/foodsafety/publications/biotech/20questions/en/index.html> (accessed April 20, 2006).

suppression of scientific
findings, 2: 466–67
therapeutic cloning, 1: 269
Butterflies, 2: 369
Byssus, 3: 703–4, 704 (ill.)

C

C polysaccharide, 1: 81
C-reactive protein, 1: 79–82,
81 (ill.)
Caffeine, 3: 715
Calcium, 1: 169, 2: 375, 3: 567
Calcium carbonate, 1: 48
Calcium-fortified food, 3: 713, 715
Calendula, 3: 719
Calgene, 2: 427, 510, 512–13,
3: 682
California, 3: 732
Callus cells, 2: 460
Calne, Roy, 1: 7
Cambium, 2: 460
Cameras, biorobotic, 3: 611
Campbell Soup Company,
2: 512–13
Canada
bioleaching, 3: 572
genetically engineered
crops, 3: 681 (ill.)
saccharin, 2: 504
spruce budworm, 2: 369
Cancer
aspirin for, 1: 18
bone marrow
transplantation for, 1: 42
bovine growth hormone
and, 2: 353
causes, 1: 56, 61
monoclonal antibodies for,
1: 57 (ill.), 58, 60
Cancer drugs, 1: 56–60, 57
(ill.), 61–64, 62 (ill.)
Canned food, 2: 415–18
Canola
biodiesel from, 2: 325, 528
genetically engineered,
1: 154 (ill.), 3: 720
herbicide-tolerant, 2: 447
oil-seed crops, 3: 717, 718,
718 (ill.)
vegetable oil, 2: 527

Capek, Karel, 3: 610
Capsules, lipid-based, 3: 696
Capture fishing, 2: 313
Carbohydrates, 2: 408
Carbon, 2: 331, 3: 663
Carbon 14, 3: 663–64
Carbon cycle, 3: 653
Carbon dioxide
beer-making, 2: 321
biodegradable packaging,
3: 558–59
carbon cycle and, 3: 653
ethanol production, 3: 650
fermentation, 3: 646–47
food bioprocessing, 2: 410
hybrid plants for, 2: 452
liquid biofuels, 2: 325
solid biofuels, 2: 331
wine-making, 2: 534, 536
Carbon monoxide, 2: 331
Carbon nanotubes, 3: 708
Cardiovascular disease, 1: 81
Carlisle, Anthony, 3: 675–76
Carlsson, Arvid, 3: 544
Carrel, Alexis, 1: 287, 3: 550
Carrier detection, 1: 144
Cars
bionic, 3: 590
bioplastics in, 3: 597
liquid biofuels, 2: 324
race, 3: 652, 653
robots, 3: 611
Castile soap, 2: 489
Castor oil, 2: 525, 528, 3: 717
Catabolic reactions, 1: 195
Catalysts, 3: 645–46, 696
Catechin, 3: 687
Catholic Church, 1: 188
Cattle. See Cows
Caucasia, 2: 534
Cauliflower mosaic virus, 2: 480
CDC. See Centers for Disease
Control and Prevention
cDNA, 1: 21, 2: 470
Celebrex. See Celecoxib
Celecoxib, 1: 216
Celera Genomics, 1: 159
Cell lines, stem cell, 1: 247–51,
259–60

Cell-surface receptors,
1: 10–11, 13
CellCept. See Mycophenolate
mofetil
Cellera, 1: 178
Cellophane, 3: 596
Cells
in bioreactors, 3: 601
described, 1: 241–42
in tissue engineering, 1: 277
Cellular metabolism, 1: 195–96
Cellulose, 1: 262, 3: 596, 654
Cellulose-based biomass, 2: 325
Cellulosic fermentation, 3: 654
Center for Food and Nutrition
Policy, 3: 692
Center for Science in the Public
Interest, 2: 408
Center for the Engineering of
Living Tissues, 1: 278
Center of Advanced Materials,
3: 687
Centers for Disease Control
and Prevention (CDC)
biosafety level laboratories,
3: 619–20
C-reactive protein, 1: 81
irradiated food, 2: 418–19
Central Intelligence Agency
(CIA), 3: 742
Cephalosporins, 1: 223
Ceramics, 3: 567–68
Cereal, 2: 412, 3: 713
Cerebral palsy, 1: 189
CFTCR (Cystic fibrosis
transmembrane
conductance regulator),
1: 161–62
Chain, Ernst Boris, 1: 224,
3: 668
Chain termination method,
1: 108–9
Chakrabarty, Anada, 3: 726
(ill.), 727
Champagne, 2: 536
Channel-catfish, 2: 315
Characteristics, acquired,
2: 464–65
Charcot, Jean-Martin, 1: 201,
203